Telecourse Study Guide

for use with

Understanding Business

Sixth Edition

William G. Nickels
University of Maryland

James M. McHugh
St. Louis Community College at Forest Park

Susan M. McHugh
Applied Learning Systems

Prepared by
Christopher W. Rogers
Miami Dade Community College

McGraw-Hill Irwin

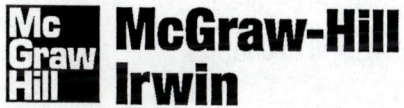

Boston Burr Ridge, IL Dubuque, IA Madison, WI New York San Francisco St. Louis
Bangkok Bogotá Caracas Kuala Lumpur Lisbon London Madrid Mexico City
Milan Montreal New Delhi Santiago Seoul Singapore Sydney Taipei Toronto

McGraw-Hill Higher Education

A Division of The McGraw-Hill Companies

Telecourse Study Guide for use with
UNDERSTANDING BUSINESS
William G. Nickels, James M. McHugh and Susan M. McHugh

Published by McGraw-Hill/Irwin, an imprint of the McGraw-Hill Companies, Inc., 1221 Avenue of the Americas, New York, NY 10020. Copyright © 2002 1999 by the McGraw-Hill Companies, Inc.
All rights reserved.
No part of this publication may be reproduced or distributed in any form or by any means, or stored in a database or retrieval system, without the prior written consent of The McGraw-Hill Companies, Inc., including, but not limited to, in any network or other electronic storage or transmission, or broadcast for distance learning.

1 2 3 4 5 6 7 8 9 0 QSR/QSR 0 9 8 7 6 5 4 3 2 1

ISBN 0-07-245574-8

www.mhhe.com

TABLE OF CONTENTS

Introduction		p v
Lesson 1	Introducing Business	p 1
Lesson 2	Responding to Change	p 8
Lesson 3	Defining Economic Systems	p 16
Lesson 4	Accommodating Business Law	p 28
Lesson 5	Contending with Government Involvement	p 39
Lesson 6	Promoting Social Responsibility	p 45
Lesson 7	Competing in a Global Environment	p 54
Lesson 8	Managing Business Information	p 68
Lesson 9	Selecting a Form of Business Ownership	p 80
Lesson 10	Highlighting Small Business	p 92
Lesson 11	Managing a Business	p 103
Lesson 12	Establishing a Business Organization	p 115
Lesson 13	Managing Human Resources	p 128
Lesson 14	Managing the Work Environment	p 142
Lesson 15	Handling Labor Relations	p 157
Lesson 16	Marketing Products	p 168
Lesson 17	Defining Products	p 180
Lesson 18	Managing Operations	p 191
Lesson 19	Pricing Products	p 203
Lesson 20	Promoting Products	p 210
Lesson 21	Distributing Products	p 221
Lesson 22	Understanding Money	p 234
Lesson 23	Managing Short-Term Financing	p 247
Lesson 24	Managing Long-Term Financing	p 258
Lesson 25	Accounting for Management	p 274
Lesson 26	Managing Risk	p 290

INTRODUCTION

This course may be one of the most important learning experiences of your life. It is meant to help you understand business so that you can use business principles in your own life. But you don't have to be in business to use business principles. You can use *marketing* principles to get a job and to sell your ideas to others. You can use your knowledge of *investments* to make money in the stock market. Similarly, you'll be able to use the *management skills* and general business knowledge wherever you go and in whatever career you pursue.

We all want to find a rewarding career and to be successful and happy. We just find it difficult to decide what that career should be. Even many of those who have relatively successful careers tend to look for something more fulfilling, more challenging, and more interesting. One purpose of this course is to introduce you to the wide variety of careers available in business and management. You'll learn about production, marketing, finance, accounting, management, economics, and more.

When you're finished, you should have a much better idea about what kind of career would be best for you. Not only that, you'll be prepared to use basic business terms and concepts that are necessary to be a success in any organization – including government agencies, charities, and social causes – or in your own small business.

The Videos

The videos for this course bring to life many of the key concepts and abstract ideas presented in the text. The videos are an interesting and, at times, entertaining tool for learning about these concepts, but they aren't like watching *Friends*. Don't let yourself slip into passive viewing—you need to concentrate on more active watching. If you are watching the videos on television at home and have a VCR, you can tape the programs to watch at a more convenient time or to review. If you are watching the videos in the learning center on campus and have an audio recorder, you can record the program so that you can review while you commute back and forth to work, while you exercise, etc.

The Text

The text that accompanies this study guide is *Understanding Business, 6th edition*, by Nickels, McHugh and McHugh, published by McGraw-Hill/Irwin. The text is an integral part of this learning experience. It provides background information and elaborates on the concepts presented in the videos.

Telecourse Study Guide

The purpose of this study guide is to help you integrate the course videos with the above text. Each lesson in this book contains:

- **Assignments** that outline the reading and viewing requirements for the lesson.
- **Learning Goals** identify what you should learn from the lesson.
- **Lesson Overview** provides a detailed outline of the text material for easy review.
- **Learning the Language of Business** activities are matching exercises that will help you develop a business vocabulary.
- **Self-Tests** are short multiple-choice quizzes to help you evaluate your knowledge of the material presented in the text and study guide.
- **Answer Keys** provide the answers for the Learning the Language of Business exercises and the Self-Tests.

How to Take a Telecourse

To complete a telecourse successfully, you need to plan when to watch, read, and study. If you enjoy watching the video with other people, hold off discussion until after the program so that you don't miss important concepts. Successful telecourse students have told us that the following activities helped them master the course:

- Read the text before watching the video.
- If possible, tape the video while you are watching it for review later.
- Review the text after watching the video. The Lesson Overview in this study guide will help you review the text.
- Complete the exercises in this study guide. They are a great way to prepare for tests.
- Keep on schedule with the lessons. Don't fall behind and try to catch up by doing too many lessons in too short a time.
- Call your course mentor or faculty advisor at the campus where you are enrolled if you have problems of any kind. This person makes time available to help you succeed in this course.

LESSON 1

INTRODUCING BUSINESS

ASSIGNMENTS

1. Review the Learning Goals and read the Lesson Overview for this lesson.

2. Read Chapter 1 pp. 1-10, the **Legal Briefcase** box on pp. 11 and pp. 22-24 in *Understanding Business,* 6th edition by Nickels, McHugh, and McHugh.

3. Watch the video Introducing Business.

4. Review the textbook material.

5. Match the key terms with the correct definitions in the Learning the Language of Business exercise.

6. Take the Self-Test.

7. Use the Answer Key to check your answers and review when necessary.

LEARNING GOALS

After you watch the video, read the textbook, and study this lesson, you should be able to:

1. Describe how businesses and nonprofit organizations add to a country's standard of living and quality of life.

2. Explain the importance of entrepreneurship to the wealth of an economy and show the relationship of profit to risk assumption.

3. Describe the factors of production.

4. Analyze what businesses must do to meet the global challenge.

LESSON NOTES

The PROFILE at the beginning of this chapter explores GETTING TO KNOW JENNY MING FROM OLD NAVY. Jenny Ming is the president of Old Navy, a part of Gap, Inc. Her experience as a buyer and her education fueled her reputation, which landed her a buyers job at Gap's Old Navy stores. Her excellent performance led to her rapid promotion, which culminated in her becoming president in 1999. Ming realizes that fashion and shopping methods change rapidly and only stores that keep up with both will prosper.

I. WHAT IS A BUSINESS?

   A. A **BUSINESS** is any activity that seeks profit by providing goods and services to others.
      1. **PROFIT** is money that a business earns above and beyond what it spends on salaries, expenses, and other costs.

   B. BUSINESSES CAN PROVIDE WEALTH AND A HIGH QUALITY OF LIFE FOR ALMOST EVERYONE
      1. An **ENTREPRENEUR** is a person who risks time and money to start and manage a business.
      2. Entrepreneurs may not only become wealthy themselves, but also provide employment for other people.
      3. Businesses are a part of an economic system that helps to create the higher standard of living and quality of life for everyone.
      4. The **STANDARD OF LIVING** of a country refers to the amount of goods and services people can buy with the money they have.
      5. The **QUALITY OF LIFE** of a country refers to the general well being of a society.

   C. NONPROFIT ORGANIZATIONS USE BUSINESS PRINCIPLES
      1. Nonprofit organizations such as government agencies, public schools, charities and social causes help make a country more responsive to all the needs of its citizens.
      2. A **NONPROFIT ORGANIZATION** is an organization whose goals don't include making a profit for its owners.
      3. You need the same skills to work in nonprofit organizations that you need in business. Skills needed include information management, leadership, marketing, and financial management.
      4. Businesses, nonprofit organizations, and volunteer groups often work to accomplish the same objectives.

II. ENTREPRENEURSHIP VERSUS WORKING FOR OTHERS

   A. ENTREPRENEURSHIP
      1. In making choices regarding your career you could decide to become part of an organization and work your way up, or take a higher risk and open your own business.
      2. A lot can be learned by studying entrepreneurs and from job experience, but an education is the best place to start.

   B. OPORTUNITIES FOR ENTREPRENEURS
      1. The United States is a prosperous place for entrepreneurs from many cultures.
         a. The number of Latino-owned businesses in the United States grew by 76% in the 1990s.
         b. There have also been significant increases in the number of businesses owned by Asians, Pacific Islanders, American Indians, and Alaskan Natives.

C. MATCHING RISK WITH PROFIT
   1. A **LOSS** occurs when a business's costs and expenses are more than its **REVENUE**, the money a business earns by selling its products.
   2. **RISK** is the chance an owner takes of losing time and money on a business that may not prove profitable.
   3. Not all companies make the same profit.
      a. Those companies that take the most risk may make the most profit.
      b. As a potential business owner, you should do research to find the right balance between risk and profit.

D. THE FACTORS NEEDED TO CREATE WEALTH
   1. The **FACTORS OF PRODUCTION**, the resources businesses use to create wealth are:
      a. land (and other natural resources).
      b. labor (workers).
      c. capital (e.g., money, machines, tools and buildings).
      d. Entrepreneurship.
      e. knowledge (information).
   2. Some experts believe that the most important factor of production is knowledge.
   3. Entrepreneurship and knowledge are key components in enriching today's countries.
   4. Entrepreneurship also helps make some states and cities rich while others remain relatively poor.

III. THE GLOBAL ENVIRONMENT

   A. The global environment of business effects all other environmental influences.
      1. The number one global environmental change today is the growth of international competition and the increase in free trade among nations.
      2. U.S. manufacturers have implemented the most advance quality methods, after analyzing the best practices around the world.
      3. U.S. workers in many industries are more productive than are workers in Japan and other countries.
      4. **PRODUCTIVITY** is the volume of goods and services that one worker can produce in a given period of time.
      5. Businesses have gone beyond simply competing with organizations in other countries to learning to cooperate with international firms.

   B. HOW GLOBAL CHANGES AFFECT YOU
      1. Many think that new fair trade agreements will lead to many career opportunities for American college graduates.
      2. Students must prepare themselves to compete in the challenging global environments.

LEARNING THE LANGUAGE OF BUSINESS

Match each of the following key terms with the appropriate definition.

A. business
B. entrepreneur
C. factors of production
D. loss
E. nonprofit organization
F. productivity
G. profit
H. quality of life
I. revenue
J. risk
K. standard of living

____ 1. The level of ability to buy goods and services.

____ 2. The chance you take of losing time and money on a business that may not prove profitable.

____ 3. A person who takes the risk of starting and managing a business.

____ 4. Earnings above and beyond what a business spends for salaries, expenses, and other costs.

____ 5. When a business's costs and expenses are more than its revenues.

____ 6. The general well-being of a society.

____ 7. The resources used to create wealth: land, labor, capital, entrepreneurship, and knowledge.

____ 8. The total output of goods and services in a given period of time divided by work hours (output per work hour).

____ 9. An organization whose goals do not include making a personal profit for its owners.

____ 10. Any activity that seeks profit by providing needed goods and services to others.

____ 11. The value of what is received for goods sold services rendered and other sources.

SELF-TEST

1. Public schools, charities and government agencies are not classified as businesses because they:
   A) have not been incorporated.
   B) do not seek to earn a profit.
   C) provide services rather than goods.
   D) do not have any stockholders.

2. Which of the following is the most accurate statement about the impact of business on society?
   A) When businesses earn a profit for their owners, they usually do so at the expense of the rest of society.
   B) While businesses often improve the standard of living within a society, they can do little to improve the quality of life.
   C) Businesses often improve the quality of life, but can do little to improve the standard of living of most people.
   D) Businesses can have a significant impact on both the standard of living and the quality of life within a society.

3. A key characteristic of entrepreneurs is that they:
   A) are willing to accept the risks involved in starting and managing a business.
   B) have a high level of scientific and technical expertise.
   C) posses a great deal of personal wealth.
   D) have experience in running large, complex organizations.

4. Last year, MacTeck Enterprises had total revenues of $24 million while its total costs and expenses were $22 million. This implies that MacTeck:
   A) earned a profit of $2 million.
   B) earned a profit of $24 million.
   C) suffered a loss of $2 million.
   D) suffered a loss of $22 million.

5. _____ is the chance a business owner will lose the time and money invested in a business that proves to be unprofitable.
   A) Depreciation
   B) Risk
   C) Fallibility
   D) Redundancy

6. Which of the following statements about factors of production is the most accurate?
   A) The four major factors of production are energy, capital, labor, and money.
   B) Most poor nations are hampered chronic shortages of labor.
   C) All resources are equally important in creating wealth.
   D) The two factors of production that seem to contribute most to creating wealth are entrepreneurship and knowledge.

7. As a factor of production, the term capital includes:
   A) stocks and bonds issued by corporations.
   B) natural resources such as land and water.
   C) tools, machinery, and buildings.
   D) services provided by the government that enable businesses to be more productive.

8. Nadiria is a small and poor nation, but its current president has a genuine desire to create more wealth for Nadiria's citizens. The president has received recommendations from several advisors. Some of the suggestions she is considering are listed below. Which of these policies is likely to create the most wealth for Nadiria?
   A) Acquire more land by invading a neighboring country that is even poorer and weaker than Nadiria.
   B) Use foreign aid from other nations to produce or purchase more tools and machinery.
   C) Establish a business environment that promotes and rewards entrepreneurship.
   D) Establish barriers to trade to protect Nadirian businesses from foreign competition.

9. Cooperation among firms from different nations is:
   A) likely to become a thing of the past as competition among nations heats up.
   B) illegal and unethical.
   C) a way to expand world markets and achieve greater world prosperity.
   D) likely to result in a loss of jobs in poor nations as production shifts to wealthier countries.

10. Elizabeth Alexander has started up a new printing business. The printers, computers, and copying machines she has bought and leased are examples of:
    A) natural resources.
    B) intangible resources.
    C) current assets.
    D) capital.

ANSWER KEY

LEARNING THE LANGUAGE OF BUSINESS

1. K
2. J
3. B
4. G
5. D
6. H
7. C
8. F
9. E
10. A
11. I

SELF-TEST

ANSWER	PAGE #
1. B	Page: 5
2. D	Page: 4
3. A	Page: 4
4. A	Page: 7
5. B	Page: 7-8
6. D	Page: 9
7. C	Page: 9
8. C	Page: 6
9. C	Page: 23
10. D	Page: 9

LESSON 2

RESPONDING TO CHANGE

ASSIGNMENTS

1. Review the Learning Goals and read the Lesson Overview for this lesson.

2. Read Chapter 1 pp. 10-22 and 24-27 in *Understanding Business,* 6th edition by Nickels, McHugh, and McHugh.

3. Watch the video Responding to Change

4. Review the textbook material.

5. Match the key terms with the correct definitions in the Learning the Language of Business exercise.

6. Take the Self-Test.

7. Use the Answer Key to check your answers and review when necessary.

LEARNING GOALS

After you watch the video, read the textbook, and study this lesson, you should be able to:

1. Examine how the economic environment and taxes affect businesses.

2. Illustrate how the technological environment has affected businesses.

3. Identify various ways in which businesses can meet and beat competition.

4. Demonstrate how the social environment has changed and what the reaction of the business community has been.

5. Review how trends from the past are being repeated in the present and what such trends will mean for the service sector.

LESSON NOTES

I. THE BUSINESS ENVIRONMENT
The five key environmental factors critical to the success of business are the: (1) economic environment, including taxes and regulation; (2) technological environment; (3) competitive environment; (4) social environment; and (5) global business environment (discussed in Lesson 1).

   A. THE ECONOMIC ENVIRONMENT
      1. People are willing to take the risk of starting businesses if they feel that the risk isn't too great.
      2. Entrepreneurs are looking for high **RETURN ON INVESTMENT (ROI)**, including the investment of their time.
      3. If government takes away too much money in the form of taxes, entrepreneurs may feel the ROI is not worth the risk. This is true regardless of whether the country is rich or poor.
      4. Governments can lessen the risk of starting a business thereby increasing entrepreneurship and wealth by:
         a. allowing private ownership of business.
         b. passing laws that enable business people to write contracts that are enforceable in court.
         c. establishing a tradable currency.
         d. eliminating corruption in business and government.

   B. THE TECHNOLOGICAL ENVIRONMENT
      1. HOW THE INTERNET IS CHANGING EVERYTHING
         a. The Internet is a powerful communication medium, which allows businesses to operate without borders.
      2. THE E-COMMERCE EXPLOSION
         a. The buying and selling of products and services over the Internet is **E-COMMERCE**.
         b. A **DOT-COM COMPANY** is a business that uses the Internet exclusively.
         c. The reasons for the surge in the number of dot-com businesses are:
            1. low transaction costs.
            2. large purchases per transaction.
            3. integration of business processes.
            4. flexibility.
            5. large catalogs.
            6. improved customer interaction.
         d. The two major types of e-commerce businesses are B2C, business to consumer, and B2B, business to business.
      3. HOW E-COMMERCE IS CHANGING THE ROLES OF INTERMEDIARIES
         a. E-commerce has changed the roles of retailers and wholesalers, eliminating them entirely in some cases.
      4. USING TECHNOLOGY TO BE RESPONSIVE TO CUSTOMERS
         a. Technology has made it possible for businesses to become more responsive to customers.
         b. A **DATABASE**, is an electronic storage file where information is kept, it can be used to store vast amounts of information about customers.
         c. Bar codes on products allow the retailer to record in their database all sorts of pertinent information about the purchase.
         d. Businesses routinely trade databases, thus sharing consumer information to more effectively manage inventory and consumer directed efforts.

C. THE COMPETITIVE ENVIRONMENT
 1. Making quality products is not enough to stay competitive in world markets. Now you have to offer quality products and outstanding service at competitive prices.
 2. COMPETING BY PLEASING THE CUSTOMER
    a. Successful companies must listen to customers to determine their wants and needs and then adjust their products, policies, and practices to meet these demands.
 3. COMPETING WITH SPEED
    a. In today's dynamic environment companies that provide speedy service are those that are winning.
    b. In this dynamic environment people must keep up with the changes by returning to school periodically to learn the latest techniques.
 4. COMPETING BY MEETING COMMUNITY NEEDS
    a. **STAKEHOLDERS** are all the people who are affected by the policies and activities of an organization.
    b. Stakeholders include customers, employees, stockholders, suppliers, dealers, bankers, environmentalists and elected officials.
    c. The challenge for companies in the 21st century will be to ensure that all stakeholders' needs are considered and satisfied.
 5. COMPETING BY RESTRUCTURING AND MEETING THE NEEDS OF EMPLOYEES
    a. To meet the needs of customers, firms must give their front line workers more freedom to respond quickly to customer requests.
    b. In many companies this has led to the **EMPOWERMENT** of the employees and usage of self-managed cross-functional teams.
    c. It sometimes takes years to restructure and organize so managers are willing to give up some of their authority.
 6. COMPETING BY CONCERN FOR THE NATURAL ENVIRONMENT
    a. Environmental issues include the potential benefits and hazards of nuclear power, recycling, the management of forests, the ethical treatment of animals, and the protection of the air we breathe and the water we drink.
    b. Environmentalism must be a major focus of everyone, and is becoming increasingly so.

D. THE SOCIAL ENVIRONMENT
 1. **DEMOGRAPHY** is the statistical study of the human population to learn its size, density, and other characteristics.
 2. DIVERSITY AND ITS ADVANTAGES FOR BUSINESS
    a. The U.S. of 2050 will be very different from what it is today.
       1) Our population will increase by 50%. As the population grows, there will be a greater need for goods and services, creating more jobs.
       2) The Hispanic, Asian and African American populations will increase.
    b. **MULTICULTURALISM** and **DIVERSITY** describe the process of optimizing the contributions of people from different cultures in the workplace.
    c. As American workers learn to work with people of all nations, they gain an advantage when it comes to negotiating and working with people in global markets.
    d. A diverse population is a strong population – there is strength in different views and perspectives.
 3. THE INCREASE IN THE NUMBER OF OLDER AMERICANS
    a. By 2030, the 76 million baby boomers will be senior citizens.
    b. Think of the career opportunities of providing goods and services for older adults. What opportunities do a wealthy, older market offer retailers, recreation specialists, etc.?
 4. TWO-INCOME FAMILIES

a. The high costs of housing and maintaining a comfortable lifestyle have made it difficult for many households to live on just one income.
b. Many companies are implementing programs to assist two-income families.
   1) Many employers provide childcare benefits of some type, some through cafeteria benefits packages.
   2) Other companies provide parental leave, flexible work schedules, and eldercare programs.
c. Some companies are increasing the number of part-time workers, allowing workers more time to stay home with their children.
d. Some companies allow workers to **TELECOMMUTE**, these workers send their work from home by telecommunications.
5. SINGLE PARENTS
   a. There has been a rapid increase in the number of single parent families.
   b. Businesses have implemented programs such as family leaves and flextime to accommodate single parents.

II. THE EVOLUTION OF AMERICAN BUSINESS

A. Businesses in the U.S. have become so productive that fewer workers are needed to produce **GOODS**, or tangible products.
B. PROGRESS IN THE AGRICULTURAL AND MANUFACTURING INDUSTRIES
   1. The use of technology allowed the agricultural industry to become so productive that the number of farmers dropped from about a third of the population to less than 2 percent.
   2. Agriculture is still a major industry in the U.S., but fewer and larger farms have replaced millions of small farms.
   3. Farmers who lost their jobs often went to work in factories.
   4. Technology made manufacturing more productive, thus some factory workers, like farmers, lost their jobs.
C. PROGRESS IN SERVICE INDUSTRIES
   1. Many workers who lost their manufacturing jobs found jobs in service industries.
   2. **SERVICES** are intangible products.
   3. Since the mid-1980s, the service sector has generated almost all of our economy's increases in employment.
   4. Projections are that the service sector will grow more slowly in the coming decades, but remain the largest growth area.
D. YOUR FUTURE IN THE GLOBAL ECONOMY
   1. The service era is quickly losing out to a new global information revolution that is breaking down barriers between nations.
   2. The information-based global revolution will alter the way business is done in the future.
   3. Most of the concepts and principles that make business more effective are applicable in government agencies and nonprofit organizations.

LEARNING THE LANGUAGE OF BUSINESS

Match each of the following key terms with the appropriate definition.

A. database
B. demography
C. diversity, multiculturalism
D. dot-com company
E. e-commerce
F. empowerment
G. goods
H. return on investment (ROI)
I. services
J. stakeholders
K. telecommute

____ 1. Those people who stand to gain or lose by the policies or activities of an organization.

____ 2. A business that sells goods and services over the Internet exclusively.

____ 3. To work at home via computer and modem.

____ 4. Giving frontline workers the responsibility and freedom to respond quickly to customer requests.

____ 5. Tangible products such as houses, food, and clothing.

____ 6. Intangible products such as education, health care, and insurance.

____ 7. The statistical study of human population to learn its size, density, and other characteristics.

____ 8. Electronic storage file for information.

____ 9. The return an owner gets for risking their money and time.

____ 10. The process of optimizing the contributions of people from differing cultures.

____ 11. The industry of using the Internet to buy and sell products and services.

SELF-TEST

1. Taxes and government regulations are part of the _____ environment of business.
   A) economic
   B) competitive
   C) social
   D) technological

2. All of the following policies would tend to foster entrepreneurship except:
   A) establishing a currency that is tradable on world markets.
   B) establishing more regulations to protect the environment.
   C) developing policies to reduce corruption in business and government.
   D) allowing private ownership of businesses.

3. _____ is the buying and selling of products and services by businesses and consumers over the Internet.
   A) E-commerce
   B) Intrapreneurship
   C) Telecommuting
   D) I-commerce

4. When businesses sell to other businesses over the Internet, these transactions are known as:
   A) telecommuting.
   B) Intertailing.
   C) B2B transactions.
   D) intermediate e-commerce transactions.

5. Summit Gifts, Inc., is a mail order firm that specializes in expensive and unusual gifts for all occasions. Summit keeps a large file of information on all of its regular customers, including names, addresses, the types of gifts they have ordered in the past, and the size and frequency of their orders. The electronic file in which this information is stored in an example of a(n):
   A) spreadsheet.
   B) ASCII file.
   C) PERT file.
   D) database.

6. Jack is a salesperson for Bi-State Direct. One thing he really likes about his job is the amount of freedom and flexibility Bi-State gives its sales people to meet the needs of their customers. Jack's experience suggests that Bi-State has adopted the philosophy of:
   A) centralized management.
   B) outsourcing.
   C) enfranchisement.
   D) empowerment.

7. Which of the statements about demography is most accurate? Demographic studies:
   A) focus on factors that have great political relevance, but little relevance to business firms.
   B) suggest that the number of two-income families will decline in the future.
   C) provide business and individuals key insights into business and career opportunities of the future.
   D) are an important source of information about weather and climate.

8. Jill Redden is looking into the possibility of opening up a day care center in her community, because she is aware of many two-income families that need a place for their children to stay while the parents work. However, she is concerned about the long-term prospects for such a business. Jill believes the future of her center will depend on whether birth rates and the number of two-income families remain high. These concerns illustrate how businesses can be affected by:
   A) econometric trends.
   B) demographic trends.
   C) holographic trends.
   D) psychometric trends.

9. Since the beginning of the 1900s, the agricultural sector of the United States has:
   A) seen the number of family farms more than double.
   B) become less and less competitive in the global economy.
   C) seen relatively little change in the amount of output per farm.
   D) experienced a big drop in employment, mainly because of tremendous improvements in efficiency.

10. Appliance repair firms, tax consultants, law firms, and insurance companies are all business firms that are part of the:
    A) skilled sector.
    B) management sector.
    C) neo-industrial sector.
    D) service sector.

ANSWER KEY

LEARNING THE LANGUAGE OF BUSINESS

1. J
2. D
3. K
4. F
5. G
6. I
7. B
8. A
9. H
10. C
11. E

SELF-TEST

Answer	Page #
1. A	Page: 8
2. B	Page: 11-12
3. A	Page: 13
4. C	Page: 14
5. D	Page: 15
6. D	Page: 20
7. C	Page: 21
8. B	Page: 21-22
9. D	Page: 24
10. D	Page: 25

LESSON

DEFINING ECONOMIC SYSTEMS

ASSIGNMENTS

1. Review the Learning Goals and read the Lesson Overview for this lesson.
2. Read Chapter 2 pp. 33-53 in *Understanding Business,* 6th edition by Nickels, McHugh, and McHugh.
3. Watch the video Defining Economic Systems.
4. Review the textbook material.
5. Match the key terms with the correct definitions in the Learning the Language of Business exercise.
6. Take the Self-Test.
7. Use the Answer Key to check your answers and review when necessary.

LEARNING GOALS

After you watch the video, read the textbook, and study this lesson, you should be able to:

1. Compare and contrast the economics of despair with the economics of growth.
2. Explain the nature of capitalism and how free markets work.
3. Discuss the major differences between socialism and communism.
4. Explain the trend toward mixed economies.
5. Use key terms (e.g., GDP, CPI, PPI, productivity, inflation, and recession) to explain the U.S. economic condition.

LESSON NOTES

The PROFILE at the beginning of this chapter compares the efforts of a pair of entrepreneurs in Europe with a similar pair in the U.S. Both duos had similar plans for an on-line vacation-booking site. The willingness of investors and employees to take risks is contrasted. The pair of entrepreneurs in the U.S. was far more successful at obtaining money and employees. Their company eventually bought the European company and later sold for almost eight times the original investment.

I. THE IMPORTANCE OF THE STUDY OF ECONOMICS

    A. Any change in the U.S. economic or political system has a major influence on the success of the business system.
        1. The world economic situation and world politics have a major influence on U.S. business.
        2. The three basic objectives of this chapter are to teach:
            a. How free markets work.
            b. How free markets differ from government-controlled markets.
            c. Some basic economic terms and concepts that you will read in business periodicals.

    B. WHAT IS ECONOMICS?
        1. **ECONOMICS** is the study of how society chooses to employ resources to produce various goods and services and to distribute them for consumption among various competing groups and individuals.
        2. Economist normally work from one of two perspectives:
            a. The part of economic study that focuses on the nation's economy as a whole is called **MACROECONOMICS**.
            b. The part of economic study that focuses on the behavior of people and organizations in a specific market is called **MICROECONOMICS**.
        3. There aren't enough known resources among all nations.
        4. **RESOURCE DEVELOPMENT** is the study of how to increase the known resources of the world and to create conditions that will make better use of those resources.

    C. THE ECONOMICS OF DESPAIR
        1. English economist Thomas Malthus theorized over 200 years ago that the population would exceed the supply of food and other resources.
        2. Other economists see a large population as a valuable resource.
        3. Technological advances have made many people the world over better off then they were in the past.
        4. Economists are challenged to find and implement policies and programs that will increase prosperity for all countries of the world.

    D. GROWTH ECONOMICS AND ADAM SMITH
        1. Adam Smith advocated creating wealth through entrepreneurship.
            a. Rather than divide fixed resources, Smith envisioned creating more resources so that everyone could be wealthier.
            b. In 1776, Smith wrote a book called <u>The Wealth of Nations</u> in which he outlined steps for creating prosperity.
        2. What are the forces that drive wealth according to Adam Smith? They are:
            a. The freedom to keep the profits from what you produce and sell and freedom to own land.
            b. The incentive to work long hours and to work hard when one gets to keep the profit from the labor. The more an individual works the more that gets produced, thus, the more for others.
        3. Adam Smith is considered the father of modern economics.

E. THE INVISIBLE HAND
1. Adam Smith called the mechanism for creating wealth and jobs an **INVISIBLE HAND**, which turns self-directed gain into social and economic benefits for all.
2. Basically, what this meant was that a person working hard to make money for his or her own personal interest would (like an invisible hand) also benefit others.
   a. For example, a farmer trying to make money would grow as many crops as possible.
   b. This provides needed food for others.
   c. If everyone worked hard in his or her own self interest, Smith said, society, as a whole would prosper.
3. Many U.S. businesspeople are becoming concerned about social issues and their obligation to return to society some of what they've earned.

II. UNDERSTANDING FREE-MARKET CAPITALISM

A. **CAPITALISM** is an economic system in which all or most of the means of production and distribution are privately owned and operated for profit.
   1. In capitalist countries, businesspeople decide how to use their resources and how much to charge
   2. No country is purely capitalist, but the foundation of the U.S. is capitalism.

C. THE FOUNDATION OF CAPITALISM
The four basic rights of capitalism are:
1. The right to private property.
2. The right to own a business and to keep all of that business's profits.
3. The right to freedom of competition.
4. The right to freedom of choice.

C. HOW FREE MARKETS WORK
1. In a free-market system, decisions about what to produce and in what quantities are made by the market itself.
2. Consumers send signals to producers about what to make, how many, and so on.
3. In the U.S., the price tells producers how much to produce, reducing the chances of a long-term shortage of goods.

D. HOW PRICES ARE DETERMINED
1. In a free-market prices are determined by buyers and sellers negotiating in the marketplace

E. THE ECONOMIC CONCEPT OF SUPPLY
1. **SUPPLY** refers to the quantity of products that manufacturers or owners are willing to sell at different prices at a specific time.
2. The amount supplied will increase as the price increases.
3. The quantity producers are willing to supply at certain prices are illustrated on a supply curve

F. THE ECONOMIC CONCEPT OF DEMAND
1. **DEMAND** refers to the quantity of products that people are willing to buy at different prices a specific time.
2. The quantity demanded will decrease as the price increases.
3. The quantity consumers are willing to buy at certain prices are illustrated on a demand curve

G. THE EQUILIBRIUM POINT, OR MARKET PRICE
1. The equilibrium price or **MARKET PRICE** is the price at which the quantity demanded and the quantity supplied are equal.
2. The point of equilibrium is the point where the supply and demand curves cross.

H. COMPETITION WITHIN FREE-MARKETS
1. Competition exists in different degrees. The four basic degrees are:
   a. Perfect competition.
   b. Monopolistic competition.
   c. Oligopoly.
   d. Monopoly.
2. **PERFECT COMPETITION** exists when there are many sellers in the market and no seller is large enough to dictate the price of a product.
   a. Sellers produce products that appear to be identical.
   b. There are no true examples of perfect competition, but agricultural products are often used as an example.
3. **MONOPOLISTIC COMPETITION** exists when a large number of sellers produce products that are very similar but are perceived by buyers to be different.
   a. Product differentiation, making buyers think similar products are different, is a key to success.
   b. Under monopolistic competition, price competition is present.
   c. The fast food industry is an example.
4. An **OLIGOPOLY** is a form of competition in which just a few sellers dominate a market.
   a. The initial investment is usually high.
   b. Prices tend to be close to the same.
   c. Examples include breakfast cereal, beer, automobiles, and soft drinks.
5. A **MONOPLOY** occurs when there is only one seller for a product or service.
   a. In the U.S., laws prohibit the creation of monopolies, but do permit approved monopolies such as public utilities.
   b. New legislation is likely to result in fewer, larger utilities and lower prices.

I. LIMITATIONS OF THE FREE-MARKET SYSTEM
1. Capitalism brought prosperity to the U.S. and much of the world, but it brought inequality as well.
2. When some countries introduced capitalist principles, inequality increased dramatically.

III. UNDERSTANDING SOCIALISM

A. **SOCIALISM** is an economic system based on the premise that most basic businesses should be owned by the government.
   1. Advocates of socialism acknowledge the major benefits of capitalism, but believe that wealth should be more evenly distributed.
   2. Socialism became the economic platform for many countries in Europe, Africa, and much of the world.
   3. Socialist nations rely heavily on the government to provide education, health care, retirement, and care for those not able to work.

B. THE BENEFITS OF SOCIALISM
   1. The major benefit of socialism is equality.
   2. Income is taken from the wealthier members of society and given to the poorer.

C. THE NEGATIVE CONSEQUENCES OF SOCIALISM
   1. Socialism creates more equality, but takes away some work incentives.
   2. Marginal tax rates (the rate you pay on the additional money earned after a certain income level) in some socialist nations once reached 85%.
   3. Socialism does not create the jobs or wealth that capitalism does.

IV. UNDERSTANDING COMMUNISM

   A. Under communism the state owns the businesses and makes all of the economic decisions.
      1. Karl Marx decided that workers should take over ownership of businesses and share in the wealth.
         a. He wrote The Communist Manifesto in 1848, becoming the father of communism.
         b. **COMMUNISM** is a system where all economic decisions are made by the state and the state owns all major forms of production.
      2. Communist countries include China, North Korea and Cuba.
      3. Communism does not inspire businesspeople to work hard, and is slowly disappearing as an economic form.

V. THE TREND TOWARD MIXED ECONOMIES

   A. There are two economic systems vying for dominance in the world:
      1. **FREE-MARKET ECONOMIES** (capitalism) -- the marketplace largely determines what goods and services get produced, who gets them, and how the economy grows.
      2. **COMMAND ECONOMIES** (socialism and communism) -- the government largely decides what goods and services will be produced, who'll get them, and how the economy will grow.

   B. No one economic system is perfect by itself.
      1. Free-market mechanisms weren't responsive enough to a nation's social and economic needs.
      2. Socialism and communism didn't create enough jobs or wealth to keep the economy growing quickly enough.
      3. No country is purely capitalist, rather some mix of the two systems.
      4. However, the long-term global trend is toward a blend of capitalism and socialism.

   D. **MIXED ECONOMIES** exist where there is some allocation of resources made by the market and some by the government.

   D. The U.S. has a mixed economy.
      1. There is a debate about the role of government in many parts of the economy.
      2. The basic principles of freedom and opportunity remain so that economic growth is sustainable.
      E. In the U.S., the government serves as a means to supplement the basic system.

VI. UNDERSTANDING THE ECONOMIC SYSTEM OF THE UNITED STATES

   A. While most of the world has been moving toward fee-markets, in recent years the U.S. has been moving toward more social programs.
      1. There was much conflict between business leaders and government leaders on issues such as taxes, regulations, and social programs.
      2. Currently the U.S. economic system is in a state of flux.

   B. KEY ECONOMIC INDICATORS
      1. The text discusses three major indicators of an economy's health: GDP, unemployment rate and price indexes.
      2. **GROSS DOMESTIC PRODUCT (GDP)** is the total value of a country's output of goods and services in a given year.
         a. The high GDP in the U.S. has led to a high standard of living.
      3. The **UNEMPLOYMENT RATE** refers to the number of civilians, 16 years old or older, who are unemployed and tried to find a job within the prior four weeks.

a. There are four categories of unemployment.
   1) Frictional unemployment - refers to those people who have quit work because they did not like the job, the boss, or working conditions.
   2) Structural unemployment - refers to unemployment caused by a mismatch between the skills (or location) of job seekers and the requirements (or location) of available jobs (i.e. coal miners in areas where mines have been closed).
   3) Cyclical unemployment - unemployment caused by a recession or similar downturn in the business cycle.
   4) Seasonal unemployment - unemployment which occurs when the demand for labor varies over the year (i.e. harvesting of crops).
4. THE PRICE INDEXES
   a. The **CONSUMER PRICE INDEX (CPI)** consists of monthly statistics that measure the pace of inflation (consumer prices going up) or deflation (consumer prices going down).
      1) Some government benefits, wages, and interest rates are based on the CPI.
   b. The **PRODUCER PRICE INDEX (PPI)** measures prices at the wholesale level.

C. DISTRIBUTION OF GDP - The percentage of GDP taken by all levels of government in the U.S. is around 36 percent. When you add in all the fees and sales taxes, the government's share can exceed 50 percent.

D. PRODUCTIVITY IN THE UNITED STATES
   1. The same amount of labor producing more goods and services is known as an increase in productivity.
   2. The higher productivity goes the lower prices could go.

E. PRODUCTIVITY IN THE SERVICE SECTOR
   1. The service sector uses machines such as word processors and computers to increase productivity. Actually these machines may add to the quality of the services, but they do not increase the output per worker which is the definition of productivity.
   2. New measures of productivity for the service economy need to be developed that include quantity as well as quality of output.

F. INFLATION AND THE CONSUMER PRICE INDEX

   1. **INFLATION** refers to a general rise in the price level of goods and services over time.
      a. The CPI measures the price of an average market basket of goods for an average family over time.
      b. **DISINFLATION** describes a condition where the increase in prices is slowing (the inflation rate is declining).
      c. **DEFLATION** means that prices are actually declining, which occurs when countries produce so many goods that people cannot afford to buy them all.

G. RECESSION VERSUS INFLATION
   1. A **RECESSION** is two or more consecutive quarters of decline in the GDP.
   2. A **DEPRESSION** is a severe recession.

LEARNING THE LANGUAGE OF BUSINESS

Match each of the following key terms with the appropriate definition.

A. capitalism
B. command economies
C. communism
D. consumer price index (CPI)
E. demand
F. deflation
G. depression
H. disinflation
I. economics
J. free-market economics
K. gross domestic product (GDP)
L. inflation
M. invisible hand
N. macroeconomics
O. market price
P. microeconomics
Q. mixed economies
R. monopolistic competition
S. monopoly
T. oligopoly
U. perfect competition
V. producer price index (PPI)
W. recession
X. resource development
Y. socialism
Z. supply
AA. unemployment rate

____ 1. A severe recession.

____ 2. The term coined by Adam Smith to describe the mechanism for creating wealth and jobs.

____ 3. Monthly statistics that measure changes in the prices of about 400 goods and services that consumers buy.

____ 4. The study of how society chooses to employ scarce resources to produce various goods and services and distribute them for consumption among various competing groups and individuals.

____ 5. Economic systems in which the government largely decides what goods and services will be produced, who will get them, and how the economy will grow.

____ 6. The quantity of products that people are willing to buy at different prices at a specific time.

____ 7. The total value of goods and services produced in a country in a given year.

____ 8. The number of civilians who are unemployed and tried to find a job with the prior four weeks.

____ 9. When there are two or more consecutive quarters of decline in the GDP.

____ 10. The quantity of products that manufacturers or owners are willing to sell at different prices at a specific time.

____ 11. Economic systems in which decisions about what to produce and in what quantities are decided by the market; that is, by buyers and seller negotiating prices for goods and services.

____ 12. A general rise in the prices of goods and services over time.

____ 13. Economic systems in which some allocation of resources is made by the market and some is made by the government.

____ 14. An economic system in which all or most of the means of production and distribution are privately owned and operated for profit.

____ 15. An economic system based on the premise that most basic businesses should be owned by the government, so that profits can be distributed evenly among the people.

____ 16. A market in which there is only one seller.

____ 17. A situation where prices are actually declining.

Lesson 3

_____ 18. A system in which the state makes all economic decisions and owns all the major forms of production.

_____ 19. A condition where price increases are slowing (the inflation rate is declining).

_____ 20. A form of competition where the market is dominated by just a few sellers.

_____ 21. The market situation where there are a large number of sellers that produce similar products, but the products are perceived by buyers as different.

_____ 22. The market situation where there are many sellers of nearly identical products and no seller is large enough to dictate the price of the product.

_____ 23. A price that is determined by supply and demand, which coincides with the point of intersection between the supply and demand curves.

_____ 24. An index that measures prices at the wholesale level.

_____ 25. The part of economic study that focuses on the nation's overall economy.

_____ 26. The study of how to increase resources and optimize their usage.

_____ 27. The part of economic study that focuses on the behavior of people and organizations in specific markets.

SELF-TEST

1. The study of how to increase the amount of available resources and create conditions that will make better use of these resources is known as:
   A) human resource management.
   B) microeconomics.
   C) econology.
   D) resource development.

2. Adam Smith believed that countries would prosper if individuals within the country prospered, since the way to make money was to provide needed goods and services to others through trade. This was called the:
   A) kinked demand theory.
   B) invisible hand.
   C) stored trade multiplier.
   D) demand accelerator.

3. A typical supply curve suggests that if the price of a good increases, the quantity sellers are willing and able to supply will:
   A) decrease.
   B) increase.
   C) remain constant.
   D) initially decrease, but eventually will start to increase.

4. The markets for breakfast cereal, beer, and automobiles all are dominated by just a few sellers. These markets are best described as:
   A) monopolistic competition.
   B) perfect competition.
   C) an oligopoly.
   D) a monopoly.

5. Under a socialist economic system:
   A) tax rates are kept at extremely low levels.
   B) a major goal of the government is to reduce the inequality in the distribution of wealth.
   C) a major goal of the government is to create incentives to encourage entrepreneurs to create jobs and wealth.
   D) the basic philosophy is that only those that create wealth should be allowed to share in that wealth.

6. Which of the following statements would a follower of Karl Marx likely make?
   A) "Over time, capitalism will become the world's dominant economic system."
   B) "The main problem with capitalism is that it is incapable of generating enough wealth."
   C) "Businesses should be owned by their workers, so that they can share in the wealth the businesses create."
   D) "It is sometimes necessary to accept great disparities in the distribution of wealth in order to create incentives for the creation of even more wealth."

7. A major trend in the world today is that:
   A) free-market economies are moving more toward socialism and socialist economies are moving more toward capitalism.
   B) productivity in the service sector is increasing much more rapidly than productivity in agriculture and manufacturing.
   C) governments in socialist economies are increasing their use of social programs and relying on higher tax rates to finance these programs.
   D) governments in countries with capitalist economies are paying less attention to environmental concerns and issues involving social equality.

8. Perry Stroica, the president of the nation of Ruritania, has announced a plan to shift his economy away from socialism toward a more capitalistic system. Perry realizes that such a change will entail some hardships, and that some citizens will be unhappy with the changes in the economy. The most likely source of unhappiness associated with a move toward capitalism is:
   A) less wealth will be created.
   B) people will have less economic freedom.
   C) tax rates will have to increase.
   D) the distribution of wealth will become less equal.

9. Three major indicators of the economic condition of the United States are the gross domestic product (GDP), the unemployment rate, and the:
   A) debt to equity ratio (DER).
   B) Gross resource utilization index (GRUI).
   C) Consumer price index (CPI).
   D) Index of capital formation (ICF).

10. Kathleen manages a manufacturing plant for ScanRite, Inc., a producer of scanners and other input devices connected to computers. About six months ago, Kathleen asked an assistant to keep track of both work hours and output at her plant. She has compared these figures, and has found that while work hours remained relatively steady over the past six months, the plant's output increased significantly. This indicates that:
    A) the productivity of workers at the ScanRite plant has increased.
    B) the ScanRite plant must have sold off some of its excess inventory.
    C) ScanRite prices have increased faster than the wages it pays to its workers.
    D) Kathleen should hire more workers.

ANSWER KEY

LEARNING THE LANGUAGE OF BUSINESS

1. G
2. M
3. D
4. I
5. B
6. E
7. K
8. AA
9. W
10. Z
11. J
12. L
13. Q
14. A
15. Y
16. S
17. F
18. C
19. H
20. T
21. R
22. U
23. O
24. V
25. N
26. X
27. P

SELF-TEST

Answer	Page #
1. D	Page: 35
2. B	Page: 36
3. B	Page: 39-40
4. C	Page: 41-42
5. B	Page: 43
6. C	Page: 44
7. A	Page: 45-46
8. D	Page: 46
9. C	Page: 49-50
10. A	Page: 52

LESSON

ACCOMMODATING BUSINESS LAW

ASSIGNMENTS

1. Review the Learning Goals and read the Lesson Overview for this lesson.

2. Read the Appendix: Working within the Legal Environment of Business pp. 116-131 in *Understanding Business*, 6th edition by Nickels, McHugh, and McHugh.

3. Watch the video Accommodating Business Law.

4. Review the textbook material.

5. Match the key terms with the correct definitions in the Learning the Language of Business exercise.

6. Take the Self-Test.

7. Use the Answer Key to check your answers and review when necessary.

LEARNING GOALS

After you watch the video, read the textbook, and study this lesson, you should be able to:

1. Distinguish between statutory and common law.

2. Explain the tort system.

3. Identify the purposes and conditions of patents and copyrights.

4. Describe warranties and negotiable instruments as covered in the Uniform Commercial Code.

5. List and describe the conditions necessary to make a legally enforceable contract and describe the possible consequences if such a contract is violated.

6. Summarize several laws that regulate competition in the United States.

7. Distinguish between the various types of bankruptcy as outlined by the Bankruptcy Code.

LESSON NOTES

I. THE NEED FOR LAWS

 A. Laws are an essential part of a civilized nation.

 B. The **JUDICIARY** is the branch of government chosen to oversee the legal system.

 C. Government has stepped in to make laws governing behavior because businesspeople have not taken sufficient steps to make more ethical decisions on their own.

 D. **BUSINESS LAW** refers to the rules, statutes, codes, and regulations established to provide a legal framework within which business may be conducted and that is enforceable in court.

 E. A businessperson should be familiar with the laws regarding product liability, sales, contracts, fair competition, consumer protection, taxes, and bankruptcy.

 F. STATUTORY AND COMMON LAW
  1. **STATUTORY LAW** includes state and federal constitutions, legislative enactments, treaties, and ordinances (written laws).
  2. **COMMON LAW** is the body of the law that comes from judges' decisions.
   a. Also known as unwritten law.
   b. A decision based upon a previous case is called a **PRECEDENT** and is used to guide judges in their handling of new cases.

 G. ADMINISTRATIVE AGENCIES
  1. Branches of government called administrative agencies issue rules, regulations, and orders.
  2. **ADMINISTRATIVE AGENCIES** are institutions created by Congress with delegated power to pass rules and regulations within its mandated area of authority.
  3. Administrative agencies hold quasi-legislative, quasi-executive, and quasi-judicial powers.
   a. The agency is allowed to pass rules and regulations within its area of authority, conduct investigations, and hold hearings when rules and regulations have been violated.
   b. They issue more rulings and settle more disputes than courts.

II. TORT LAW

 A. A **TORT** is a wrongful conduct that causes injury to another person's body, property, or reputation.
  1. An intentional tort is a willful act purposely inflicted that results in injury.
  2. **NEGLIGENCE** deals with questionable but unintentional behavior that causes harm or injury.
  3. Product liability is one of the more controversial areas of tort law,

 B. PRODUCT LIABILITY
  1. **PRODUCT LIABILITY** is covered under tort law and holds businesses liable for negligence in the production, design, sale, or use of products it markets.
  2. **STRICT PRODUCT LIABILITY** means without regard to fault; that is, a company could be liable for damages caused by placing a product on the market with an unknown defect.
  3. The rule of strict liability has caused serious problems for some manufacturers.
  4. Manufacturers of chemicals and drugs are lobbying Congress to set damage limits.

III. LAWS PROTECTING IDEAS: PATENTS, COPYRIGHTS, AND TRADEMARKS

    A. A **PATENT** gives inventors exclusive rights to their inventions for 20 years.
       1. Patents owners may sell or license the use of the patent to others.
       2. Patents are filed with the U.S. Patent Office.
       3. Penalties for violating a patent can be severe. Kodak lost millions of dollars for infringing on a Polaroid patent.
       4. Some 60% of patent applications are approved, costing the inventor a minimum of $6,600, fees over the life of the patent.
       5. Critics argue that some inventors use a submarine patent, intentionally delaying a patent application and waiting for others to develop the technology.

    B. A **COPYRIGHT** protects an individual's rights to materials such as books, articles, photos, and cartoons.
       1. Copyrights are filed with the Library of Congress and involve a minimum of paperwork.
       2. They last for the lifetime of the author or artist plus 50 years.

    C. A **TRADEMARK** gives exclusive legal protection to a name, symbol, or design (or combination them) that identifies one seller's goods or services from those of competitors. Trademarks generally belong to the owner forever.

IV. SALES LAW: THE UNIFORM COMMERCIAL CODE

    A. The **UNIFORM COMMERCIAL CODE (UCC)** is a comprehensive commercial law adopted by states; it covers sales laws and other commercial law.
       1. The 11 articles of the UCC cover sales; commercial paper; bank deposits and collections; letters of credit; bulk transfers; warehouse receipts, bills of lading, and other documents of title; investment securities; and secured transactions.
       2. The text discusses two of these articles: article 2 (warranties) and article 3 (negotiable instruments).

    B. WARRANTIES
       1. **EXPRESS WARRANTIES** are specific representations by the seller regarding the goods.
       2. **IMPLIED WARRANTIES** are guarantees legally imposed on the seller.
       3. A full warranty requires a seller to replace or repair a product at no charge if the product is defective.
       4. Limited warranties typically limit the problems that are covered.

    C. NEGOTIABLE INSTRUMENTS
       1. **NEGOTIABLE INSTRUMENTS** are forms of commercial paper (such as checks) that are transferable among businesses and individuals.
       2. Negotiable instruments must be:
          a. written and signed by the maker.
          b. made payable on demand at a certain time.
          c. made payable to the bearer or to order.
          d. contain an unconditional promise to pay a specified amount of money.
       3. Checks or other forms of negotiable instruments are transferred when the payee ENDORSES, signs the back of the check.

V. CONTRACT LAW

    A. TERMS
       1. A **CONTRACT** is a legally enforceable agreement between two or more parties.
       2. **CONTRACT LAW** specifies what a legally enforceable agreement is.

B. A contract is legally binding if the following conditions are met:
1. An offer is made.
2. There must be voluntary acceptance of the offer.
3. Both parties must give **CONSIDERATION** (something of value).
4. Both parties must be competent.
5. The contract must be legal.
6. The contract must be in a proper form.

C. BREACH OF CONTRACT
1. **BREACH OF CONTRACT** means that one party fails to follow the terms of the contract.
2. Consequences of a breached contract are:
   a. Specific performance - The person violating the contract may be required to live up to the agreement if no monetary award is adequate.
   b. Payment of damages - The monetary settlement, or **DAMAGES**, is awarded to a person who is injured by a breach of contract.
   c. Discharge of the obligation.
3. It is best to have a contract in writing. A contract should: (1) be in writing, (2) specify the consideration, and (3) be clearly offered and accepted.

VI. LAWS TO PROMOTE FAIR AND COMPETITIVE PRACTICES

A. Businesses once operated under relatively free market conditions and were able to drive smaller competitors out of business with little recourse.

B. THE HISTORY OF ANTITRUST LEGISLATION
1. The Sherman Antitrust Act of 1890, forbids contracts, combinations, or conspiracies in restraint of trade and actual monopolies or attempts to monopolize any part of trade or commerce.
2. Legal clarification of the concepts of the Sherman Act:
   a. The Clayton Act of 1914, prohibits exclusive dealing, tying contracts, interlocking directorates, and buying large amounts of stock in competing corporations.
   b. The Federal Trade Commission Act of 1914, prohibits unfair methods of competition in commerce and created the Federal Trade Commission.
   c. The Robinson-Patman Act of 1936, prohibits price discrimination.

VII. LAWS TO PROTECT CONSUMERS

A. **CONSUMERISM** is a social movement that seeks to increase and strengthen the rights and powers of buyers.

B. President John F. Kennedy identified four basic rights of consumers:
1. The right to safety.
2. The right to be informed.
3. The right to choose.
4. The right to be heard.

VIII. TAX LAWS

A. **TAXES** are government's way of raising money.

B. Taxes are also government's way of discouraging citizens from doing what it considers harmful (for example, sin taxes on cigarettes and alcohol).

C. Government encourages businesses to hire new employees or purchase new equipment by offering a tax credit.

D. Taxes are levied from a variety of sources.
1. Income, sales, and property are the major bases of tax revenue.
2. The tax policies of states and cities are taken into consideration when businesses seek to locate operations.

IX. BANKRUPTCY LAW

A. **BANKRUPTCY** is the legal process by which a person or business, unable to meet financial obligations, is relieved of those debts by having the court divide any assets among creditors, freeing the debtor to begin anew.

B. AMENDMENTS TO THE BANKRUPTCY LAW
1. The Bankruptcy Amendments of 1984 allow a person who is bankrupt to keep part of the equity in a house.
2. The Bankruptcy Reform Act of 1994 creates reforms that speed up and simplify the process

C. In 1999 over 1.3 million Americans filed for bankruptcy over 90% of filings each year are by individuals.

D. Bankruptcy can be either voluntary or involuntary.
1. **VOLUNTARY BANKRUPTCY** involves legal procedures filed by a debtor.
2. **INVOLUNTARY BANKRUPTCY** involves bankruptcy procedures initiated by a debtor's creditors.

E. Bankruptcy procedures are filed under one of the following sections of the bankruptcy code:
1. Chapter 7 - Straight bankruptcy or liquidation; used by businesses and individuals.
2. Chapter 11 - Reorganization; used by businesses and some individuals.
3. Chapter 13 - Repayment; used by individuals.

F. Chapter 7 calls for straight bankruptcy, which requires the sale of nonexempt assets of debtors.
1. Cash from the sale is divided among creditors.
2. First, creditors with secured claims are paid and then the unsecured claims are paid.
3. The text lists the order that unsecured claims are paid.

G. Chapter 11 allows a company to reorganize and continue operations while paying only a limited proportion of its debts.
1. The Bankruptcy Reform Act of 1994 extends a fast track procedure for small businesses filing under Chapter 11.
2. Under Chapter 11 a company continues to operate, but has court protection against creditor lawsuits while it tries to work out a debt repayment plan.
3. Less than 25% of Chapter 11 companies emerge healthy.
4. In 1991 the U.S. Supreme Court ruled that individuals have the right to file bankruptcy under Chapter 11.

H. Chapter 13 permits individuals, including small-business owners, to pay back creditors over a three to five year period.

X. DEREGULATION

A. **DEREGULATION** means that the government withdraws certain laws and regulations that seem to hinder competition.

B. Business and government need to continue to work together to create a competitive environment that is fair and open.
C. There have recently been calls for new regulations in some industries it seems that some regulation of business is necessary to assure fair and honest dealings with the public.
D. If businesses do not want additional regulation, they must accept and respond to the responsibilities they have to society.

LEARNING THE LANGUAGE OF BUSINESS

Match each of the following key terms with the appropriate definition.

A. administrative agencies
B. bankruptcy
C. breach of contract
D. business law
E. common law
F. consideration
G. consumerism
H. contract
I. contract law
J. copyright
K. damages
L. deregulation
M. express warranties
N. implied warranties
O. involuntary bankruptcy
P. judiciary
Q. negligence
R. negotiable instruments
S. patent
T. precedent
U. product liability
V. statutory law
W. strict product liability
X. taxes
Y. tort
Z. trademark
AA. Uniform Commercial Code (UCC)
BB. voluntary bankruptcy

____ 1. Exclusive rights for inventors to their inventions for 17 years.
____ 2. Bankruptcy procedures filed by a debtor's creditors.
____ 3. A social movement that tries to increase the rights and powers of buyers in relation to sellers.
____ 4. Laws that specify what constitutes a legally enforceable agreement.
____ 5. The branch of government chosen to oversee the legal system.
____ 6. The body of law that comes from judges' decisions; also known as "unwritten law."
____ 7. A legally protected name, or design (or combination of these) that identifies the goods or services of one seller and distinguishes them from those of competitors.
____ 8. State and federal constitutions, legislative enactments, treaties, and ordinances (written laws).
____ 9. The legal process by which a person or business, unable to meet financial obligations, is relieved of those debts by having the court divide any assets among creditors, freeing the debtor to begin anew.
____ 10. A comprehensive commercial law adopted by every state in the United States; it covers sales laws and other commercial law.
____ 11. The monetary settlement awarded to a person who is injured by a breach of contract.
____ 12. Guarantees legally imposed on the seller.
____ 13. Wrongful conduct that causes injury to another person's body, property, or reputation.
____ 14. Institutions created by Congress with delegated power to pass rules and regulations within its mandated area of authority.
____ 15. Rules, statutes, codes, and regulations established to provide a legal framework within which business may be conducted and that is enforceable in court.
____ 16. Something of value; it is one of the requirements of a legal contract.
____ 17. Exclusive rights to materials such as books, articles, photos, and cartoons.
____ 18. Specific representations by the seller regarding the goods.
____ 19. Forms of commercial paper (such as checks) that are transferable among businesses and individuals.
____ 20. Federal, state, and local governments way of raising money.
____ 21. A legally enforceable agreement between two or more parties.
____ 22. Holds businesses liable for negligence in the production, design, sale, or use of products it markets.
____ 23. Government withdrawal of certain laws and regulations that seem to hinder competition (for example, airline regulations).
____ 24. Legal procedures initiated by a debtor.
____ 25. Violation when one party fails to follow the terms of a contract.
____ 26. A behavior that causes unintentional harm or injury.
____ 27. A decision made by a judge in an earlier case used to guide the handling of a new case.
____ 28. The legal responsibility for harm or injury caused by a product regardless of fault.

SELF-TEST

1. The government regulates business activities even though businesses would prefer to set their own standards of behavior. Government has intervened because:
   A) the relationships between businesses and other parties are more complex.
   B) business has not been perceived as implementing acceptable practices fast enough for the public.
   C) the judiciary branch of the government reflects the needs and changes in society.
   D) there has been an increase in the number and compensation of lawyers.

2. Usually, the remedy for a tort is:
   A) imprisonment.
   B) a breach of contract.
   C) bankruptcy.
   D) monetary compensation.

3. The intent of a patent is to:
   A) increase competition in the marketplace.
   B) reward innovation and hard work of inventors.
   C) slow the growth of monopolies.
   D) encourage copycat inventions.

4. You promise to pay your sister tomorrow the $25 that you owe her. This promise is not a negotiable instrument because:
   A) it is not in writing.
   B) it is not payable at a specific time.
   C) it is not a promise to pay a specific amount.
   D) it does not contain an unconditional promise.

5. Which of the following claims receive priority when assets are distributed among creditors in a bankruptcy case?
   A) Wages, salaries, and commissions.
   B) Refunds to customers.
   C) Costs involved in the bankruptcy case.
   D) Employee benefit plan contributions

6. The purpose of the Sherman Antitrust Act was to:
   A) prevent large organizations from dominating a market.
   B) avoid the problem of small business failures.
   C) encourage the growth of large-scale efficiency found in big businesses.
   D) minimize the inconsistency of multiple dealers of a single product.

7. The *Griggs v. Duke Power Company* (1971) case established a precedent on the need to use job-related tests in employment practices. Similar court cases have been decided on the basis of this decision. This is an example of:
   A) common law.
   B) statutory law.
   C) administrative law.
   D) criminal law.

8. A software development firm based in Florida and conducting business in Texas is unsure about the differences in state laws regarding business transactions. What body of laws standardizes regulations dealing with business transactions?
   A) Uniform Commercial Code
   B) Universal Business Regulations
   C) National Commercial Rules
   D) Unified Commercial Regulations

9. You and your boss agree to terminate your employment contract because you desire to devote more time to school. This breach of contract would likely be resolved by:
   A) a specific performance requirement.
   B) the payment of damages.
   C) a judge.
   D) a discharge of obligation

10. Without the permission of the inventor, Cheatum Automobile Manufacturing copied the engine design of an innovative competitor. Cheatum is guilty of:
    A) corporate liability.
    B) trademark infringement.
    C) innovative product research.
    D) patent infringement.

ANSWER KEY

LEARNING THE LANGUAGE OF BUSINESS

1. S
2. O
3. G
4. I
5. P
6. E
7. Z
8. V
9. B
10. AA
11. K
12. N
13. Y
14. A
15. D
16. F
17. J
18. M
19. R
20. X
21. H
22. U
23. L
24. BB
25. C
26. Q
27. T
28. W

SELF-TEST

Answer	Page #
1. B	Page: 116
2. D	Page: 118
3. B	Page: 120
4. A	Page: 121-122
5. C	Page: 128
6. A	Page: 123
7. A	Page: 117
8. A	Page: 121
9. D	Page: 123
10. D	Page: 120

LESSON 5

CONTENDING WITH GOVERNMENT INVOLVEMENT

ASSIGNMENTS

1. Review the Learning Goals and read the Lesson Overview for this lesson.

2. Read Chapter 2 pp. 53-56 in *Understanding Business,* 6th edition by Nickels, McHugh, and McHugh.

3. Watch the video Contending with Government Involvement.

4. Review the textbook material.

5. Match the key terms with the correct definitions in the Learning the Language of Business exercise.

6. Take the Self-Test.

7. Use the Answer Key to check your answers and review when necessary.

LEARNING GOALS

After you watch the video, read the textbook, and study this lesson, you should be able to:

1. Describe monetary policy and its importance to the economy.

2. Discuss fiscal policy and its importance to the economy.

LESSON NOTES

I. MONETARY POLICY

    A. **MONETARY POLICY** is the management of the money placed into the economy and the management of interest rates.
        1. The Federal Reserve System is responsible for managing the money supply. Its goal is to keep the economy growing without causing inflation.
            a. The Federal Reserve System is responsible for managing the money supply.
            b. The Federal Reserve System operates independently of the president and Congress and has the goal of keeping the economy growing without causing inflation.

    B. Tight versus loose monetary policy
        1. Fed can curb inflation by decreasing the money available and discouraging borrowing.
            a. It does this by cutting the money supply and raising interest rates.
            b. Production is cut back slowing the economy and lowering inflation.

II. FISCAL POLICY

    A. **FISCAL POLICY** is the government efforts to keep the economy stable by increasing or decreasing taxes and/or government spending.
        1. For many years, federal expenses have been exceeding federal revenues – the result is an increasing federal debt.
        2. The money paid for interest on the debt is so high that it drains money from the economy.
        3. In the late 1990s the government had a surplus, when the revenues exceeded the spending.
            a. There is much debate as to what to do with a surplus.

    B. The **NATIONAL DEBT** is the sum of all the federal deficits over time.

LEARNING THE LANGUAGE OF BUSINESS

Match each of the following key terms with the appropriate definition.

A. fiscal policy
B. monetary policy
C. national debt

____ 1. The sum of all the federal deficits over time.

____ 2. The management of the amount of money placed into the economy by the government and the management of interest rates

____ 3. Government efforts to keep the economy stable by increasing or decreasing taxes or government spending.

SELF-TEST

1. In the United States, the control of the money supply is the responsibility of the:
   A) United States Treasury.
   B) Federal Reserve System.
   C) Department of State.
   D) Federal Deposit Insurance Corporation.

2. Efforts by the Federal Reserve System to control the money supply and interest rates are known as:
   A) fiscal policy.
   B) incomes policy.
   C) monetary policy.
   D) securities policy.

3. When the government attempts to keep the economy stable by increasing or decreasing taxes and/or government spending, its efforts are referred to as:
   A) monetary policy.
   B) incomes policy.
   C) fiscal policy.
   D) cyclical policy.

4. The main reason the federal government ran a budget surplus in the late 1990s was that:
   A) it made dramatic cuts in spending for social programs in the mid and late 1990s.
   B) it passed the largest tax increase in history in 1998.
   C) the economy grew very rapidly.
   D) it switched to a new accounting system that identified additional sources of government revenue.

5. When the federal government spends more in a year than it receives in tax revenues, the result is called a:
   A) federal reserve allowance.
   B) GDP deflator.
   C) balance of payments deficit.
   D) federal deficit.

6. When the government attempts to keep the economy stable by increasing or decreasing taxes and/or government spending, it is engaging in:
   A) monetary policy.
   B) incomes policy.
   C) fiscal policy.
   D) physical policy

7. Senator Bud Jette is alarmed at the state of the economy. Unemployment is high and GDP is low. Senator Jette has called for Congress to take decisive action to increase its expenditures and cut taxes in order to stimulate the economy. The actions called for by Senator Jette are examples of the government's use of:
   A) monetary policy.
   B) fiscal policy.
   C) incomes policy.
   D) social investment policy.

8. When the government runs a budget deficit it adds to the:
   A) national debt.
   B) balance of payments deficit.
   C) treasury deficit.
   D) aggregate federal liability.

9. Your local newspaper has a story in its business section that reports that government spending will again exceed tax revenues. This means that the:
   A) national debt will increase.
   B) balance of payments will experience yet another deficit.
   C) rate of inflation is likely to fall.
   D) monetary policies pursued by the Fed have been too loose.

10. The Federal Reserve System operates:
    A) independently of the president and Congress.
    B) under the direction of the executive branch of the government.
    C) under the direction of the Banking Oversight Committee of Congress.
    D) as a special branch of the U.S. Treasury.

ANSWER KEY

LEARNING THE LANGUAGE OF BUSINESS

1. C
2. B
3. A

SELF-TEST

Answer	Page #
1. B	Page: 53
2. C	Page: 53
3. C	Page: 54
4. C	Page: 54
5. D	Page: 54
6. C	Page: 54
7. B	Page: 54
8. A	Page: 54
9. A	Page: 54
10. A	Page: 54

LESSON 6

PROMOTING SOCIAL RESPONSIBILITY

ASSIGNMENTS

1. Review the Learning Goals and read the Lesson Overview for this lesson.

2. Read Chapter 4 pp. 94-112 in *Understanding Business,* 6th edition by Nickels, McHugh, and McHugh.

3. Watch the video Promoting Social Responsibility.

4. Review the textbook material.

5. Match the key terms with the correct definitions in the Learning the Language of Business exercise.

6. Take the Self-Test.

7. Use the Answer Key to check your answers and review when necessary.

LEARNING GOALS

After you watch the video, read the textbook, and study this lesson, you should be able to:

1. Explain why legality is only the first step in behaving ethically.

2. Ask the three questions one should answer when faced with a potentially unethical action.

3. Describe management's role in setting ethical standards.

4. Distinguish between compliance-based and integrity-based ethics codes, and list the six-steps in setting up a corporate ethics code.

5. Define social responsibility and examine corporate responsibility to various stakeholders.

6. Analyze the role of American businesses in influencing ethical behavior and social responsibility in global markets.

LESSON NOTES

The Profile at the beginning of this chapter focuses on Judy and Chuck Ruggeri, owners of Fantastic Sams hair salons in Pennsylvania. The Ruggeris volunteer their services in hospitals and preschools, and have their stylists go to the homes of the elderly. Active in numerous charities and community services the Ruggeris are a great example of the "good neighbor," socially responsible business.

I. MANAGING BUSINESS ETHICALLY AND RESPONSIBLY

    A. Ethical behavior can influence your success in business.

    B. **SOCIAL RESPONSIBILITY** means that a business shows concern for the welfare of society as a whole.

    C. LEGALITY IS ONLY THE FIRST ETHICAL STANDARD
       1. Moral and ethical behavior is not the same as following the dictates of the law.
          a. Social responsibility and moral and ethical behavior go beyond the law.
          b. **ETHICS** refers to the standards of moral behavior; that is, behavior that is accepted by society as right or wrong.
          c. Legality only refers to laws we have written to protect ourselves from immoral acts.

    D. PERSONAL ETHICS BEGIN AT HOME
       1. Society as a whole is not too socially minded.
          a. A recent study revealed that most Americans have some issues of morality.
          b. Nearly one-third said they never contributed to a charity.
          c. Seventy percent of U.S. high school students said they had cheated on an exam within the last year.
       2. Three ethics check questions can help individuals and organizations be sure their decisions are ethical:
          a. Is it legal?
          b. Is it balanced?
              1) Will I win everything at the expense of another party?
              2) An ethics-based manager tries to make decisions that benefit all parties involved.
          c. How will it make me feel about myself?
       3. Individuals and companies that develop a strong ethics code and have a better chance than most of behaving ethically.

    E. ETHICS IS MORE THAN AN INDIVIDUAL CONCERN
       1. Some managers think ethics is a personal matter, and that they are not responsible for an individual's misdeeds.
       2. Individuals do not usually act alone they need the implied, if not the direct, cooperation of others to behave unethically in a corporation.
       3. After experiencing numerous ethical problems with their automotive services, Sears replaced 23,000 pages of policies and procedures with a simple common sense booklet called Freedoms & Obligations.

    F. ORGANIZATIONAL ETHICS BEGINS AT THE TOP
       1. People learn their standards and values from observing what others do, not from what they say.
       2. Corporate values are instilled in employees by the leadership and example of strong top managers.

3. In companies such as IBM and Xerox a high value system has become pervasive, and employees feel part of a corporate mission that is socially beneficial.
4. There are many reasons why a business should be managed ethically.
    a. To maintain a good reputation, keep existing customers, attract new customers, or avoid lawsuits.
    b. To reduce turnover or avoid government intervention.
    c. To please customers, employees, and society.
    d. Because it is the right thing to do.

II. SETTING CORPORATE ETHICAL STANDARDS

   A. Although ethics codes vary greatly, they can be classified into two major categories: compliance-based and integrity-based.
      1. **COMPLIANCE-BASED ETHICS CODES** emphasize preventing unlawful behavior by increasing control and by penalizing wrongdoers.
      2. **INTEGRITY-BASED ETHICS CODES** define the organization's guiding values, create an environment that supports ethically sound behavior, and stress a shared accountability among employees.

   B. A long-term improvement of business ethics calls for a six-step approach to enforcing ethics codes.
      1. Top management must adopt and unconditionally support an explicit corporate code of conduct.
      2. Employees must understand that expectations for ethical behavior begin at the top and that senior management expects all employees to act accordingly.
      3. Managers and others must be trained to consider the ethical implications of all business decisions.
      4. An ethics office must be set up. Phone lines should be established so those employees who don't want to be seen with an ethics officer can inquire about ethical matters anonymously.
      5. Outsiders such as suppliers, subcontractors, distributors, and customers must be told about the ethics program.
         a. Often pressure to put aside ethical considerations comes from the outside.
         b. It helps employees resist such pressure when everyone knows what the ethical standards are.
      6. The ethics code must be enforced.
         a. One important step is the selection of an ethics officer.
         b. This officer will communicate to employees and set a positive tone.

III. CORPORATE SOCIAL RESPONSIBILITY

   A. The social performance of a company has several dimensions:
      1. **CORPORATE PHILANTHROPY** includes charitable donations to nonprofit organizations.
      2. **CORPORATE RESPONSIBILITY** includes everything from minority hiring to the making of safe products, and more.
      3. **CORPORATE POLICY** refers to the position a firm takes on issues that affect the firm and society.

   B. Impact of corporations on society
      1. Many people get a negative view of the impact that companies have on society.
      2. Many companies have made commitments to volunteerism.
      3. In a recent survey, two-thirds of the MBA students surveyed said that they would take a lower salary to work for a socially responsible company.

4. Social responsibility is seen differently through the eyes of various stakeholders to whom businesses are responsible.

C. RESPONSIBILITY TO CUSTOMERS
1. Business is responsible to satisfy customers with goods and services of real value.
2. Pleasing the customer is not as easy as it seems.
3. Three out of five new businesses fail perhaps because their owners failed to please their customers.
4. Socially conscious behaviors could bring in new customers.

D. RESPONSIBILITY TO INVESTORS
1. Milton Friedman has said that corporate social responsibility means making money for stockholders.
2. Some believe that before you can do good, you must do well; others believe that by doing good, you can also do well.
3. Many people believe that it makes financial as well as moral sense to invest in companies that are planning ahead to create a better environment.
4. Some investors commit **INSIDER TRADING** when they use private company information to make gains.

E. RESPONSIBILITY TO EMPLOYEES
1. Businesses have a responsibility to create jobs.
2. Business has an obligation to see to it that hard work and talent is fairly rewarded.
3. If a business treats the employees with respect the employees will respect the business.

F. RESPONSIBILITY TO SOCIETY
1. A major responsibility of business to society is to create new wealth.
    a. Most nonprofits own shares of publicly held companies.
    b. As those share prices increase, funds are available to benefit society.
2. Businesses are responsible for promoting social justice.
    a. For its own well being, business depends on its employees being active in civil society such as politics, law, churches, arts and charities.
    b. Many companies use group volunteer projects to improve their communities.
3. Business is responsible for contributing to making its own environment a better place.
4. Many corporations are publishing reports that document their net social contribution.

G. SOCIAL AUDITING
1. How can you know how well organizations are making social responsiveness an integral part of top management's decision making?
2. A **SOCIAL AUDIT** is a systematic evaluation of an organization's progress toward implementing programs that are socially responsible and responsive.
3. Problems related to social auditing:
    a. It is difficult to define what socially responsible and being responsive are.
    b. Business activities and their effects on society are difficult to measure.
4. Some suggest that positive actions should be added up, then negative effects be subtracted to get a net social contribution.
5. Four groups serve as watchdogs regarding how well companies enforce their ethical and social responsibility policies:
    a. Socially conscious investors, who insist that companies extend the company's own high standards to all their suppliers.
    b. Environmentalists, who apply pressure by naming companies that don't abide by the environmentalists' standards.
    c. Union officials, who hunt down violations and force companies to comply in order to avoid, negative publicity.

d. Customers, who take their business elsewhere if a company demonstrates socially irresponsible practices.

IV. INTERNATIONAL ETHICS AND SOCIAL RESPONSIBILITY

   A. Ethical problems are not unique to the United States.
      1. The text gives the examples of the recent "influence peddling" in Japan, South Korea, and China.
      2. What is new in international ethics is that leaders are being held to new, higher standards.

   B. Many American businesses are demanding socially responsible behavior from international suppliers.
      1. They make sure their suppliers do not violate U.S. human rights and environmental standards.
      2. In contrast there are companies such Nike that have often been criticized for the low pay and long hours of factory workers in Asia.
      3. Should international suppliers be required to adhere to American ethical standards? What about countries where child labor is an accepted part of society? What about multi-national corporations?
         a. None of these questions are easy to answer.
         b. They show how complex social responsibility issues are in international markets.

LEARNING THE LANGUAGE OF BUSINESS

Match each of the following key terms with the appropriate definition.

A. compliance-based ethics codes
B. corporate philanthropy
C. corporate policy
D. corporate responsibility
E. ethics
F. insider trading
G. integrity-based ethics codes
H. social audit
I. social responsibility

____ 1. A business's concern for the welfare of society as a whole.

____ 2. A systematic evaluation of an organization's progress toward implementing programs that are socially responsible and responsive.

____ 3. Dimension of social responsibility that includes charitable donations.

____ 4. Standards of behavior, or behavior society see as right.

____ 5. Ethical standards that emphasize preventing unlawful behavior by increasing control and by penalizing wrongdoers.

____ 6. Dimension of social responsibility that includes everything from minority hiring practices to the making of safe products.

____ 7. Dimension of social responsibility that refers to the position a firm takes on social and political issues.

____ 8. Ethical standards that define the organization's guiding values, create an environment that supports ethically sound behavior, and stress a shared accountability among employees.

____ 9. When investors use private company information for their personal financial gain.

SELF-TEST

1. The laws we have written establish the standards of _____ behavior.
   A) ethical
   B) legal
   C) moral
   D) socially responsible

2. Three "ethics check questions" often help individuals and organizations in deciding if their decisions are ethical. All of the following are "ethics check questions" **except**:
   A) Is it legal?
   B) Is it balanced?
   C) Has it been done before?
   D) How will it make me feel about myself?

3. Bill is concerned that his firm is suffering from low morale as a result of a recent television news report showing his firm using immigrant labor in unsafe, sweatshop conditions. Which ethics-based question would have helped Bill avoid this self-esteem problem?
   A) Is it legal?
   B) Is it balanced?
   C) How will it make me feel about myself?
   D) Is it consistent with our stockholders' goals?

4. Jako Corporation has recently instituted a new corporate ethics code. Diane Jako, president of the company, knows that ethical relationships are based on:
   A) trust and cooperation.
   B) strict penalties for illegal activities.
   C) a well-developed corporate code of ethics.
   D) government observers within the company.

5. Corporate values are :
   A) a personal matter to be determined by each employee.
   B) taught by attending company-sponsored seminars.
   C) instilled by the leadership of outside consultants.
   D) learned by observing the actions of others in the organization.

6. Which of the following would be a unique focus of an integrity-based ethics code?
   A) Increased control over employee actions.
   B) Shared accountability among employees.
   C) Penalties for wrongdoers.
   D) Awareness of the relevant laws.

7. In an effort to help employees resist the pressure to make an unethical decision, the Johnston Petroleum Company has communicated their code of ethics statement to outsiders. Suppliers, subcontractors, distributors, and customers have been told of the firm's core values. This approach is consistent with:
   A) an integrity-based ethics code.
   B) a compliance-based ethics code.
   C) government regulatory mandates.
   D) corporate philanthropy.

8. XYZ Distributing feels that money is the answer to all social responsibility issues. The firm believes the more they give, the better corporate citizen they are. XYZ is most concerned with:
   A) corporate responsibility.
   B) corporate philanthropy.
   C) corporate structure and function.
   D) corporate profits.

9. The vice president of human resources at Ato Enterprises feels strongly that workers need to see that hard work, skill, and talent pay off. This is consistent with which of the following:
   A) the firm's responsibility to customers.
   B) the firm's responsibility to investors.
   C) the firm's responsibility to society.
   D) A the firm's responsibility to employees.

10. Recently, it has come to the public's attention that political leaders in Japan and South Korea have been involved in "influence peddling." This realization has likely:
    A) been ignored by the citizens of the countries.
    B) caused the public to demand higher standards of their leaders.
    C) encouraged others to participate in this practice.
    D) increased the desire for international trade with these countries.

ANSWER KEY

LEARNING THE LANGUAGE OF BUSINESS

1. I
2. H
3. B
4. E
5. A
6. D
7. C
8. G
9. F

SELF-TEST

Answer	Page #
1. B	Page: 96
2. C	Page: 98
3. C	Page: 98-99
4. A	Page: 101-103
5. D	Page: 99
6. B	Page: 101
7. A	Page: 101
8. B	Page: 103
9. D	Page: 106
10. B	Page: 110

LESSON 7

COMPETING IN A GLOBAL ENVIRONMENT

ASSIGNMENTS

1. Review the Learning Goals and read the Lesson Overview for this lesson.

2. Read Chapter 3 pp. 62-90 in *Understanding Business*, 6th edition by Nickels, McHugh, and McHugh.

3. Watch the video *Competing in a Global Environment*

4. Review the textbook material.

5. Match the key terms with the correct definitions in the Learning the Language of Business exercise.

6. Take the Self-Test.

7. Use the Answer Key to check your answers and review when necessary.

LEARNING GOALS

After you watch the video, read the textbook, and study this lesson, you should be able to:

1. Discuss the growing importance of the global market and the roles of comparative advantage and absolute advantage in international trade.

2. Explain the importance of importing and exporting, and understand key terms used in international business.

3. Describe the current status of the United States in global business.

4. Illustrate the strategies used in reaching global markets.

5. Evaluate the forces that affect trading in world markets.

6. Debate the advantages and disadvantages of trade protectionism.

7. Explain the role of multinational corporations in global markets.

8. Explain how technology affects global e-commerce.

LESSON NOTES

The PROFILE at the beginning of this chapter focuses on Mary Lou Wilson of Enrich International. Her foresight and enthusiasm had her suggest that Japan be chosen for a target in Enrich International's global market expansion. Wilson believed that to succeed in Japan you had to know Japanese culture. She immersed herself in the Japanese culture. Her company's herbal beauty products have Japanese sales of over $13 million a month. Many U.S. business people like Mary Lou Wilson are finding vast opportunities in the global market.

I. THE DYNAMIC GLOBAL MARKET.

   A. A few statistics can help illustrate the importance of international markets:
      1. Whereas there are 280 million people in the U.S., there are over 6 billion potential customers in the world.
      2. Of these, approximately 75% live in developing areas.
      3. The U.S. is the largest importer in the world. It is often the world's largest exporter as well.
         a. **IMPORTING** is buying products from another country.
         b. **EXPORTING** is selling products to another country.
      4. Competition is intense; the U.S. must compete against aggressive exporters.

   B. The purpose of this chapter is to discuss the potential and problems of international business.

II. WHY TRADE WITH OTHER NATIONS?

   A. Reasons for trading with other nations include:
      1. No nation can produce all the products it needs.
      2. Nations demand trade with countries to meet the needs of their people.
      3. Trade relations enable countries to produce what they can and buy the rest in a mutually beneficial exchange.

   B. **FREE TRADE** is the movement of goods and services among nations without political or economic obstruction.

   C. THE THEORIES OF COMPARATIVE AND ABSOLUTE ADVANTAGE
      1. **COMPARATIVE ADVANTAGE THEORY** states that a country should produce and sell to other countries those products that it produces most efficiently and should buy from other countries those products it cannot produce as effectively or efficiently.
      2. **ABSOLUTE ADVANTAGE** exists when a country has a monopoly on producing a product or is able to produce it at a cost below that of all other countries.

III. GETTING INVOLVED IN GLOBAL TRADE

   A. The real potential in global markets may be with small businesses, which generate about half of the private sector commerce, but account for only 20% of exports.

   B. Getting started in global trade is often a matter of observation, determination, and risk.

   C. IMPORTING GOODS AND SERVICES
      1. Foreign students attending U.S. schools often notice some products widely available in their countries are not available here.
      2. Importing these goods into the U.S. can be quite profitable.

D. EXPORTING GOODS AND SERVICES
1. Exporting is selling products to another country.
2. What can you sell to other countries?
   a. Just about anything of quality you can sell in the United States.
   b. The text offers the example of snowplows sold to Saudi Arabia for cleaning sand from their driveways.
3. Selling in global markets involves many hurdles.
4. The text supplies several sources for information about exporting including a government pamphlet, a trade magazine, and the SBA.

E. MEASURING GLOBAL TRADE
1. **BALANCE OF TRADE** is the relationship of exports to imports.
2. **TRADE DEFICIT** is buying more goods from other nations than are sold to them.
3. **BALANCE OF PAYMENTS** is the difference between money coming into a country (from exports) and money leaving the country (for imports plus money flows from other factors such as tourism, foreign aid, and military expenditures).
   a. A favorable balance of payments means more money is flowing into than flowing out of the country.
   b. Likewise, an unfavorable balance of payments means more money is leaving than coming into the country.
4. **DUMPING** is the practice of selling products for less in a foreign country than is charged in the producing country.
   a. The U.S. has laws against dumping by foreign firms.
   b. Dumping can take time to prove as some governments subsidize certain industries to sell goods in global markets for less.

IV. TRADING IN GLOBAL MARKETS: THE U.S. EXPERIENCE

A. Even though 95% of the world's population lives outside of the U.S., America has never been very good at exporting.
   1. In the early 1980s, no more than 10% of American businesses exported products.
   2. Now a majority of large businesses are involved in global trade and growing numbers of small businesses are going global.

B. Although the United States is the world's largest exporter, it does not export a significant percentage of its products.
   1. The U.S. buys more goods from other nations that it sells to other nations called a trade deficit or unfavorable balance of trade.

C. During the 1980s, it was widely reported that the United States had become a debtor nation, that is, a country that owes more money to other nations than they owe it.
   1. This is not necessarily a bad sign when foreign businesses invest here.
   2. There is a trend emerging toward more foreign direct investment in the U.S.

V. STRATEGIES FOR REACHING GLOBAL MARKETS

A. LICENSING
   1. **LICENSING** involves granting to a foreign company the right to manufacture its product or use its trademark on a fee basis.
   2. The advantages of licensing are:
      a. A business can gain additional revenues from a product it would not have normally produced domestically.
      b. A business can gain additional revenues from the sale of startup supplies, component materials, and consulting services from the licensing firm.

      c. Licensor spends little or no money to produce and market the product.
  3. The disadvantages of licensing are:
     a. Often a firm must grant licensing rights to its product for an extended period.
     b. If a product experiences remarkable growth in the foreign market, the bulk of the revenues go to the licensee.
     c. If the foreign licensor learns the technology, it may break the agreement and begin to produce a similar product on its own. The licensing firm loses its trade secrets, plus the royalties.

B. EXPORTING
  1. Export assistance centers (EACs) were created to provide hands-on exporting assistance and trade-finance support for small and medium-sized businesses.
  2. Export trading companies serve the role of matching buyers and sellers from different countries.
  3. An export trading company is a good place to get career training in international trade.

C. FRANCHISING
  1. Franchising is popular both domestically and in global markets.
  2. Franchisers must adapt in the countries they serve.
  3. Domino's Pizza found that Germans like small individual pies and Japanese enjoyed squid and sweet mayonaisse pizza.

D. CONTRACT MANUFACTURING
  1. **CONTRACT MANUFACTURING**, also referred to as outsourcing, involves the production of private-label goods by a foreign company to which a company then attaches its brand name or trademark.
  2. Through contract manufacturing a company can often experiment in a new market without heavy start-up costs.

E. INTERNATIONAL JOINT VENTURES AND STRATEGIC ALLIANCES
  1. A **JOINT VENTURE** is a partnership in which companies (often from different countries) join to undertake a major project.
  2. The text offers the example of the 37-year joint venture between Xerox Corporation and Fuji Photo Film Co.
  3. The advantages of joint venture include:
     a. shared technology,
     b. shared marketing expertise,
     c. entry into markets where foreign goods are not allowed unless produced locally, and
     d. shared risk.
  4. The disadvantages are:
     a. One partner can learn the technology and practices of the other and leave to become a competitor,
     b. The technology may become obsolete; and
     c. The partnership may be too large to be as flexible as needed.
  5. A longer-term partnership, called a **STRATEGIC ALLIANCE** may help both companies build competitive market advantages.

F. FOREIGN SUBSIDIARIES
  1. A **FOREIGN SUBSIDIARY** is a company owned by another company (parent company) in a foreign country.
  2. The legal requirements of both the home and the host country must be observed.
  3. The advantages of foreign subsidiaries include that the company maintains complete control over any technology or expertise it may possess.
  4. The major disadvantage is that the firm's assets could be taken over by the foreign government if relations with the host country fail.

G. FOREIGN DIRECT INVESTMENT
1. **FOREIGN DIRECT INVESTMENT** occurs when a business buys permanent property and businesses in foreign nations.
    a. Japanese purchases in the U.S. occurred because they were the best investment alternatives at the time.

VI. FORCES AFFECTING TRADING IN GLOBAL MARKETS

A. SOCIOCULTURAL FORCES
1. American businesspeople are notoriously bad at adapting to cultural differences among nations.
2. American businesspeople have been accused of ethnocentricity, feeling that our culture is superior to all others and our job is to teach others the American way.
    a. Religion is an important part of any society's culture and can have a significant impact on business operations.
    b. Sociocultural differences can also have an impact on business functions such as human resource management.
    c. Learning about cultural perspectives, about time, change, competition, natural resources, achievement, and even work itself can be of great assistance.
3. Cultural differences affect not only management behaviors but global marketing strategies.
    a. Global marketing is used to describe selling the same product in essentially the same way everywhere in the world.
    b. Brand names such as Intel, Nike, Ford, and IBM have widespread global appeal and recognition.

B. ECONOMIC AND FINANCIAL FORCES
1. The global market does not have a universal currency. Currencies fluctuate in value daily.
2. The **EXCHANGE RATE** is the value of one currency relative to the currencies of other countries.
    a. Global markets operate under a system of floating exchange rates, in which currencies float according to supply and demand in the currency market.
    b. **DEVALUATION** is lowering the value of a nation's currency relative to other currencies.
3. Changes in currencies can cause other problems. Labor costs can vary considerably as currency values shift.
4. Understanding currency fluctuations and financing opportunities is vital to success in the global market.
5. Currency problems are especially bad in developing nations.
6. Trading in developing nations is often done through bartering.
    a. Bartering is the exchange of merchandise for merchandise or service for service with no money involved.
    b. **COUNTERTRADING** is more complex, in that several countries may be involved.
    c. Approximately 25% of the international exchanges involve countertrading.
    d. The text uses the example of Ford trading vehicles in Jamaica for bauxite.

C. LEGAL AND REGULATORY FORCES
1. In global markets, several groups of laws and regulations may apply.
2. Businesspeople find global markets governed by a myriad of laws and regulations that are often inconsistent.
3. American businesspeople are bound to follow U.S. laws and regulations. The Foreign Corrupt Practices Act of 1978 prohibits questionable or dubious payments to foreign officials to secure business contracts.

D. PHYSICAL AND ENVIRONMENTAL FORCES
   1. In some countries transportation is difficult and inefficient.
      a. Product storage facilities are poor.
      b. Unclean water can pose a problem.
   2. Exporters must be aware of the technological differences between nations.

VII. TRADE PROTECTIONISM

   A. **TRADE PROTECTIONISM** is the use of government regulations to limit the import of goods and services.
      1. Countries often use trade protectionism measures to protect their industries against dumping and foreign competition.
      2. Another barrier to international trade is the overall political atmosphere between nations.

   B. For centuries businesspeople advocated an economic principle called mercantilism.
      1. Mercantilism is selling more goods to other nations than you bought from them; that is, to have a favorable balance of trade.
      2. Governments charged a **TARIFF** on imports, making them more expensive.

   C. There are two kinds of tariffs:
      1. Protective tariffs are import taxes designed to raise the price of imported products, so domestic products are more competitive.
      2. Revenue tariffs are import taxes designed to raise money for the government.

   D. There is much debate about the degree of protectionism a government should practice.
      1. One form, the **IMPORT QUOTA**, describes limiting the number of products in certain categories that can be imported.
      2. **EMBARGO** is a complete ban on the import or export of certain products.
      3. Some say that as much as half of all trade is limited by nontariff barriers.

   E. THE GENERAL AGREEMENT ON TARIFFS AND TRADE, AND THE WORLD TRADE ORGANIZATION
      1. In 1948, the General Agreement on Tariffs and Trade (GATT) was established.
      2. This agreement among 23 countries provided a forum for negotiating mutual reductions in trade restrictions.
      3. The 1986 Uruguay Round of GATT talks was convened to renegotiate trade agreements.
         a. After eight years, 124 nations agreed to a new GATT agreement.
         b. The U.S. House of Representatives and Senate approved the pact in 1994.
      4. The new GATT agreement:
         a. Lowers tariffs on average by 38% worldwide.
         b. Extends GATT rules to new areas such as agriculture, services and the protection of patents.
      5. On January 1, 1995 the **WORLD TRADE ORGANIZATION (WTO)** assumed the primary purpose of GATT and was assigned the primary task of mediating trade disputes.

   F. COMMON MARKETS
      1. A **COMMON MARKET** is a regional group of countries that have no internal tariffs, a common external tariff, and the coordination of laws to facilitate exchange among countries.
      2. The European Union (EU) is a group of nations in Western Europe that dissolved their economic borders in the early 1990s.
      3. The path to unification has been slow and difficult, yet significant progress has been made.

G. THE NORTH AMERICAN FREE TRADE AGREEMENT (NAFTA)
1. The primary concerns of NAFTA opponents revolve around the issues of U.S. employment, exports, and the environment.
2. Proponents predict a vast new market for exports that would create jobs and opportunities in the long term.
3. The combination of the United States, Canada, and Mexico created a market of over 370 million people with a gross domestic product of over $7 trillion.
4. NAFTA creates a free trade area where nations can trade freely with each other without tariffs or other trade barriers.
5. The emergence of economic blocs like NAFTA has changed the landscape of global trade.

VIII. MULTINATIONAL CORPORATIONS

A. A **MULTINATIONAL CORPORATION (MNC)** is an organization that does manufacturing and marketing in many different countries; it has multinational stock ownership and multinational management.

B. The more multinational a company is, the more it attempts to operate without being influenced by restrictions from various governments.

IX. THE FUTURE OF GLOBAL TRADE: GLOBAL E-COMMERCE

A. New markets present new opportunities for trade and development, particularly in the emerging nations in Asia.

B. Technology has made global markets instantly accessible.
1. The Internet and e-commerce have enabled businesses worldwide to bypass the traditional channels of distribution and reach the global market.

C. GLOBALIZATION AND YOU
1. Those students who are prepared to manage global operations will have an advantage over other graduates.
2. Students are encouraged to study foreign languages, foreign cultures, and international business.

LEARNING THE LANGUAGE OF BUSINESS

Match each of the following key terms with the appropriate definition.
A. absolute advantage
B. balance of payments
C. balance of trade
D. common market
E. comparative advantage theory
F. contract manufacturing
G. countertrading
H. devaluation
I. dumping
J. embargo
K. exchange rate
L. exporting
M. foreign direct investment
N. foreign subsidiary
O. free trade
P. import quota
Q. importing
R. joint venture
S. licensing
T. multinational corporation (MNC)
U. strategic alliance
V. tariff
W. trade deficit
X. trade protectionism
Y. World Trade Organization (WTO)

____ 1. Buying products from another country.

____ 2. Selling products to another country.

____ 3. Lowering the value of a nation's currency relative to other currencies.

____ 4. The movement of goods and services among nations without political or economic obstruction.

____ 5. A partnership in which companies (often from two or more different countries) join to undertake a major project.

____ 6. When a country has a monopoly on producing a product or is able to produce it at a cost below that of all other countries.

____ 7. Production of private-label goods by a company to which another company then attaches its brand name or trademark.

____ 8. A company owned by another company (parent company) in a foreign country.

____ 9. Buying of permanent property and businesses in foreign nations.

____ 10. Agreement in which a producer allows a foreign company to produce its product in exchange for royalties.

____ 11. A regional group of countries that have no internal tariffs, a common external tariff, and a coordination of laws to facilitate exchange; an example is the European Union.

____ 12. Theory, which asserts that a country should produce and sell to other countries those products that, it produces most efficiently.

____ 13. A complete ban on the import or export of certain products.

____ 14. The difference between money coming into a country (from exports) and money leaving the country (from imports) plus money flows from other factors such as tourism, foreign aid, military expenditures, and foreign investment.

____ 15. Selling products for less in a foreign country than is charged in the producing country.

____ 16. An organization that does manufacturing and marketing in many different countries; it has multinational stock ownership and multinational management.

____ 17. The value of one currency relative to the currencies of other countries.

____ 18. The use of government regulations to limit the import of goods and services; based on the theory that domestic producers can survive and grow, producing more jobs.

____ 19. The relationship of exports to imports.

____ 20. Limiting the number of products in certain categories that can be imported.

____ 21. Bartering among several countries.

____ 22. Buying more goods from other nations than are sold to them.

____ 23. A long-term partnership between two or more companies, established to help each company build competitive advantages.

____ 24. The international organization that replaced GATT and was assigned the primary duty to mediate trade disputes among nations.

____ 25. A tax imposed on imported products.

SELF-TEST

1. Which theory states that a nation should produce and sell goods to other countries that it produces most efficiently, and buy goods produced more efficiently by other countries?
   A) Comparative advantage.
   B) Absolute advantage.
   C) Mercantilism.
   D) Bilateral advantage.

2. Last year, the nation of Wolfbranch imported goods totaling $400 million and exported products totaling $386 million. Wolfbranch evidently has a(n):
   A) unfavorable balance of trade.
   B) favorable balance of trade.
   C) trade surplus.
   D) surplus in trading in the global market.

3. An evaluation of the role of the United States in global markets would find that, in recent years, the U.S has:
   A) had a merchandise trade surplus with the rest of the world.
   B) had large trade deficits with Japan and China.
   C) avoided becoming a debtor nation.
   D) attracted very little foreign direct investment.

4. Pillsbury is a firm that operates throughout the United States, even though it is wholly owned by a British company, Grand Metropolitan. Pillsbury is an example of a:
   A) licensed venture.
   B) joint venture.
   C) export trading company.
   D) foreign subsidiary.

5. McHugh Corporation of Ireland and Enomoto Enterprises of Japan have undertaken the production of a new electric car with rechargeable batteries that can be driven at high speeds for long distances. They have shared the investment, and each has contributed important technological expertise to the effort. These two firms have entered into a(n):
   A) international joint venture.
   B) multinational cartel.
   C) industrial countertrade agreement.
   D) multinational limited partnership.

6. Differences in electrical power and transportation systems can present special problems for U.S. firms when attempting to enter global markets. These represent _____ differences that global managers must take into account.
   A) physical and environmental
   B) legal and regulatory
   C) economic
   D) governmental

7. Responding to pressure from political lobbyists representing the steel industry, the U.S. government levies a tax on steel products imported from Europe. This is an example of a(n):
   A) protective tariff.
   B) revenue tariff.
   C) quota.
   D) embargo.

8. Traders in the 18th century were encouraged to do their best in selling their nation's goods in the market to create a favorable balance of trade. Nations attempted to sell more goods to other nations than they bought from other nations. This approach to global trading is called:
   A) ethnocentrism
   B) mercantilism.
   C) protectionism.
   D) isolationism.

9. Exxon Corporation refines and markets its petroleum products in many different nations. In addition, Exxon's stockholders and managers come from many different nationalities. Exxon is an example of a true:
   A) meganational.
   B) multinational corporation.
   C) joint international venture.
   D) international bureaucracy.

10. The only deposits of a rare mineral known as longnectite are found in the nation of Swanland. Since no other nation has deposits of longnectite, Swanland has a(n)_____ in the production of this mineral.
    A) bilateral advantage.
    B) universal advantage.
    C) absolute advantage.
    D) internal advantage.

ANSWER KEY

LEARNING THE LANGUAGE OF BUSINESS

1. Q
2. L
3. H
4. O
5. R
6. A
7. F
8. N
9. M
10. S
11. D
12. E
13. J
14. B
15. I
16. T
17. K
18. X
19. C
20. P
21. G
22. W
23. U
24. Y
25. V

SELF-TEST

Answer	Page #
1. A	Page: 65
2. A	Page: 68
3. B	Page: 70
4. D	Page: 74
5. A	Page: 73
6. A	Page: 81
7. A	Page: 82
8. B	Page: 82
9. B	Page: 86
10. C	Page: 66

LESSON 8

MANAGING BUSINESS INFORMATION

ASSIGNMENTS

1. Review the Learning Goals and read the Lesson Overview for this lesson.

2. Read Chapter 17 pp. 520-544 in *Understanding Business,* 6th edition by Nickels, McHugh, and McHugh.

3. Watch the video *Managing Business Information.*

4. Review the textbook material.

5. Match the key terms with the correct definitions in the Learning the Language of Business exercise.

6. Take the Self-Test.

7. Use the Answer Key to check your answers and review when necessary.

LEARNING GOALS

After you watch the video, read the textbook, and study this lesson, you should be able to:

1. Outline the changing role of business technology.

2. Compare the scope of the Internet, intranets, and extranets as tools in managing information.

3. List the steps in managing information, and identify the characteristics of useful information.

4. Review the hardware most frequently used in business, and outline the benefits of the move toward computer networks.

5. Classify the computer software most frequently used in business.

6. Evaluate the human resource, security, privacy and stability issues in management that are affected by information technology.

7. Identify the careers that are gaining or losing workers due to the growth of information technology.

LESSON NOTES

The PROFILE at the beginning of this chapter focuses on Rina Delmonico of Ren Consulting, Inc. Rina, although eccentric is an Information Technology (IT) expert. She has succeeded as the Chief Information Officer at more than one firm. What seem to be the keys to her success are innovation and a willingness to try new technological applications. For firms to succeed in the 21st century they must be able to manage and use information technology.

I. THE ROLE OF INFORMATION TECHNOLOGY

    A. Business technology is continuously changing names and changing roles.
        1. In the 1970s, business technology was known as **DATA PROCESSING (DP)**.
            a. Data are raw, unanalyzed, and unsummarized facts and figures.
            b. Information is the processed and summarized data that can be used for managerial decision making.
            c. Its role was to support existing business through improving the flow of information.
        2. In the 1980s, business technology became known as **INFORMATION SYSTEMS (IS)**.
            a. Its role was changed from supporting business to doing business (for example ATMs and voice mail).
            b. As business used technology more, it became more dependent on it.
        3. In the late 1980s, business technology became known as **INFORMATION TECHNOLOGY (IT)**.
            a. Business shifted from using new technology on old methods, to using it on new methods.
            b. Information technology's role became, to change business.

    B. HOW INFORMATION TECHNOLOGY CHANGES BUSINESS
        1. Time and place have always been at the center of business.
            a. Today IT allows businesses to delivery products and services whenever and wherever it is convenient for the customer.
            b. As IT breaks time and location barriers, it creates organizations and services that are independent of location.
        2. **VIRTUALIZATION** means that you don't have a physical place to go to work, but everything is accessible through technology.
            a. The technology allows you to access people and information as if you were in an actual office.
            b. Virtual communities are forming as people communicate over computer networks.
        3. The way business works has drastically changed due to technology.

    C. MOVING FROM INFORMATION TECHNOLOGY TOWARD KNOWLEDGE TECHNOLOGY
        1. In the mid-1990s, we started moving from information technology toward **KNOWLEDGE TECHNOLOGY (KT)** information charged with enough intelligence to make it relevant and useful.
        2. KT adds a layer of intelligence to filter appropriate information and deliver it when it is needed.
        3. KT changes the traditional flow of information from an individual going to the database to the data coming to the individual.
        4. KT "thinks" about the facts based on an individual's needs so businesspeople can spend more time deciding about how to react to problems and opportunities.

II. THE ROAD TO KNOWLEDGE: THE INTERNET, INTRANETS, EXTRANETS, AND VIRTUAL PRIVATE NETWORKS

   A. Knowledge, more than physical assets, is now the key to successful competition.
      1. Knowledge has become one of the more important factors of production.
      2. Business is realizing that it needs to manage knowledge like any other asset.
      3. This need is leading to new technologies that support contact among staff, suppliers, and customers.

   B. Internets and intranets
      1. The Internet is a network of computer networks.
      2. An **INTRANET** is a company-wide network closed to public access, which uses Internet-type technology.
         a. Some companies use intranets only to publish information for employees.
         b. Others create interactive intranets, allowing employees to input information.
         c. One-half to two-thirds of all businesses are running intranets.
         d. To limit access, companies can construct a firewall between themselves and the outside world to protect corporate information from unauthorized users.
      3. An extranet is a semiprivate network that uses Internet technology so more than one company can access the same information.
      4. A **VIRTUAL PRIVATE NETWORK (VPN)** is a private data network that creates secure connections through regular Internet lines.
         a. The VPN is much cheaper because it doesn't require a dedicated line.

   C. BROADBAND TECHNOLOGY
      1. With no changes in capacity, however, the more people use Internet technology, the slower it becomes.
         a. The traffic on the information superhighway has become so intense that early Net users have been squeezed off the crowded Internet.
         b. Their answer is to create another Internet, reserved for research purposes only.
      2. **BROADBAND TECHNOLOGY** allows users a continuous connection.
         a. This wideband technology allows for voice and video.
         b. The data speed can reach 50 times the speed of traditional 56k modems.

   D. The new system, **INTERNET 2**, will run more than 22,000 times faster than the 56k modem and will support heavy-duty applications.
      1. A key element is a network called VBNS, or very high-speed backbone network service, set up in 1995 to link government supercomputer centers and a select group of universities.
      2. The system had expanded by 2000 to include 172 member universities.
      3. The designers of Internet 2 are planning to filter Internet 2 technology out in such a way that there is plenty of room for everyone.

III. MANAGING INFORMATION

   A. Managers have always had to sift through mountains of information to find what they need.
      1. Today businesspeople also have voice mail, the Internet, faxes, and e-mail.
      2. Businesspeople refer to this information overload as infoglut.

   B. Identifying the four or five key goals helps eliminate unnecessary information.

   C. The usefulness of management information depends on four characteristics:
      1. Quality - The information must be accurate and reliable.

2. Completeness - There must be enough data to make a decision, but not too much to confuse.
3. Timeliness - Information must reach managers quickly.
4. Relevance - Managers must know the questions to ask to get the answers they need.
D. Sorting out the useful information and getting it to the right people is the goal in solving information overload.
1. Software programs can filter information so that users can get the customized information they need.
2. Known as **PUSH TECHNOLOGY**, they push the information to you, delivering customized news to your computer.

E. MANAGING KNOWLEDGE
1. Knowledge can lead to profits, so businesses find ways to mine the knowledge of their employees.
2. **KNOWLEDGE MANAGEMENT** is the sharing, organizing, and disseminating of information in a simple relevant manner.

IV. THE ENABLING TECHNOLOGY: HARDWARE

A. The most powerful computer hardware today may be obsolete by the time you study this.
1. Chairman of Intel Corp., Gordon Moore, has remarked that the capacity of computer chips should double every year or so (Moore's law).
2. Gordon has recently revised his law by saying that his prediction cannot hold good for much longer because the finite size of atomic particles will prevent infinite miniaturization.
3. This will be a simple overview of the kind of computer technology available now.

B. Hardware includes computers, pagers, cellular phones, scanners, printers, fax machines, etc.
1. All-in-one devices that address all your communications needs are now available.
2. Researchers are working on a human computer interface that combines a video camera and computer.

C. CUTTING THE CORD: WIRELESS INFORMATION APPLIANCES
1. Some experts believe we are moving out of the PC era and into the Internet appliance era.
   a. These appliances get people to the Internet and e-mail.
2. The biggest move is to handheld wireless devices.

D. COMPUTER NETWORKS
1. The most dynamic change in recent years is the move away from mainframe computer processing toward network systems that allow many users to access information at the same time.
   a. In the new **NETWORK COMPUTING SYSTEM** (also called **CLIENT/SERVER COMPUTING**), the tasks such as searching sales records are handled by personal computers called "clients."
   b. The information needed to complete the tasks is stored in huge databases controlled by the server.
2. The major benefits of networks are:
   a. Saving time and money.
   b. Easy links across functional boundaries.
   c. People can see their products more clearly.
      1) In traditional organizations, information is summarized so many times that it often loses its meaning.
      2) Networks catch raw information.

3. The major drawbacks of networks are:
   a. PC repair costs.
   b. System maintenance costs.

E. Mainframes are not dead
   1. The new hybrid mainframe and network computing are options.
      a. The thin-client network uses machines that look like PCs but lack processing power.
   2. A second option is to lease software from an applications service provider (ASP).
      a. The ASP maintains and upgrades the software.
      b. The Internet provides the access.

V. SOFTWARE

A. Computer software provides the instructions that enable you to tell the computer what to do.
   1. It is important to find the right software to do the job, before finding the right hardware.
      a. Some programs are easier to use than others.
      b. Some programs are more sophisticated with more functions.
      c. A businessperson must decide what functions he or she wants performed then choose the appropriate software.
   2. Most software is distributed commercially through suppliers.
      a. There is some software, called **SHAREWARE**, which is copyrighted but distributed to potential customers free of charge.
      b. **PUBLIC DOMAIN SOFTWARE (FREEWARE)** is software that is free for the taking.
   3. Businesspeople most frequently use software for six major purposes:
      a. Writing (word processors).
      b. Manipulating numbers (spreadsheets).
      c. Filing and retrieving data (databases).
      d. Presenting information visually (graphics).
      e. Communicating (e-mail, instant messaging).
      f. Accounting.
   4. Many functions have been combined into one kind of program known as integrated software or suites.
   5. A new class of software program, called groupware, has emerged for use on networks.

VI. EFFECTS OF INFORMATION TECHNOLOGY ON MANAGEMENT

A. HUMAN RESOURCE ISSUES
   1. Computers will tend to eliminate middle management functions and thus flatten organization structures.
   2. Computers and the increased use of the Internet and intranets will allow employees to stay home and do their work from there, telecommuting.
   3. Advantages of telecommuting:
      a. Telecommuting involves less travel time and costs, and often increases productivity.
      b. It helps companies save money by retaining valuable employees and by tempting experienced employees out of retirement.
      c. Companies can get by with smaller, less expensive office space.

d. Telecommuting enables men and women to stay home with small children and is a tremendous boon for disabled workers.
   e. Studies show that it is more successful among self-starters and those whose work doesn't require face-to-face interaction with co-workers.
 4. The major disadvantages of telecommuting are:
   a. Long-distance work can give workers a dislocated feeling of being left out of the office loop.
   b. Some feel a loss of energy people can get through social interaction.
   c. Often people working from home don't know when to turn the work off.
   d. Some companies are using telecommuting as a part-time alternative.
 5. Electronic communication could never replace human communication for creating enthusiasm and esprit de corps.
 6. Computers are tools, not a total replacement for managers or workers.

B. SECURITY ISSUES
 1. Hackers, people who break into computer systems for illegal purposes, are a problem.
 2. Computer security today is more complicated than in the past.
   a. When information was processed in a mainframe environment, the single data center was easier to control.
   b. Today computers are not only accessible in all areas of the company, but also from other companies.
 3. A **VIRUS** is a piece of programming code inserted into other programming to cause some unexpected and undesirable event.
   a. Viruses are spread by downloading infected programming over the Internet or by sharing an infected diskette.
   b. Some viruses are playful, but some can erase data or crash a hard drive.
   c. Software programs such as Norton's AntiVirus inoculate the computer so that it doesn't catch a known virus.
   d. It is important to keep your antivirus protection program up-to-date and practice safe computing.
 4. Existing laws do not address some Internet issues such as:
   a. Copyright and pornography.
   b. Intellectual property and contract disputes.
   c. Online sexual and racial harassment.
   d. Crooked sales schemes.

C. PRIVACY ISSUES
 1. A major problem with privacy has developed as more and more personal information is stored in computers and people are able to access that data illegally.
   a. The Internet allows Web surfers to access all sorts of information about you.
   b. One of the key issues is: Isn't this personal information already public anyway?
 2. Web sites have gotten downright nosy by secretly tracking users' movements online.
   a. Web surfers seem willing to swap personal details for free access to online information.
   b. Web sites often send **COOKIES** to your computer that stay on your hard drive.
   c. These often simply contain your name and password.
   d. Others track your movements around the Web and then blend that information with their databases and tailor the ads you receive accordingly.
   e. You need to decide how much information about yourself you are willing to give away.

D. STABILITY ISSUES
 1. The instability of technology can cost business money and lost profits. Frequent issues are:

        a. Human errors.
        b. Malfunctioning software.
        c. Complex software and hardware configurations.

VII. TECHNOLOGY AND YOU

    A. It may be occupational suicide to be computer illiterate since most workers come in contact with computers to some degree.
       1. The U.S. Commerce Department estimated that by 2006, 50% of Americans would be employed in positions directly associated with information technology.

       2. The Commerce Department has warned that the U.S. is facing an increasing shortage of information technology workers.
          a. In 2000, there was a shortage of 850,000 skilled (IT) workers.
          b. A chief information officer with more than four years of experience could then earn about $500,000 annually.

    B. Researchers who have studied computerphobia (fear of computers) found that 55% of Americans have the disorder.
       1. Gender, age, and income level don't appear to lead to computerphobia the key variable is exposure.
       2. As information technology eliminates old jobs while creating new ones, it is up to you to learn the skills you need to be certain you aren't left behind.

LEARNING THE LANGUAGE OF BUSINESS

Match each of the following key terms with the appropriate definition.

A. Broadband technology
B. cookies
C. data processing (DP)
D. information systems (IS)
E. information technology (IT)
F. Internet 2
G. Intranet
H. knowledge management
I. knowledge technology (KT)
J. network computing system (client/server computing)
K. public domain software (freeware)
L. push technology
M. shareware
N. virtual private network (VPN)
O. virtualization
P. virus

_____ 1. Sharing, organizing and disseminating information in the simplest and most relevant way possible for the users of the information.

_____ 2. Technology that helps companies *do business* (includes such tools as ATMs and voice mail).

_____ 3. A private data network that creates secure connections over regular Internet lines.

_____ 4. Computer software that is copyrighted but distributed to potential customers free of charge. It is expected that users will send a fee to the developer if the software is found useful.

_____ 5. Technology that supported existing business (primarily used to improve the flow of financial information).

_____ 6. Technology that delivers voice, video and data through the Internet.

_____ 7. Accessibility through technology that allows business to be conducted independent of location.

_____ 8. Pieces of information data, such as registration data or user preferences, sent by a Web site over the Internet to a Web browser that the browser software is expected to save and to send back to the server whenever the user returns to that Web site.

_____ 9. Computer systems that allow personal computers (clients) to obtain needed information from huge databases in a central computer (server).

_____ 10. Technology that helps companies *change business* by its applications to new methods of doing business.

_____ 11. Technology that adds a layer of intelligence to filter appropriate information and deliver it when it is needed.

_____ 12. The new Internet system that links government supercomputer centers and a select group of universities.

_____ 13. A company-wide network, closed to public access, that uses Internet-type technology.

_____ 14. Software that is free for the taking.

_____ 15. Web software that delivers information tailored to a previously defined user profile; it pushes the information to users so they don't have to pull it out.

_____ 16. A piece of programming code inserted into other programming to cause some unexpected, and for the victim, usually undesirable event.

SELF-TEST

1. The major impact of information technology has been to:
   A) encourage the growth of giant corporations.
   B) create organizations that are independent of location.
   C) reduce the demand for skilled labor.
   D) increase overall costs of production.

2. The organizations that benefit the most from an intranet are the ones that:
   A) publish information on the intranet that all employees can access.
   B) operate the intranet over a mainframe system.
   C) base the intranet interface on one of the popular web browsers.
   D) develop interactive intranet applications.

3. For the past several years, scientists and engineers at Equatech, Inc., have relied on the Internet to keep in touch with their peers at various universities and research organizations. In recent years these researchers have become frustrated because the increasing congestion on the Internet has disrupted their attempts to communicate and collaborate with colleagues at other institutions. Which of the following developments would be most likely to help Equatech's researchers overcome this problem? Equatech should:
   A) set up an intranet.
   B) allow its scientists and engineers to telecommute.
   C) assign each employee a second e-mail address.
   D) gain access to Internet 2.

4. Joan Carlson is a marketing manager for a chain of clothing stores. She recently received a newsletter that contained some timely and reliable information about trends in men's clothing for next season. Unfortunately, Joan's store sells only women's clothes. The information in the newsletter was not useful to Joan because it lacks:
   A) redundancy.
   B) accuracy.
   C) relevance.
   D) selectivity.

5. The Edutext Company has adopted a system that allows its employees to use Windows based applications. Each user has a machine that resembles a desktop PC. However, these desktop machines lack the processing power to perform all the tasks themselves, so they are connected to a server that stores the programs and data and provides the actual processing power. Edutext is using a system known as a(n):
   A) an extranet.
   B) server computer.
   C) thin-client network.
   D) central processing system.

6. Software programs that search thousands of news sources and send customized news to a user's computer desktop are examples of:
   A) push technology.
   B) wide-area network search and retrieval (WANSAT) technology.
   C) target information provider (TIP) technology.
   D) filtered information forwarding (FIF) technology.

7. Mike Antonucci is a college instructor who wants to use computer software to organize information about student grades on tests and papers, and compute the total and percentage grades earned by each student at the end of the semester. Mike wants to record all of the grade information in an electronic equivalent of a worksheet complete with formulas that will allow the program to do all of the computations. The type of software best suited to Mike's needs is a(n):
   A) graphics program.
   B) integrated software package.
   C) desktop publishing software.
   D) spreadsheet program.

8. Jason Hart was recently informed by his bank that someone illegally broke into the bank's computer system and gained access to information about customer account numbers and ATM access codes. The bank is recommending that Jason and other customers change their account numbers and access numbers for security reasons. The bank, and Jason, are victims of a(n):
   A) net crasher.
   B) software pirate.
   C) slammer.
   D) hacker.

9. Regina Williams works for Findabuck Finance Company, but she seldom sees the inside of Findabuck's offices. Instead, she does most of her work, on a computer located in the spare bedroom of her home. The computer is linked to Findabuck's office, so her work is distributed as quickly and efficiently as if she were at the office herself. Regina is one of the increasing number of workers who:
   A) has become an independent contractor.
   B) telecommutes.
   C) compu-commutes.
   D) uses linked-access shareware.

10. Which of the following statements about the job market for information technology workers is most accurate?
    A) There are so many college students majoring in information technology that by the year 2007, the number of new information technology workers entering the job market is likely to far exceed the number of new jobs created in this field.
    B) Pay scales for technology workers are likely to lag behind those of other types of workers over the next few years.
    C) There is a serious shortage of information technology workers at the present time, and this shortage may become even worse in the future.
    D) Though the market for information technology workers grew rapidly in the 1990s, this job market is currently in a stable equilibrium, with little change in overall employment expected until 2010 or later.

ANSWER KEY

LEARNING THE LANGUAGE OF BUSINESS

1. H
2. D
3. N
4. M
5. C
6. A
7. O
8. B
9. J
10. E
11. I
12. F
13. G
14. K
15. L
16. P

SELF-TEST

Answer	Page #
1. B	Page: 523
2. D	Page: 525-526
3. D	Page: 526
4. C	Page: 528
5. C	Page: 523
6. A	Page: 528
7. D	Page: 535
8. D	Page: 538
9. B	Page: 537
10. C	Page: 541-542

LESSON 9

SELECTING A FORM OF BUSINESS OWNERSHIP

ASSIGNMENTS

1. Review the Learning Goals and read the Lesson Overview for this lesson.

2. Read Chapter 5 pp. 132-163 in *Understanding Business,* 6th edition by Nickels, McHugh, and McHugh.

3. Watch the video *Selecting a Form of Business Ownership*

4. Review the textbook material.

5. Match the key terms with the correct definitions in the Learning the Language of Business exercise.

6. Take the Self-Test.

7. Use the Answer Key to check your answers and review when necessary.

LEARNING GOALS

After you watch the video, read the textbook, and study this lesson, you should be able to:

1. Compare the advantages and disadvantages of sole proprietorships.

2. Describe the differences between general and limited partners, and compare the advantages and disadvantages of partnerships

3. Compare the advantages and disadvantages of corporations, and summarize the differences between C corporations, S corporations, and limited liability companies.

4. Define and give examples of three types of corporate mergers and explain the role of leveraged buyouts and taking a firm private.

5. Outline the advantages and disadvantages of franchises and discuss the opportunities for diversity in franchising and the challenges of international franchising.

6. Explain the role of cooperatives.

LESSON NOTES

The PROFILE at the beginning of this chapter focuses on Rachel Bell and Sara Sutton who founded JobDirect.com an Internet based job bank in 1995. Their plan was to match employers with employees. The business progressed slowly until they decided to incorporate and issue shares of stock. With the added financial strength, they expanded and excelled. By 1999 they had 24 employees and over $3 million in client contact bookings. The corporate form of ownership allowed them to raise money and hire experts to execute their vision. They learned that a business can start as one form and change to another as conditions dictate.

I. BASIC FORMS OF BUSINESS OWNERSHIP

   A. How you decide to form your business can make a difference in your long-term success.

   B. The three major forms of business ownership are:
      1. A **SOLE PROPRIETORSHIP** is an organization that is owned, and usually managed, by one person; it is the most common form.
      2. A **PARTNERSHIP** is a legal form of business co-owned by two or more owners.
      3. A **CORPORATION** is a legal entity with authority to act and have liability separate from its owners.

   C. Each form of business ownership has its advantages and its disadvantages.

II. SOLE PROPRIETORSHIPS

   A. ADVANTAGES OF SOLE PROPRIETORSHIPS
      1. Ease of starting and ending the business.
      2. Being your own boss.
      3. Pride of ownership.
      4. Leaving a legacy.
      5. Retention of profit.
      6. No special taxes.

   B. DISADVANTAGES OF SOLE PROPRIETORSHIPS
      1. **UNLIMITED LIABILITY** means that any debts or damages incurred by the business are your debts and you must pay them.
      2. Limited financial resources.
      3. Management difficulties.
      4. Overwhelming time commitment.
      5. Few fringe benefits.
      6. Limited growth.
      7. Limited life span.

III. PARTNERSHIPS

   A. TYPES OF PARTNERSHIPS
      1. **GENERAL PARTNERSHIP**: a partnership in which all owners share in operating the business and in assuming liability for the business's debts.
      2. **LIMITED PARTNERSHIP**: a partnership with one or more general partners and one or more limited partners.
         a. A **GENERAL PARTNER** is an owner who has unlimited liability and is active in managing the firm.

- b. A **LIMITED PARTNER** risks an investment in the firm, but enjoys limited liability and cannot legally help manage the company.
- c. **LIMITED LIABILITY** means that limited partners are not responsible for the debts of the business beyond the amount of their investment.
3. A **MASTER LIMITED PARTNERSHIP (MLP)** is a new form of partnership that acts like a corporation and is traded on the stock exchange, but is taxed like a partnership avoiding the corporate income tax.

B. Uniform Partnership Act (UPA)
1. All states except Louisiana have adopted the Uniform Partnership Act to replace laws relating to partnerships.
2. The UPA defines the three key elements of any general partnership:
   a. Common ownership.
   b. Shared profits and losses.
   c. The right to participate in managing the operations of the business.

C. ADVANTAGES OF PARTNERSHIPS
1. More financial resources.
2. Shared management and pooled knowledge.
3. Longer survival.

D. DISADVANTAGES OF PARTNERSHIPS
1. Unlimited liability
   a. Each general partner is liable for the debts of the firm, no matter who was responsible for causing those debts.
   b. You are liable for your partners' mistakes as well as your own.
   c. Many states are now allowing partners to form a **LIMITED LIABILITY PARTNERSHIP (LLP)**.
   d. An LLP limits a partner's liability based upon their own acts or omissions, or on those of someone they supervise.
2. Division of profits
3. Disagreements among partners
   a. Disagreements can arise over division of authority, purchasing decisions, and money.
   b. Because of such potential conflicts, all terms of partnership should be spelled out in writing to protect all parties.
4. Difficult to terminate

E. Many businesspeople try to avoid the disadvantages of the sole proprietorship and partnership by forming corporations.

IV. CORPORATIONS

A. A **CONVENTIONAL C CORPORATION** is a state-chartered legal entity with authority to act and have liability separate from its owners.
1. The corporation's owners (stockholders) are not liable for the debts of the corporation beyond the money they invest.
2. A corporation also enables many people to share in the ownership of a business without working there.

B. ADVANTAGES OF CORPORATIONS
1. More money for investment
   a. To raise money, a corporation sells ownership (stock) to anyone interested.
   b. Corporations may also find it easier to obtain loans.
2. Limited liability

  a. Limited liability is probably the most significant advantage of corporations.
  b. Limited liability means that the owners of a business are responsible for losses only up to the amount they invest.
 3. Size
  a. Corporations have the ability to raise large amounts of money.
  b. They can also hire experts in all areas of operation.
  c. They can buy other corporations in other fields to diversify their risk.
  d. Corporations have the size and resources to take advantage of opportunities anywhere in the world.
 4. Perpetual life
  a. The death of one or more owners does not terminate the corporation.
 5. Ease of ownership change
 6. Ease of drawing talented employees
 7. Separation of ownership from management
  a. Owners/shareholders are separate from the managers and employers.
  b. The owners thus have some say in who runs the corporation, but no control.

C. DISADVANTAGES OF CORPORATIONS
 1. Initial cost
  a. Incorporation may cost thousands of dollars and involve expensive lawyers and accountants.
  b. There are less expensive ways of incorporating in certain states.
 2. Extensive paperwork
  a. A corporation must process many forms.
  b. A corporation must prove all its expenses and deductions are legitimate.
  c. A corporation must keep detailed records.
 3. Two tax returns must be filed, both a corporate tax return and an individual tax return.
 4. Size
  a. Large corporations sometimes become inflexible and too tied down in red tape.
 5. Difficulty of termination
 6. Double taxation
  a. Corporate income is taxed twice.
  b. The corporation pays tax on income before it can distribute any to stockholders.
  c. The stockholders pay tax on the income they receive from the corporation.
  d. States often tax corporations more harshly than other enterprises.
 7. Possible conflicts with board of directors
  a. Since the board chooses the company's officers, an entrepreneur can be forced out of the very company he founded.

D. INDIVIDUALS CAN INCORPORATE
 1. By incorporating, individuals such as doctors and lawyers can save on taxes and receive other benefits of incorporation.

E. S CORPORATIONS
 1. An **S CORPORATION** is a unique government creation that looks like a corporation, but is taxed like sole proprietorships and partnerships.
  a. S corporations have shareholders, directors, and employees, but the profits are taxed as the personal income of the shareholders.
  b. The benefits of S corporations change every time the law changes.
 2. S corporations must:
  a. Have no more than 75 shareholders.
  b. Have shareholders who are individuals or estates and are citizens or permanent residents of the U.S.
  c. Have only one class of outstanding stock.

d. Not have more than 25% of income derived from passive sources (rents, royalties, interest, etc.)
3. DISADVANTAGES OF S CORPORATIONS
   a. The top tax rate for S corporations is almost five points higher than the highest corporation rate.
   b. Fast-growing small businesses that don't intend to pay dividends to owners are switching to C corporation status to avoid the higher taxes.

F. LIMITED LIABILITY COMPANIES
   1. A **LIMITED-LIABILITY COMPANY (LLC)** is similar to an S corporation without the special eligibility requirements.
      a. Limited liability companies are so new that many states have just recently passed legislation regarding them.
      b. By the fall of 1996, all fifty states and the District of Columbia recognized LLCs.
   2. The Uniform Limited Liability Company Act was prepared for the National Conference of Commissioners on Uniform State Laws in an effort to provide uniform legislation regarding limited liability companies.
   3. LLCs are best for many new businesses for the following reasons:
      a. Personal-asset protection.
      b. Choice to be taxed as partnership or as corporation.
      c. Flexible ownership rules.

V. CORPORATION EXPANSION: MERGERS AND ACQUISITIONS

A. In 1998, 9 of the 10 largest merger transactions of all times took place.
   1. A **MERGER** is the result of two firms forming one company.
   2. An **ACQUISITION** is when one company buys another company.

B. There are three major types of corporate mergers: vertical, horizontal, and conglomerate.
   1. **VERTICAL MERGER** is the joining of two firms involved in different stages of related businesses.
   2. **HORIZONTAL MERGER** joins two firms in the same industry and allows them to diversify or expand their products.
   3. **CONGLOMERATE MERGER** unites completely unrelated firms.

C. Rather than merge or sell to another company, some corporations decide to maintain control of the firm internally.
   1. Taking a firm private involves the efforts of a group of stockholders or management to obtain all the firm's stock for themselves.
   2. A **LEVERAGED BUYOUT (LBO)** is an attempt by employees, management, or a group of investors to purchase an organization primarily through borrowing.
      a. The funds borrowed are used to buy out the stockholders in the company.
      b. Employees, managers, or group of investors now become the owners of the firm.
   3. Merger mania has also involved foreign companies purchasing U.S. companies.

VI. SPECIAL FORMS OF BUSINESS OWNERSHIP

A. In addition to the three basic forms of business ownership, we shall discuss two special forms of ownership, franchises and cooperatives.

VII. FRANCHISES

A. A **FRANCHISE AGREEMENT** is an arrangement whereby someone with a good idea for a business (the **FRANCHISOR**) sells the rights to use the business name and to sell a product or service (the **FRANCHISE**) to others (the **FRANCHISEE**) in a given territory.
B. Some people would like to own their own businesses but want more assurance of success. Franchising may be an alternative for such people.
   1. Franchising accounts for 40% of the national retail sales.
   2. The most popular businesses for franchising are restaurants, retail stores, hotels and motels, and automotive parts and service centers.
   3. Some entrepreneurs have had great success taking American franchises overseas.

C. ADVANTAGES OF FRANCHISES
   1. Management and marketing assistance, including an established product, help in choosing a location, and assistance in all phases of operation.
   2. Personal ownership, you are still your own boss, although you must follow the rules, regulations, and procedures of the franchise.
   3. Nationally recognized name, you get instant recognition and support.
   4. Financial advice and assistance
      a. Franchisees get assistance arranging financing and learning to keep records.
      b. Some franchisors will even provide financing to potential franchisees.
   5. Lower failure rate
      a. Historically, the failure rate for franchises has been lower than that of other business ventures.
      b. Studies show that you should carefully research any franchise before buying.

D. DISADVANTAGES OF FRANCHISES
   1. Large start-up costs
      a. Most franchises will demand a fee to obtain the rights to the franchise.
      b. Start-up costs can be over $4 million for a Holiday Inn.
   2. Shared profit, the franchisor often demands a large share of the profits, or royalty, based on sales, not profit.
   3. Management regulation
      a. Some franchisees may feel burdened by the company's rules and regulations.
      b. In recent years franchisees have been banding together to resolve their grievances with franchisors.
   4. Coattail effects
      a. The actions of other franchisees have an impact on the franchise's future growth and level of profitability.
      b. Franchisees must also look out for competition from fellow franchisees.
   5. Restrictions on selling
      a. Many franchisees face restrictions in the reselling of their franchises.
      b. Franchisors often insist on approving the new owner, who must meet their standards.
   6. Fraudulent franchisors
      a. Most franchisors are not large systems.
      b. There has been an increase in complaints to the FTC about franchisors that delivered little or nothing that they promised.

E. DIVERSITY IN FRANCHISING
   1. In 2000, women owned 80 percent of all new businesses, while women own only 24 percent of franchises.
   2. When women find it difficult to obtain financing to expanding their businesses, they often turn to finding franchisees to sidestep expansion costs.
   3. Franchising opportunities fit the needs of many aspiring minority businesspersons.

        4. The Commerce Department's Federal Minority Business Development Agency provides minorities with training in how to run franchises.

  F. HOME-BASED FRANCHISES
      1. Home-based businesses offer advantages but leave owners with a feeling of isolation.
      2. Home-based franchisees feel less isolated.

  G. E-COMMERCE IN FRANCHISING
      1. Internet users of today are able to obtain online retail franchises.
         a. Before jumping into this venture, check out all the facts.
         b. Website conflicts are possible; some franchisors prohibit franchisee-sponsored websites.

  H. USING TECHNOLOGY IN FRANCHISING
      1. Franchisors are using technology to meet the needs of customers and franchisees.
      2. Franchise Websites can streamline communication with employees, customers, and vendors.
      3. Using the Internet every franchisee has immediate access to every subject that involves the franchise operation.

  I. FRANCHISING IN INTERNATIONAL MARKETS.
      1. More than 450 of the 3,000 franchisers in America have outlets overseas. Canada is by far the most popular target because of proximity and language.
      2. Franchisers find the costs of franchising high in these markets, but the costs are counterbalanced by less competition and rapidly expanding consumer base.
      3. Franchisers must be careful to adapt to the region.

VIII. COOPERATIVES

  A. **COOPERATIVES** are organizations that are owned by members/customers who pay an annual membership fee and share in any profit-making.
      1. There are 47,000 cooperatives in the U.S.
      2. Members democratically control these businesses by electing a board of directors that hires professional management.

  B. Some cooperatives give a group more economic power than they would have as individuals (i.e. farm cooperatives.)
      1. The farm cooperative started with farmers joining together to get better prices for their food products.
      2. The organization expanded so that farm cooperatives now buy and sell other products needed on the farm.
      3. In spite of debt and mergers, cooperatives are still a major force in agriculture today.

IX. WHICH FORM OF OWNERSHIP IS FOR YOU?
There are risks to every form of business ownership. The miracle of free enterprise is that the freedom and incentives of capitalism make risks acceptable to many people.

LEARNING THE LANGUAGE OF BUSINESS

Match each of the following key terms with the appropriate definition.

A. acquisition
B. conglomerate merger
C. conventional C corporation
D. cooperative
E. corporation
F. franchise
G. franchise agreement
H. franchisee
I. franchisor
J. general partner
K. general partnership
L. horizontal merger
M. leveraged buyout (LBO)
N. limited liability
O. limited-liability company (LLC)
P. limited liability partnerships (LLP)
Q. limited partner
R. limited partnership
S. master limited partnership (MLP)
T. merger
U. partnership
V. S corporation
W. sole proprietorship
X. unlimited liability
Y. vertical merger

____ 1. A unique government creation that looks like a corporation but is taxed like sole proprietorships and partnerships.

____ 2. A person who buys a franchise.

____ 3. The responsibility of a business's owners for losses only up to the amount they invest.

____ 4. The result of two firms forming one company.

____ 5. The responsibility of business owners for all of the debts of the business; making the personal assets of the owners vulnerable to claims against the business

____ 6. The joining of firms in completely unrelated industries.

____ 7. A company similar to an S corporation but without the special eligibility requirements.

____ 8. A legal entity with authority to act and have liability separate from its owners.

____ 9. An owner (partner) who has unlimited liability and is active in managing the firm.

____ 10. A partnership with one or more general partners and one or more limited partners.

____ 11. The joining of two companies involved in different stages of related businesses.

Lesson 9

____ 12. A partnership in which all owners share in operating the business and in assuming liability for the business's debts.

____ 13. An organization owned by members/customers who pay an annual membership fee and share in any profits (if it is a profit-making organization).

____ 14. A legal form of business with two or more owners.

____ 15. An attempt by employees, management, or a group of investors to purchase an organization primarily through borrowing.

____ 16. A partnership that limits partners' risk of losing their personal assets to only their own acts and omissions and to the acts and omissions of people under their supervision.

____ 16. An arrangement whereby someone with a good idea for a business sells the rights to use the business name and sell its products or services to others in a given territory.

____ 17. A company's purchase of the property and obligations of another company.

____ 18. The right to use a specific business's name and sell its products or services in a given territory.

____ 19. A company that develops a product concept and sells others the rights to make and sell the products.

____ 20. A partnership that looks much like a corporation in that it acts like a corporation and is traded on the stock exchanges like a corporation, but is taxed like a partnership and thus avoids the corporate income tax.

____ 21. The joining of two firms in the same industry.

____ 22. Owner who invests money in the business but does not have any management responsibility or liability for losses beyond the investment.

____ 23. A business that is owned, and usually managed, by one person.

____ 24. A state chartered legal entity with authority to act and have liability separate from its owners.

SELF-TEST

1. Leanne wants to start a business. Right now she is leaning toward forming a sole proprietorship, but she is also looking at other possibilities. She has very limited personal wealth and wants to ensure adequate financing for her new business, while minimizing her personal risk. Forming a sole proprietorship would:
   A) achieve her goals better than any other form of ownership.
   B) give her easy access to additional financing, but result in a high level of personal risk.
   C) protect her from personal risk, but limit access to financial resources.
   D) be a poor choice, since it would limit her access to financing while exposing her to unlimited liability.

2. When comparing partnerships to sole proprietorships, an advantage of partnerships is that they:
   A) are less risky, because each partner is responsible for only a specified fraction of the firm's debts.
   B) are easier to terminate.
   C) cost less to organize.
   D) give the firm a stronger financial foundation.

3. Homer and Marge have decided to open a floral design shop, which they intend to run as co-owners. Both intend to take an active role in the management of their new business, and each will accept unlimited liability. Homer and Marge are planning to operate a:
   A) joint venture.
   B) general partnership.
   C) limited partnership.
   D) cooperative.

4. Dr. Driller is a dentist who is interested in incorporating as an individual. If he attempts to do so, Dr. Driller is likely to find that:
   A) most states do not allow individuals to incorporate.
   B) the procedures for an individual to incorporate are extremely complex.
   C) he may actually save on taxes.
   D) his business will be owned by a large number of stockholders with whom he must share his income.

5. Diverse Diversions, Inc., operates a chain of hobby shops. The company has always been a C corporation, but became interested in switching to an S corporation. It consulted a lawyer about its plans. After learning more about the company, the lawyer explained that Diverse Diversions could not qualify to become an S corporation. Which of the following characteristics of Diverse Diversions would prevent it from becoming an S corporation? Diverse Diversions:
   A) sells goods rather than services.
   B) operates stores in more than one state.
   C) has only one class of stock.
   D) has almost a thousand stockholders.

6. In a leveraged buyout, the managers of a firm, its employees, or other investors attempt to:
   A) move the company elsewhere and start over.
   B) obtain the assets of the company through bankruptcy proceedings.
   C) use borrowed funds to buy out the firm's stockholders.
   D) negotiate a merger with another firm to create a conglomerate.

7. Consolidated Shoe is looking at a possible merger with different firms in the entertainment, oil, and transportation industries. Consolidated Shoe is considering a:
   A) vertical merger.
   B) horizontal merger.
   C) conglomerate merger.
   D) domesticated merger.

8. Mary is interested in becoming a franchisee in Cactus Charley's, a very successful fast food chain specializing in food dishes from the American southwest. Which of the following problems is Mary most likely to encounter if she agrees to become a franchisee?
   A) High initial costs and fees.
   B) Poor name recognition and visibility.
   C) Lack of financing.
   D) Lack of managerial assistance.

9. Bo will retire from the U.S. Army next month. Bo was stationed in several foreign countries during his career, and enjoyed living overseas. He is thinking about opening a franchise in one of the countries where he served. Bo should note that:
   A) the key to success in a foreign market is to operate his franchise just as he would in the United States.
   B) most foreign governments do not allow U.S. franchises to operate within their borders unless the appropriate officials are bribed.
   C) starting a franchise in a foreign country often is more expensive than operating a franchise in the U.S., but competition is likely to be less intense.
   D) franchises in foreign countries are seldom profitable because standards of living are so low.

10. Twenty-six years ago, several small apple growers in Illinois joined voluntarily to market their apples in an attempt to get better prices. Over the years they expanded the organization to include other services such as buying and selling farm supplies and equipment and providing financial and technical services. The arrangement established by these apple growers is an example of a(n):
    A) closed corporation.
    B) joint venture.
    C) limited partnership.
    D) cooperative.

ANSWER KEY

LEARNING THE LANGUAGE OF BUSINESS

1. V
2. H
3. N
4. T
5. X
6. B
7. O
8. E
9. J
10. R
11. Y
12. K
13. D
14. U
15. M
16. G
17. A
18. F
19. I
20. S
21. L
22. Q
23. W
24. C
25. P

SELF-TEST

Answer	Page #
1. D	Page: 136
2. D	Page: 137
3. B	Page: 137
4. C	Page: 144-145
5. D	Page: 145
6. C	Page: 150
7. C	Page: 148
8. A	Page: 152
9. C	Page: 156
10. D	Page: 157

LESSON 10

HIGHLIGHTING SMALL BUSINESS

ASSIGNMENTS

1. Review the Learning Goals and read the Lesson Overview for this lesson.

2. Read Chapter 6 pp. 164-195 in *Understanding Business,* 6th edition by Nickels, McHugh, and McHugh.

3. Watch the video *Highlighting Small Business.*

4. Review the textbook material.

5. Match the key terms with the correct definitions in the Learning the Language of Business exercise.

6. Take the Self-Test.

7. Use the Answer Key to check your answers and review when necessary.

LEARNING GOALS

After you watch the video, read the textbook, and study this lesson, you should be able to:

1. Explain why people are willing to take the risks of entrepreneurship, list the attributes of successful entrepreneurs, describe the benefits of entrepreneurial teams and intrepreneurs, and explain the growth of home-based and Web-based businesses.

2. Discuss the importance of small business to the American economy and summarize the major causes of small-business failure.

3. Summarize ways to learn about how small businesses operate.

4. Analyze what it takes to start and run a small business.

5. Outline the advantages and disadvantages small businesses have in entering global markets.

LESSON NOTES

The PROFILE at the beginning of this chapter focuses on Andy Wilson who took the bizarre "duck," a World War II amphibious bus/truck/boat and made it into a business venture. Andy's now very successful Boston Duck Tours started off slow, but rapidly gained funds and momentum. His entrepreneurial expertise has been recognized through his selection in 1997 as, "Small Business Person of the Year for the Commonwealth of Massachusetts."

I. THE AGE OF THE ENTREPRENEUR
   A. One poll of college seniors showed that 51% of the men and 31% of the women were attracted to starting their own business rather than joining a corporation.

   B. Of the 5.6 million Americans who started businesses in 1996, one-third were 30 or younger.

   C. Colleges are responding by offering more courses on the subject of **ENTREPRENEURSHIP**.

   D. An entrepreneur is an innovator who assumes the risks of starting and managing a business.

II. THE JOB-CREATING POWER OF ENTREPRENEURS IN THE UNITED STATES

   A. One of the major issues in the U.S. today is the need to create more jobs.

   B. You can get some idea about the job-creating power of entrepreneurs when you look at some of the great American entrepreneurs from the past and the present.

   C. The text lists a number of examples including past entrepreneurs George Eastman of Kodak and Henry Ford of Ford Motor Company and contemporary entrepreneurs Steve Jobs, Michael Dell, and Mary Kay Ash.

III. WHY PEOPLE TAKE THE ENTREPRENEURIAL CHALLENGE

   A. Reasons why people are willing to take the risks of business ownership include:
      1. Opportunity.
      2. Profit.
      3. Independence.
         a. Many entrepreneurs do not enjoy working for someone else.
         b. Some have found more self-satisfaction in starting their own businesses.
      4. Challenge.
         a. Some believe that entrepreneurs are excitement junkies who flourish on taking risks.
         b. Many contend that entrepreneurs take moderate, calculated risks.
         c. In general, entrepreneurs seek achievement more than power.

   B. WHAT DOES IT TAKE TO BE AN ENTREPRENEUR?
      1. The list of entrepreneurial attributes includes:
         a. Self-directed.
         b. Self-nurturing.
         c. Action-oriented.
         d. Highly energetic.
         e. Tolerant of uncertainty.

Lesson 10

2. Most entrepreneurs don't get the ideas for their products and services from some flash of inspiration often the source of innovation is more like a flashlight.
3. An entrepreneurial test to determine if you have the entrepreneurial spirit is provided at the end of the chapter.

C. ENTREPRENEURIAL TEAMS
1. An **ENTREPRENEURIAL TEAM** is a group of experienced people from different areas of business who join together to form a managerial team with the skills needed to develop, make, and market a new product.
2. This gives the company the combination of skills needed to get the new company off to a great start.

D. MICROPRENEURS AND HOME-BASED BUSINESSES
1. Some business owners are interested in simply enjoying a better lifestyle and doing what they want, this person is called a **MICROPRENEUR**.
2. While entrepreneurs are committed to the quest for growth, micropreneurs can be happy with little expansion.
3. Many micropreneurs are home-based business owners, and many are owned by people who are trying to combine career and family.
4. Some of the reasons for the growth in home-based businesses are:
   a. Computer technology.
   b. Corporate downsizing.
   c. Changing social attitudes.
   d. New less restrictive tax laws.
5. The challenges of being micropreneurs are:
   a. Getting new customers.
   b. Time management.
   c. City ordinances.
   d. Managing risk.

E. WEB-BASED BUSINESSES
1. In 2000, 64% of small businesses took orders over the Web.
2. By 2003, the number of small businesses using the Internet should exceed 4 million.
3. There are many Internet sites to assist you in setting up a Web-based business.
   a. Be careful, many dot.com companies have failed.

F. ENTREPRENEURSHIP WITHIN FIRMS
1. **INTRAPRENEURS** are creative people who work as entrepreneurs within corporations.
2. By using company's existing financial, physical, and human resources, they launch new products and generate new profits.
3. Examples in the text focus on 3M, Hewlett-Packard, and Lockheed Corp.

IV. ENCOURAGING ENTREPRENEURSHIP - WHAT GOVERNMENT CAN DO
A. The government passed the Immigration Act in 1990 to encourage more entrepreneurs to come to the United States.
   1. It created a category of investor visas that allows 10,000 people to come to the United States each year if they invest $1 million in an enterprise that creates or preserves 10 jobs.
   2. Some believe that the more entrepreneurs that can be lured to the U.S., the more jobs will be created.

B. One way to encourage entrepreneurship is through enterprise zones that feature low taxes and government support.
   1. The government could encourage entrepreneurship by offering investment tax credits to businesses that invest in creating jobs.
   2. The government could also institute a plan of public investment to rebuild the nation's infrastructure.

C. Some states are becoming stronger entrepreneurial supporters.
   1. Some states provide incubators and technological centers.
   2. **INCUBATORS** are centers that offer advice, help, and low cost office space.

V. GETTING STARTED IN SMALL BUSINESS

A. The purpose of this part of the chapter is to explore small businesses, their role in the economy, and how they are started and managed.
   1. You will learn that, in general, the same principles apply to both small and large companies.
   2. All organizations demand capital, good ideas, planning, information management, budgets, accounting, marketing, employee relations, and good overall management.

B. SMALL VERSUS BIG BUSINESS
   1. **SMALL BUSINESS** is defined by the SBA as a business that is:
      a. Independently owned and operated.
      b. Not dominate in its field of operation.
      c. Meets certain standards in term of employees or annual receipts (for example, less than $2 million a year for service companies).
   2. Small businesses account for over 40% of the gross domestic product (GDP).
   3. The first jobs of about 80% of all Americans are in small business.

C. IMPORTANCE OF SMALL BUSINESS
   1. Since 75% of the nation's new jobs are in small business; they are an important source of employment.
   2. The advantages that small business' have over big companies are that they have more personal customer service and they have the ability to respond quickly to opportunities.
   3. Big businesses don't serve all the needs of the market; there is plenty of room for small businesses in niches.

D. SMALL-BUSINESS SUCCESS AND FAILURE
   1. Failure rate
      a. There is some debate about how many new small businesses fail each year.
      b. Conventional wisdom says that four out of five businesses (80%) fail in their first five years.
      c. Yet the SBA reports a 62% death rate within six years.
      d. However, a recent study by economist Bruce Kirchhoff shows that the failure rate is only 18% over the first eight years.
      e. It now seems that business failures are much lower than traditionally reported.
   2. Still nearly one out of five businesses that fails is left owing money to creditors.
   3. Many small businesses fail because of managerial incompetence and inadequate financial planning.
   4. Choosing the right type of business is critical to success.
      a. Many businesses with the lowest failure rates require advanced training to start.
      b. In general it seems that the easiest businesses to start are the ones that tend to have the least growth and the greatest failure rate.

VI. LEARNING ABOUT SMALL-BUSINESS OPERATIONS

A. LEARN FROM OTHERS
1. Investigate local community colleges for small business classes.
2. Talk to others who have already done it.

B. GET SOME EXPERIENCE
1. Go to work for others and learn all you can.
2. Forty-two percent of small-business owners got the idea for their business from their prior jobs.
3. The general rule is that one should have 3 years of experience in a comparable business before going out on your own.

C. TAKE OVER A SUCCESSFUL FIRM
1. After many years, some small business owners' feel stuck in their businesses.
2. The text describes a method of becoming successful small business managers.
   a. The first step is to find a businessperson running a successful small business.
   b. For a year or so, work hard to learn all about the business.
   c. At the end of two years, offer to become assistant manager.
   d. After another year or two, offer to manage the business when the owner retires or decides to only work part-time.
   e. You can establish a profit-sharing plan for yourself plus a salary.
   f. The owner benefits by keeping ownership and earning profits without working.
3. If profit sharing doesn't appeal to the owner, you may want to buy the business outright.

VII. MANAGING A SMALL BUSINESS

A. Ninety percent of all failures are a result of poor management.
1. This could mean poor planning, poor record keeping, poor inventory control, poor promotion, or poor employee relations.
2. It could likely include poor capitalization.
3. This section explores the major functions of business as they pertain to small business:
   a. Planning your business (business plan).
   b. Funding your business (finance).
   c. Knowing your customers (marketing).
   d. Managing your employees (human resource development).
   e. Keeping records (accounting).

B. BEGIN WITH PLANNING
1. A **BUSINESS PLAN** is a detailed written statement that describes the nature of the business, the target market, the advantages the business will have in relation to competition, and the resources and qualifications of the owner(s).
   a. A business plan is mandatory for talking with bankers or other investors.
   b. Michael Celello, president of the People's Commercial Bank, says that fewer than 10% of prospective borrowers come to a bank adequately prepared and offers several tips.
2. WRITING A BUSINESS PLAN
   a. One of the most important parts of the business plan is the executive summary, which has to catch the reader's interest.
   b. There are computer software programs now available to help you get organized.
   c. Getting the completed business plan in the right hands is almost as important as getting the right information into the plan.

C. GETTING MONEY TO FUND A SMALL BUSINESS
1. New entrepreneurs have several sources of capital: personal savings, relatives, former employers, banks, finance companies, venture capital organizations, government agencies, and more.
   a. Technology-minded entrepreneurs often have the best shot at attracting start-up capital.
   b. Other than personal savings, individual investors are the primary source of capital for most entrepreneurs.
   c. **VENTURE CAPITALISTS** may ask for a hefty stake (as much as 60%) in your company in exchange for the cash to start your business.
2. THE SMALL BUSINESS ADMINISTRATION (SBA)
   a. The SBA may provide the following types of financial assistance:
      1) Direct loans.
      2) Guaranteed loans.
      3) Participation loans.
      4) Loans from Minority Enterprise Small Business Investment Companies (MESBICs).
      5) Women's Prequalified Pilot Loan Program.
      6) Microloans.
   b. The SBA's microloan program awards loans on the basis of belief in the borrowers' integrity and the soundness of their business idea.
   c. You may also want to consider requesting funds from **SMALL BUSINESS INVESTMENT COMPANY PROGRAM (SBICs).** SBICs are private investment companies, which the Small Business Administration licenses to lend money to small businesses.
   d. Small business development centers (SBDCs), funded jointly by the federal government and individual states, can help evaluate the feasibility of your idea, develop your business plan, and complete your funding application.
3. Obtaining money from banks, venture capitalists, and government sources is very difficult for most small businesses.

D. KNOWING YOUR CUSTOMERS
1. A **MARKET** consists of people with: (1) unsatisfied wants and needs, (2) with the resources, and (3) the willingness to buy.
2. The goal of a businessperson is to find a need and fill it.
3. In order to fill these needs, one must first identify the wants and needs of potential customers.
4. You will gain more insights about markets in Chapters 13 and 14.

E. MANAGING EMPLOYEES
1. If you talk to small business owners, you will find that one of their most difficult chores is to find, hire, train, and motivate good employees.
   a. Nonetheless, employees of small companies are often more satisfied with their jobs than their counterparts in large companies.
   b. They find they are more challenged, their ideas are more accepted, and their bosses treat them with more respect.
2. As the business grows, it becomes necessary to delegate authority.
   a. This is touchy especially in businesses with employees who have been with the company since its start.
   b. These long-term employees may not have the necessary managerial skills.
3. Attitudes such as you "can't fire family" or you must promote someone because "They're family" can hinder growth.
4. You'll learn more about managing employees in Chapters 7 through 12.

F. KEEPING RECORDS
1. A businessperson that sets up an accounting system early will save much grief later.
2. Computers make record keeping easier and let the business owner follow the progress of the business.
3. A good accountant is invaluable in setting up record keeping systems and providing tax planning, financial forecasting, and choosing sources of financing.
4. You will learn more about accounting in Chapter 18, which focuses on accounting.

G. LOOKING FOR HELP
1. Small businesspeople need help setting up their businesses early in the process.
2. A necessary aide is a competent, experienced lawyer who knows and understands small businesses.
3. A marketing consultant with small business experience can help with marketing decisions.
4. Two other valuable experts are a commercial loan officer and an insurance agent.
5. The **SERVICE CORPS OF RETIRED EXECUTIVES (SCORE)** consists of 13,000 volunteers who provide consulting services for small businesses free of charge.
6. The SBA also sponsors the **ACTIVE CORPS OF EXECUTIVES (ACE),** volunteers who counsel small businesses.
7. Other helpful contacts: other small business owners, chambers of commerce, the Better Business Bureau, and trade associations.

VII. GOING INTERNATIONAL: SMALL-BUSINESS PROSPECTS

A. The global market is potentially a more lucrative market for small businesses that the U.S. alone.
1. However, most small businesses still do not think internationally.
2. Only 20% of small business' executives say they export.

B. Many potential international businesspeople do not enter the global market because:
1. Financing is difficult to arrange.
2. They don't know how to get started.
3. They don't understand the cultural differences.
4. The bureaucratic paperwork is overwhelming.

C. There are many good reasons for small business people to consider going international (global).
1. Most of the world's market lies outside the U.S.
2. Exporting can absorb excess inventory.
3. It can soften downturns in the U.S. market.
4. It can extend the life of products.

D. Small businesses have several advantages over large businesses.
1. Overseas buyers enjoy dealing with individuals rather than with large corporate bureaucracies.
2. Small companies can usually begin shipping much faster.
3. Small companies provide a wide variety of suppliers.
4. Small companies can give more personal service and more attention.

E. Sources of information about international business can be obtained from the Department of Commerce's Bureau of Export Administration, and the SBA.

LEARNING THE LANGUAGE OF BUSINESS

Match each of the following key terms with the appropriate definition.

A. Active Corps of Executives (ACE)
B. business plan
C. entrepreneurial team
D. entrepreneurship
E. incubators
F. intrepreneurs
G. market
H. micropreneurs
I. Service Corps of Retired Executives (SCORE)
J. small business
K. Small Business Investment Company Program (SBICs)
L. venture capitalist

____ 1. Individuals or organizations which invest in new businesses in exchange for partial ownership of the company.

____ 2. A person with entrepreneurial skills who is employed in a corporation to launch new products; such people take hands-on responsibility for creating innovation of any kind in an organization.

____ 3. A detailed written statement that describes the nature of the business, the target market, the advantages the business will have over competitors, and the resources and qualifications of the owners.

____ 4. The acceptance of the risk of starting and managing a new business.

____ 5. Part of SBA made up of experienced businesspeople that provide consulting services to small businesses for free (minus expenses).

____ 6. Volunteers from industry, trade associations, and education that counsel small businesses.

____ 7. People with unsatisfied wants and needs who have both the resources and willingness to buy.

____ 8. Centers which provide "newborn" businesses (usually in technological industries) with low-cost offices and basic business services.

____ 9. A business that is independently operated, is not dominant in its field, and meets certain size standards in terms of number of employees and annual receipts.

____ 10. A group of experienced people from different areas of business who join together to form a managerial team with the skills needed to develop, make, and market new products.

____ 11. Private investment companies which the Small Business Administration licenses to lend money to small businesses.

____ 12. Those who are willing accept the risk of starting and managing the type of business that remains small, lets them do the kind of work they want to do, and offers them a balanced lifestyle.

SELF-TEST

1. An examination of the reasons people accept the risks of entrepreneurship indicates that:
   A) the desire to earn a profit is the only reason most people have for becoming entrepreneurs.
   B) many people become entrepreneurs because they do not enjoy working for someone else.
   C) the desire to become an entrepreneur is just part of human nature.
   D) contrary to popular opinion, most entrepreneurs are not interested in personal achievement.

2. Ellie is a creative person who works for the Bigdome Corporation, a large, multifaceted producer of consumer products. One of her primary duties is to initiate and develop new products to complement the firm's current line. Ellie is involved in:
   A) intrapreneuring.
   B) extrapolating.
   C) megatrending.
   D) marketeering.

3. Which of the following is included as one of the fastest-growing segments of the U.S. economy in the last decade?
   A) large scale manufacturing
   B) minority-owned businesses
   C) transportation industry
   D) farming sector

4. After looking at a variety of options, Gene has decided to start a new small manufacturing firm. Based on his decision, it appears that Gene is:
   A) more interested in earning high profits than achieving security.
   B) primarily concerned with being able to start a business with a minimum amount of hassle.
   C) not a self-motivated individual.
   D) afraid to get into a risky type of business.

5. The idea of getting advice from other small business owners is:
   A) generally not a good idea since they could be your competitors.
   B) often valuable advice since you can from learn from their experiences.
   C) not recommended since federal privacy laws could be violated.
   D) only helpful if the person giving the advice has been very successful.

6. Gregory had worked for Friday Floral for two years. During this time he had learned many of the aspects of running a successful florist. Gregory would like to start his own flower shop, but lacks the necessary capital. Gregory might be best advised to:
   A) offer to take over management of the business, allowing the owner to enjoy some time off.
   B) consider working for a major corporation while saving enough money to start his business.
   C) go to college and apply for student loans.
   D) go ahead and start his business with limited funds since he has an understanding of the business operations.

7. When seeking a loan from a bank, an entrepreneur starting a new business should realize that bankers will:
    A) expect to receive a share of ownership in the business in exchange for their loan.
    B) expect the entrepreneur to have a well prepared business plan.
    C) generally make loans only to small businesses in computer related industries.
    D) offer only very short-term financing.

8. Kathy, like many others in her extended family, works in the furniture store started by Kathy's grandfather. As the business has expanded, she has found that one area of small business management offers unique problems to family run operations is:
    A) marketing.
    B) accounting.
    C) managing inventory.
    D) managing employees.

9. Small business owner Tony has thought about selling his product in Brazil. If he decides to enter the Brazilian market, he is likely to face all of the following problems with the exception of:
    A) cultural differences between the United States and Brazil.
    B) difficulties in obtaining adequate financing.
    C) difficulty in convincing foreign buyers to deal with his small firm rather than a major corporation.
    D) a heavy burden of bureaucratic paperwork.

10. Which of the following statements best describes the opportunities available to small businesses in international markets?
    A) The world market is much larger, and potentially more lucrative, market for small businesses than the U.S. market alone.
    B) The main barrier preventing small businesses from competing internationally is the lack of support from the federal government.
    C) Most foreign buyers prefer to deal with large, well-known corporations rather than small businesses.
    D) Small businesses are almost always better off ignoring foreign markets since they lack the resources needed to compete in global markets.

ANSWER KEY

LEARNING THE LANGUAGE OF BUSINESS

1. L
2. F
3. B
4. D
5. I
6. A
7. G
8. E
9. J
10. C
11. K
12. H

SELF-TEST

Answer	Page #
1. B	Page: 167
2. A	Page: 174
3. B	Page: 176
4. A	Page: 177
5. B	Page: 179
6. A	Page: 180
7. B	Page: 181
8. D	Page: 187
9. C	Page: 190
10. A	Page: 189-190

LESSON 11

MANAGING A BUSINESS

ASSIGNMENTS

1. Review the Learning Goals and read the Lesson Overview for this lesson.

2. Read Chapter 7 pp. 202-231 in *Understanding Business,* 6th edition by Nickels, McHugh, and McHugh

3. Watch the video *Managing a Business.*

4. Review the textbook material.

5. Match the key terms with the correct definitions in the Learning the Language of Business exercise.

6. Take the Self-Test.

7. Use the Answer Key to check your answers and review when necessary.

LEARNING GOALS

After you watch the video, read the textbook, and study this lesson, you should be able to:

1. Explain how the changes that are occurring in the business environment are affecting the management function.

2. Enumerate the four functions of management.

3. Relate the planning process and decision making to the accomplishment of company goals.

4. Describe the organizing function of management, including staffing and diversity management.

5. Explain the differences between leaders and managers, and describe the various leadership styles.

6. Summarize the five steps of the control function of management.

7. Differentiate the skills needed at each level of management.

LESSON NOTES

The PROFILE at the beginning of this chapter focuses on John Chambers CEO of Cisco Systems. He has taken Cisco to the top of the Internet technology field. He has a participative management style and is a talented leader. The keys to his success are simple. He provides the best product by buying the best companies, retaining the best employees by motivating and compensating them well, and through his constant focus on customer needs.

I. THE NEW BUSINESS ENVIRONMENT

   A. A number of changes have prompted managers to reorganize their organizations and their approaches to management.
      1. Changes are necessary because of global competition, technological change, and the growing importance of pleasing customers.
      2. The need to respond better to customers is motivating businesses to reorganize to give more authority and responsibility to managers.
      3. Accelerating technological change increases the need for a new breed of worker, one who is more educated and has higher skill levels. Higher educated workers demand more freedom of operation and different managerial styles.
      4. The start of the next century is shaping up as a time to get rid of old management styles and introduce a new way of operating.

   B. MANAGERS ARE NO LONGER JUST BOSSES
      1. Managers use the art of getting things done through people and organizational resources.
      2. Bosses are changing from bossy behavior to leading, training, supporting, guiding and motivating employees.
      3. Managers in the future are much more likely to be working in teams.
      4. This approach to management will demand that a manager be a skilled communicator and team player as well as a planner, coordinator, organizer, and supervisor.

   C. FUNCTIONS OF MANAGEMENT
      1. **MANAGEMENT** is a process that is used to accomplish organizational goals through planning, organizing, leading, and controlling.
         a. **PLANNING** includes anticipating future trends and determining the best strategies and tactics to achieve organizational goals and objectives.
         b. **ORGANIZING** includes designing the organization structure, organization, and creating conditions that ensure that everyone works together to achieve the organization's goals.
         c. **LEADING** means creating a vision for the organization and guiding, training, coaching, and motivating others to work effectively to achieve the organization's goals and objectives.
         d. **CONTROLLING** is determining whether an organization is progressing toward its goals and objectives, and taking corrective action if it's not.

II. PLANNING: CREATING A VISION BASED ON VALUE

   A. Planning is the management function that involves anticipating future trends and determining the best strategies and tactics to achieve organizational objectives.
      1. Planning involves the setting of the organizational vision, goals, and objectives.
      2. A **VISION** is more than a goal; it is the larger explanation of why the organization exists and where it is trying to head.
      3. A **MISSION STATEMENT** outlines the fundamental purposes of the organization.

Lesson 11   Page 104

4. **GOALS** are the broad, long-term accomplishments an organization wishes to attain.
5. **OBJECTIVES** are specific, short-term statements detailing how to achieve the organizational goals.
6. Planning is a continuous process.
   a. **SWOT ANALYSIS** is used to analyze an organization's strengths, weaknesses, opportunities, and threats.

B. Planning answers several questions for business.
   1. What is the situation now?
   2. Where do we want to go?
   3. How can we get there from here?

C. Types of planning
   1. **STRATEGIC PLANNING** determines the major goals of the organization and the policies and strategies for obtaining and using resources to achieve those goals.
      a. Long-range planning is becoming more difficult because changes are occurring too fast for long-range thinking.
      b. The long-range goal is to be flexible and responsive to the market.
      c. Strategic planning is usually done by top management.
   2. **TACTICAL PLANNING** is the process of developing detailed, short-term decisions about what is to be done, who is to do it, and how it is to be done.
      a. Tactical planning is normally done by managers or teams of managers at lower levels of the organization.
   3. **OPERATIONAL PLANNING** is setting of work standards and schedules necessary to implement the tactical objectives.
   4. **CONTINGENCY PLANNING** is the preparation of alternative courses of action that may be used if the primary plans do not achieve the objectives of the organization.
      a. Economic and competitive environments change so rapidly that it is wise to have alternative plans of action ready in anticipation of environmental changes.
      b. The leaders of market-based companies stay flexible, listen for opportunities, and respond quickly to seize opportunities.

D. DECISION MAKING: FINDING THE BEST ALTERNATIVE
   1. **DECISION MAKING** is choosing among two or more alternatives.
      a. These are the 7 Ds of decision making:
         1) Define the situation.
         2) Describe and collect needed information.
         3) Develop alternatives.
         4) Develop agreement among those involved.
         5) Decide which alternative is best.
         6) Do what is indicated. (implementation)
         7) Determine whether the decision was a good one and follow up.
      b. The best decisions are based upon sound information.

III. ORGANIZING: CREATING A UNIFIED SYSTEM

A. After planning a course of action, managers must organize the firm to accomplish their goals.
   1. The **ORGANIZATION CHART** pictures who reports to whom and who is responsible for each task.
   2. The corporate hierarchy illustrated on the organization chart includes top, middle, and supervisory managers.

B. Levels of management
1. **TOP MANAGEMENT** is the highest level of management and consists of the president and other key company executives who develop strategic plans.
   a. Titles include chief executive officer (CEO), chief operating officer (COO), and chief financial officer (CFO), and others.
2. **MIDDLE MANAGEMENT** includes general and division managers, branch and plant managers, deans, and department heads who are responsible for tactical plans.
3. **SUPERVISORY MANAGEMENT** includes people directly responsible for assigning specific jobs to workers and evaluating their daily performance; these managers are frequently referred to as first-line managers.

C. The trend toward self-managed teams
1. The trend in the United States is toward self-managed teams, with planning, organizing, directing, and controlling delegated to lower-level managers.
2. It means developing and training employees to assume greater responsibility in planning, teamwork, and problem solving.
   a. Teamwork typically improves communication, cooperation, reduces internal competition, and maximizes employee talent.

D. THE STAKEHOLDER-ORIENTED ORGANIZATION
1. The firm must find the best way to organize to respond to the needs of customers and other stakeholders.
   a. Stakeholders include anyone who is affected by the organization and its policies and products.
   b. Most large firms are being restructured into smaller, more customer-focused units to become more responsive.
2. Companies are no longer organizing to make it easy for managers to have control. Instead, they are organizing so customers will have control.
3. Managers have to establish closer relationships with suppliers to ensure a supply of world-class materials.
4. Other relationships are also important, combined they make the entire system work well.

E. STAFFING: GETTING AND KEEPING THE RIGHT PEOPLE
1. **STAFFING** is a management function that involves the recruiting, hiring, motivating and retaining of the optimal people for achieving the company's objectives.
   a. Innovative and creative workers can make a business into a major competitor.
2. Retention of good employees is vital.
   a. People want to be treated well.
   b. People want fair compensation.
   c. People want a good balance between work and home.
3. Staffing is becoming a greater part of each manager's assignment.

F. MANAGING DIVERSITY
1. **MANAGING DIVERSITY** means building systems and a climate that unites different people in a common pursuit without undermining their individual strengths.
2. If people are to work on teams, they have to learn to deal with people who have different personalities, priorities, and lifestyles.
3. Heterogeneous (mixed) groups are more productive than homogeneous (similar) groups in the workplace.
4. It is often quite profitable to have employees who match the diversity of customers.
5. It is also beneficial to work with minority business enterprises to maintain a strong and diverse supplier network.

IV. LEADING: PROVIDING CONTINUOUS VISION AND VALUES

A. Leadership involves creating vision for others to follow, establishing corporate values and ethics, and transforming the way the organization does business so it is more effective and efficient. Management is carrying out the leadership's vision.

B. Leaders:
   1. Have a vision and rally others around that vision.
   2. Establish corporate values.
   3. Emphasize corporate ethics.
   4. Don't fear change, but embrace it and create it.

C. LEADERSHIP STYLES
   1. Research studies have not been able to identify one set of traits that are common to all leaders.
   2. There are also different leadership styles:
      a. **AUTOCRATIC LEADERSHIP** involves making managerial decisions without consulting others.
      b. **PARTICIPATIVE (democratic) LEADERSHIP** consists of managers and employees working together to make decisions.
      c. **LAISSEZ-FAIRE (free-rein) LEADERSHIP** involves managers setting objectives and employees being relatively free to do whatever it takes to accomplish those objectives.
      d. Individual leaders rarely fit neatly into just one category.
   3. When to use the various styles of leadership
      a. The best leadership style to use depends on who is being led and what the situation is.
      b. Any one manager can use a variety of leadership styles depending on who he or she is dealing with and the situation.

D. EMPOWERING WORKERS
   1. For traditional organizations, directing involves giving assignments, explaining routines, clarifying policies, and providing feedback on performance.
   2. Progressive leaders are less likely to be giving specific instructions to employees.
      a. They are more likely to use **EMPOWERMENT**, allowing them to make decisions on their own.
      b. **ENABLING** is the term used to describe giving workers the education and tools needed to assume their new decision-making powers.

E. MANAGING KNOWLEDGE
   1. Empowering employees means giving them knowledge and information to do the best job they can.
   2. **KNOWLEDGE MANAGEMENT** is finding the right information, keeping it in a readily accessible place, and making the information known to employees.
      a. This prevents "reinventing the wheel."

V. CONTROLLING: MAKING SURE IT WORKS

A. The control function is the heart of the management system because it provides the feedback that enables managers to adjust to any deviations from plans.

B. Controlling consists of the following steps:
   1. Setting clear performance standards.
   2. Monitoring and recording actual performance.
   3. Comparing results against plans and standards.

4. Communicating results and deviations to the employees involved.
5. Providing positive feedback or taking corrective action.

C. Setting standards
   1. To measure results against standards, the standards must be specific, attainable, and measurable.
   2. Clear procedures for monitoring performance should be established.

D. A NEW CRITERION FOR MEASUREMENT: CUSTOMER SATISFACTION
   1. The criterion for measuring success in a customer-oriented firm is customer satisfaction of both internal and external customers.
      a. **EXTERNAL CUSTOMERS** include dealers and ultimate customers who buy products for their own personal use.
      b. **INTERNAL CUSTOMERS** are units within the firm that receive services from other units.
   2. Other criterion of organizational effectiveness may include the firm's contribution to society and their being environmentally responsible.

E. THE CORPORATE SCORECARD
   1. A corporate scorecard measures financial progress, return on investment, and profits, in addition to customer satisfaction.
   2. Most companies would do better with a balanced approach that measures both financial growth and employee and customer satisfaction.

VI. TASKS AND SKILLS AT DIFFERENT LEVELS OF MANAGEMENT

A. The further up the managerial ladder, the greater the need for people who are visionaries, good planners, organizers, coordinators, communicators, morale builders, and motivators.

B. Managers must have three categories of skills:
   1. **TECHNICAL SKILLS** involve the ability to perform tasks of a specific department such as selling (marketing).
   2. **HUMAN RELATIONS SKILLS** include leadership, motivation, coaching, communication, morale building, training and development, help and supportiveness, and delegating.
   3. **CONCEPTUAL SKILLS** refer to a manager's ability to picture the organization as a whole and the relationship of various parts to perform tasks such as planning, organizing, controlling, systems development, problem-analysis, decision-making, coordinating, and delegating.
   4. Supervisory managers spend more time using technical and human relations skills; whereas, top managers use fewer technical skills and more conceptual and human relations skills.

C. MANAGEMENT SKILLS ARE TRANSFERABLE
   1. Studying management and leadership prepares people for a career in any organization.
   2. When selecting a career in management, a student has several decisions to make:
      a. What kind of organization is most desirable?
      b. What type of managerial position seems most interesting?
      c. What type of industry is most appealing?

LEARNING THE LANGUAGE OF BUSINESS

Match each of the following key terms with the appropriate definition.

A. autocratic leadership
B. conceptual skills
C. contingency planning
D. controlling
E. decision making
F. empowerment
G. enabling
H. external customers
I. goals
J. human relations skills
K. internal customers
L. knowledge management
M. laissez-faire (free-reign) leadership
N. leading
O. management
P. managing diversity
Q. middle management
R. mission statement
S. objectives
T. operational planning
U. organization chart
V. organizing
W. participative (democratic) leadership
X. planning
Y. staffing
Z. strategic planning
AA. supervisory management
BB. SWOT analysis
CC. tactical planning
DD. technical skills
EE. top management
FF. vision

___ 1. Leadership style that consists of managers and employees working together to make decisions.

___ 2. Specific, short-term statements detailing how to achieve the goals.

___ 3. A sense of why the organization exists and where it is heading.

___ 4. Highest level of management, consisting of the president and other key company executives who develop strategic plans.

___ 5. Management function which involves designing the organizational structure, attracting people to the organization (staffing), and creating conditions and systems that ensure that everyone and everything work together to achieve the objectives of the organization.

___ 6. Level of management, which includes plant managers, and department heads who are responsible for tactical plans.

Lesson 11 Page 109

_____ 7. Process of determining the major goals of the organization and the policies and strategies for obtaining and using resources to achieve those goals.

_____ 8. Broad, long-term accomplishments an organization wishes to attain.

_____ 9. First level of management above workers; includes people directly responsible for assigning specific jobs to employees and evaluating their daily performance.

_____ 10. The process used to accomplish organizational goals through planning, organizing, directing, and controlling people and other organizational resources.

_____ 11. Ability to picture the organization as a whole and the relationship of various parts.

_____ 12. Choosing among two or more alternatives.

_____ 13. Leadership style that involves managers setting objectives and employees being relatively free to do whatever it takes to accomplish those objectives.

_____ 14. Process of preparing alternative courses of action that may be used if the primary plans do not achieve the objectives of the organization.

_____ 15. Giving workers the education and tools needed to assume their new decision-making powers.

_____ 16. Dealers, who buy products to sell to others, and ultimate customers (or end users), who buy products for their own personal use.

_____ 17. Giving employees the authority and responsibility to respond quickly to customer requests.

_____ 18. Management function which involves checking to determine whether or not an organization is progressing toward its goals and objectives, and taking corrective action if it is not.

_____ 19. Process of developing detailed, short-term decisions about what is to be done, who is to do it, and how it is to be done.

_____ 20. Ability to lead, communicate, motivate, coach, build morale, train, support, and delegate.

_____ 21. Building systems and a culture that unites different people in a common pursuit without undermining their individual strengths.

_____ 22. Ability to perform tasks of a specific department (such as selling).

_____ 23. Units within the firm that receive services from other units.

_____ 24. Leadership style that involves making decisions without consulting others.

_____ 25. A management function that involves creating a vision for the organization and guiding, training, coaching, and motivating others to work effectively to achieve the organization's goal and objectives.

_____ 26. An outline of the fundamental purposes of the organization.

____ 27. The process of setting work standards and schedules necessary to implement the tactical objectives.

____ 28. An analysis of an organization's strengths, weaknesses, opportunities and threats.

____ 29. The management function that involves anticipating trends and determining the best strategies and tactics to achieve organizational goals and objectives.

____ 30. The process of finding the right information, keeping the information in a readily accessible place and making the information known to everyone in the firm.

____ 31. A management function that includes hiring, motivating, and retaining the best people available to accomplish the company's objectives.

____ 32. A visual device which shows the relationships and divides the organization's work.

SELF-TEST

1. How are managers today different from managers in the past?
   A) Managers today are more likely to reprimand workers.
   B) Managers in the past would use praise and gentle suggestions.
   C) Managers in the past were less loyal to their employer.
   D) Managers today emphasize teamwork.

2. Which of the following activities is part of the planning function of a manager?
   A) Assigning a particular worker to do a specific task.
   B) Looking at market forecasts to identify future business opportunities and challenges.
   C) Talking to an employee whose job performance has been unsatisfactory.
   D) Conducting a job interview with a potential new employee.

3. Jamal is part of a management group that is examining whether his company, State Engineering, should offer some important new services that would broaden its business by appealing to a different group of potential clients. Jamal's group is involved with:
   A) contingency planning.
   B) peripheral planning.
   C) strategic planning.
   D) tactical planning.

4. In today's environment the organizing efforts of managers focus on:
   A) clearly defining the relationships that exist within the firm.
   B) creating the appropriate vision for the firm.
   C) creating a unified system of several firms that work together.
   D) checking results to see if the firm is achieving its goals.

5. After thirteen years as a laborer for Hendrix Construction, Mike Jimmy was promoted to the position of foreman. He is directly responsible for assigning various jobs to his work crew and evaluating their performance on a daily basis. Jimmy is now a member of:
   A) top management.
   B) supervisory management.
   C) middle management.
   D) forward management.

6. Pam is a sales manager for Paradise Beauty Products. She has told her sales people that she expects each of them to increase their customer contacts by at least 5 percent in the next month. Pam has set a(n):
   A) procedural policy.
   B) functional objective.
   C) policy guide.
   D) performance standard.

7. Autocratic leadership is likely to be effective when:
   A) subordinates are highly trained professionals.
   B) the organization faces an emergency situation.
   C) workers enjoy expressing their opinions and having a say in what is done.
   D) the manager is uncertain about the best strategy to pursue.

8. At Channing Pharmaceuticals, research personnel are told that the company would like to develop at least three new products each year. After that, scientists and other research personnel work essentially on their own to accomplish this task. Managers at Channing seem to prefer:
   A) laissez-faire leadership.
   B) consultative leadership.
   C) projectory leadership.
   D) autocratic leadership.

9. Ricardo works as a department head at Barnes Hospital. His job requires Ricardo to spend most of his time training and coaching employees to perform their jobs more effectively and teaching other managers to be better leaders. Ricardo's job requires him to make full use of his:
   A) technical skills.
   B) conceptual skills.
   C) orientation skills.
   D) human relations skills.

10. When comparing the productivity of homogenous (similar) groups with the productivity of heterogeneous (mixed) groups, researchers have found:
    A) no difference in the productivity of the two types of groups.
    B) that heterogeneous groups tend to be more productive than homogenous groups.
    C) that homogeneous groups tend to be more productive than heterogeneous groups.
    D) that whenever groups include both men and women, productivity suffers. However, racial and ethnic diversity have no impact on productivity.

ANSWER KEY

LEARNING THE LANGUAGE OF BUSINESS

1. W
2. S
3. FF
4. EE
5. V
6. Q
7. Z
8. I
9. AA
10. O
11. B
12. E
13. M
14. C
15. G
16. H

17. F
18. D
19. CC
20. J
21. P
22. DD
23. K
24. A
25. N
26. R
27. T
28. BB
29. X
30. L
31. Y
32. U

SELF-TEST

Answer	Page #
1. D	Page: 204-205
2. B	Page: 206
3. C	Page: 209-210
4. C	Page: 214
5. B	Page: 212
6. D	Page: 222-223
7. B	Page: 217
8. A	Page: 219
9. D	Page: 224
10. B	Page: 215

LESSON 12

ESTABLISHING A BUSINESS ORGANIZATION

ASSIGNMENTS

1. Review the Learning Goals and read the Lesson Overview for this lesson.

2. Read Chapter 8 pp. 232-261 in *Understanding Business,* 6th edition by Nickels, McHugh, and McHugh.

3. Watch the video *Establishing A Business Organization.*

4. Review the textbook material.

5. Match the key terms with the correct definitions in the Learning the Language of Business exercise.

6. Take the Self-Test.

7. Use the Answer Key to check your answers and review when necessary.

LEARNING GOALS

After you watch the video, read the textbook, and study this lesson, you should be able to:

1. Explain the organizational theories of Fayol and Weber.

2. Discuss the various issues involved in structuring and restructuring organizations.

3. Describe traditional organizations and their limitations.

4. Show how matrix-style organizations and cross-functional teams help companies become more consumer oriented.

5. Define the use of various organizational tools and techniques such as networking, reengineering, and outsourcing.

6. Give examples to show how organizational culture and the informal organization can hinder or assist organizational change.

LESSON NOTES

The PROFILE at the beginning of this chapter focuses on Carleton (Carly) Fiorina who after tremendous success at AT&T and Lucent Technologies took the job of CEO at Hewlett-Packard. She reinvented the business structure at HP. She rapidly changed HPs revenues by 14% and the stock price by 36% through her actions. She cut costs and merged HPs four companies into two; she reduced the brand names used by HP from 100 down to 1. Her goal was to make the firm more responsive, and a consumer oriented industry leader.

I. THE CHANGING ORGANIZATION

  A. Moving from a boss-driven to an employee-driven company isn't easy.
    1. American companies are trying to develop an organizational design that best serves the needs of the customer.

  B. THE HISTORIC DEVELOPMENT OF ORGANIZATIONAL DESIGN
    1. Not until the 20th century and introduction of mass production did business organizations grow complex and difficult to manage.
    2. The bigger the plant, the more efficient production became, a concept called **ECONOMY OF SCALE**.
    3. The text discusses two major organizational theorists:
       a. Henri Fayol a Frenchman who wrote <u>Administration Industrielle et Generale</u> in 1919.
       b. Max Weber a German who wrote his theories at about the same time.

  C. FAYOL'S PRINCIPLES OF ORGANIZATION
    1. Fayol introduced principles such as:
       a. Unity of command – Each worker is to report to only one boss.
       b. Hierarchy of authority – One should know to whom to report.
       c. Division of labor – Functions were divided into areas of specialization.
       d. Subordination of individual interests to the general interests – Goals of the team were to be considered more important than individual goals.
       e. Authority – Managers should give orders and expect them to be followed.
       f. Degree of centralization – The decisions needed to be made by top management were depended upon the size of the organization.
       g. Clear definition of communication channels.
       h. Order – A place for everything and everything in its place.
       i. Equity – Employees should be treated fairly and justly.
       j. Esprit de corps – Employees should be proud of and loyal to the organization.
    2. These principles have been taught for years, becoming synonymous with the concept of management.
    3. These principles led to a relatively rigid organization.

  D. MAX WEBER AND ORGANIZATIONAL THEORY
    1. Weber's principles were similar to Fayol's with the addition of:
       a. Job descriptions.
       b. Written rules and decision guidelines.
       c. Consistent procedures, regulations, and policies.
       d. Staffing and promotions based upon qualifications.
    2. Max Weber promoted the pyramid-shaped organization in his book <u>The Theory of Social and Economic Organizations</u>.
       a. Weber put great trust in managers and felt that the less decision-making employees had to do, the better.
       b. Today, many firms believe that workers are the best source of ideas, and managers are there to support workers.

      c. Many firms today are going away from the pyramid structure.
      d. **DOWNSIZING** is the eliminating of many managerial and nonmanagerial positions and giving more authority to employees who deal directly with the customer.

  E. TURNING MANAGERIAL CONCEPTS INTO ORGANIZATIONAL DESIGN
    1. American companies are trying to develop organizational designs that best serve the needs of the customers.
    2. **ORGANIZATIONAL DESIGN** is the structuring of workers so that they can best accomplish all the goals of the firm.
      a. In the past, many organizations were designed so managers could control workers, using a hierarchy.
      b. A **HIERARCHY** means that there is one person at the top and many levels of managers responsible to that person.
      c. Some organizations have as many as 10 to 14 layers of management between the chief executive officer and the lowest-level employee.
    3. **BUREAUCRACY** is the term used in organizations to describe having many layers of management who set rules and regulations and participate in all decisions.
    4. Organizations are avoiding the slow service of a bureaucracy by giving employees more decision-making power.
    5. Bureaucratic organizations emphasize functional separation.
      a. Power goes top down.
      b. This encouraged specialization.
      c. This structure is not responsive to customer wants and needs.

II. ISSUES INVOLVED IN STRUCTURING AND RESTRUCTURING ORGANIZATIONS

  A. To be able to respond to customer demands more quickly, organizations are restructuring.
    1. **RESTRUCTURING** means redesigning an organization so that it can more effectively and efficiently service customers.

  B. TALL VERSUS FLAT ORGANIZATION STRUCTURES
    1. Tall organization structures have many layers of management.
      a. The organizational chart becomes very tall because of the levels of management.
    2. Flat organization structures cut out management layers and expand sideways instead.
      a. Organizations that cut out layers are more responsive to customers.

  C. CHOOSING THE APPROPRIATE SPAN OF CONTROL
    1. **SPAN OF CONTROL** refers to the optimum number of subordinates a manager supervises or should supervise.
      a. At lower levels, it is possible to implement a wide span of control.
      b. The number narrows at higher levels of the organization.
    2. Variables in span of control include:
      a. Capabilities of the manager – The more experienced and capable the manager the broader the span of control can be.
      b. Capabilities of the subordinates – The more need for supervision, the narrower the span of control.
      c. Complexity of the job:
        1) Geographical closeness – The more concentrated the work area, the broader the span of control.
        2) Functional similarity – The more similar the employees' functions are, the broader the span of control.

           3) Need for coordination – The greater the need for coordination, the narrower the span of control.
           4) Planning demands – The more planning required the narrower the span of control.
           5) Functional complexity – The more complex, the narrower the span of control.
       d. Other factors to consider include professionalism of superior and subordinates and the number of new problems that occur each day.
    3. The trend is to expand the span of control as organizations get rid of middle managers.

D. **ADVANTAGES AND DISADVANTAGES OF DEPARTMENTALIZATION**
    1. **DEPARTMENTALIZATION** is dividing organizational functions into separate units.
       a. Functional structure is the traditional technique for departmentalizing which has the grouping of workers into departments based on similar skills, expertise, or resource use.
    2. The advantages of functional departmentalization are:
       a. Skills can be developed in depth.
       b. It allows for economies of scale as resources can be centralized.
       c. There is good coordination within the function.
    3. The disadvantages of departmentalization are:
       a. Lack of communication between the departments.
       b. Employees identify with the department rather than the whole organization.
       c. Response to external change is slow.
       d. Employees become narrow specialists.
       e. People within the same department begin to think alike, and lose creativity.

E. **DIFFERENT WAYS TO DEPARTMENTALIZE**
    1. To better serve the customer businesses have tried five different ways to departmentalize.
    2. Departmentalization by product (an automobile manufacturer may have separate divisions for trucks, passenger cars, vans, etc.).
    3. Departmentalization by function (production, marketing, finance, human resources, and accounting are common).
    4. Departmentalization by customer group (a manufacturer may have one department that focuses on consumer goods, and another that focuses on industrial goods).
    5. Departmentalization by geographic location.
    6. Departmentalization by process (a coat manufacturer may have a department that cuts the material, another that dyes it, and another that sews it).
    7. Some firms use combinations of the techniques.
    8. The Internet has created new technique opportunities.

F. **CENTRALIZATION VERSUS DECENTRALIZATUON OF AUTHORITY**
The degree to which an organization allows managers at lower levels to make decisions determines the degree of decentralization.
    1. **CENTRALIZED AUTHORITY** means decision-making remains in the upper layers of management.
    2. **DECENTRALIZED AUTHORITY** means decision-making is delegated to lower level managers.
    3. The trend today is toward more decentralized authority.

III. ORGANIZATION MODELS

   A. There is several ways to structure an organization to accomplish its goals.

   B. LINE ORGANIZATIONS
      1. A **LINE ORGANIZATION** has direct two-way lines of responsibility, authority, and communication running from top to bottom, with all employees reporting to only one boss.
      2. Disadvantages:
         a. Too inflexible.
         b. Few specialists to advise employees along the line.
         c. The lines of communication are too long.
         d. Unable to handle complex decisions.

   C. LINE-AND-STAFF ORGANIZATIONS
      1. **LINE PERSONNEL** perform functions that contribute directly to the goals of the organization.
      2. **STAFF PERSONNEL** advise and assist line personnel.
      3. The advantage is having expert consultants continuously available.

   D. MATRIX-STYLE ORGANIZATIONS
      1. Both line, and line and staff organization structures suffer from a certain inflexibility.
         a. Both have established lines of authority and communication and work well in organizations with relatively unchanging environments and slow product development.
         b. The economic, technological, and competitive environments are rapidly changing.
         c. In such organizations, emphasis is on new product development, creativity, and interdepartmental teamwork.
      2. A MATRIX **ORGANIZATION** brings specialists from different parts of the organization together to work on specific projects. But, they still remain part of a line and staff structure.
         a. Matrix organization structures were developed in the aerospace industry.
         b. The structure is now used in banking, management consulting firms, ad agencies, and school systems.
      3. The advantages of the matrix-style organization are:
         a. Flexibility.
         b. Interorganizational cooperation and teamwork.
         c. Creativity.
         d. More efficient use of organizational resources.
      4. Disadvantages of matrix-style organizations:
         a. Costly and complex.
         b. Confusion in loyalties.
         c. Requires good interpersonal skills and cooperative employees and managers.
         d. It is only a temporary solution to long-term problems.
      5. Matrix-style organizations seem to violate some traditional managerial principles, but the system functions relatively effectively.

   E. CROSS-FUNCTIONAL SELF-MANAGED TEAMS
      1. **CROSS-FUNCTIONAL TEAMS** are groups of employees from different departments who work together on a semi-permanent basis (as opposed to the temporary teams established in matrix-style organizations).
         a. Often the teams are empowered to make decisions on their own without seeking the approval of management.
         b. Self-managed teams reduce the barriers between design, engineering, marketing, and other functions.

IV. GOING BEYOND ORGANIZATIONAL BOUNDERIES

A. Cross-functional teams lead to networking
   1. It is a good idea to include customers, suppliers, and distributors on cross-functional product development teams.
   2. Cross-functional teams may cross national boundaries.

B. NETWORKING AND VIRTUAL CORPORATIONS
   1. **NETWORKING**, in this context, means the linking of organizations with communications technology and other means to work together on common objectives.
   2. Networking allows the parties involved to work in **REALTIME**, which is when the things are actually taking place.
   3. This process electronically breaks down the walls between organizations, creating **TRANSPARENCY** or a clear visible organization.
   4. The networking system becomes a **VIRTUAL CORPORATION**, where firms come and go as needed.

C. EXTRANETS AND INTRANETS
   1. An **EXTRANET** is an extended Internet that connects suppliers, customers, and other organizations through secure Web sites.
   2. It is made up of **INTRANETS**, communication links within companies that travel over the Internet, but are closed to public access.
   3. Everyone in the firm is electronically linked so they can communicate and work together on projects.

V. THE RESTRUCTURING PROCESS AND TOTAL QUALITY

A. **TOTAL QUALITY MANAGEMENT (TQM)** is the practice of striving for maximum customer satisfaction by ensuring quality from all departments in an organization.
   1. **CONTINUOUS IMPROVEMENT** is the process of constantly improving the way the organization does things so that customer needs can be better satisfied.
   2. When an organization needs dramatic changes, only reengineering will do.
   3. **REENGINEERING** is the fundamental rethinking and radical redesign of organizational processes to achieve dramatic improvements in critical measures of performance.

B. HOW RESTRUCTURING AFFECTS ORGANIZATIONAL DESIGN
   1. Many firms are discovering that the key to long-term success in a competitive market is to empower front-line people to respond quickly to customer wants and needs.
   2. The most advanced service organizations have turned the traditional organizational structure upside down.
   3. An **INVERTED ORGANIZATION** has contact people at the top and the chief executive officer at the bottom.
      a. There are few layers of management, and their job is to assist and support front-line people.
      b. Companies based on this structure support front-line personnel with internal and external databanks, advanced communication systems, and professional assistance.
   4. Front-line people have to be better educated, better trained, and better paid than in the past.

C. THE MOVEMENT TOWARD OUTSOURCING
   1. In the past, each organization had a separate department for each function such as accounting, marketing, and production.

- a. Today's organizations are looking to other organizations to help them generate world-class quality.
- b. **COMPETITIVE BENCHMARKING** is rating an organization's practices, processes, and products against the world's best.
2. If the organization can't do as well as the best, the idea is to outsource the function to an organization that is the best.
   - a. **OUTSOURCING** is assigning various functions, such as accounting and legal work, to outside organizations.
   - b. Some functions, such as information management and marketing, may be too important to outsource.
3. **CORE COMPETENCIES** are those functions that the organization can do as well or better than anyone else in the world.

VI. ESTABLISHING A CUSTOMER-ORIENTED CULTURE

A. Organizational change is bound to cause some resistance, and should be accompanied by the establishment of an organizational culture that facilitates such change.
  1. **ORGANIZATIONAL (or COROORATE) CULTURE** is the widely shared values within an organization that provide coherence and cooperation to achieve common goals.
     - a. The culture of an organization is reflected in stories, traditions, and myths.
     - b. An organizational culture can also be negative.
  2. Good organizational culture emphasizes service to others, especially customers.
     - a. The atmosphere is one of friendly, caring people who enjoy working together.
     - b. Those companies have less need for close supervision of employees.

B. THE INFORMAL ORGANIZATION
  1. All organizations have two systems.
     - a. The **FORMAL ORGANIZATION** appears on the organization chart.
     - b. The **INFORMAL ORGANIZATION** is the system of relationships among employees that develop outside the formal organization.
     - c. The formal organization is the structure that details lines of responsibility, authority, and position.
     - d. The informal organization is the system of relationships that develop spontaneously as employees meet and form power centers.
  2. No organization can operate effectively without both types of organization.
     - a. The formal organization can be slow and bureaucratic, while the informal organization can adapt quickly.
     - b. The informal organization is too unstructured and emotional for decision-making, while the formal organization provides guidelines and lines of authority.
  3. It is wise to learn quickly who the important people are in the informal organization.
  4. The nerve center of the informal organization is the grapevine.
  5. Successful managers learn to work with the informal organization and use it to the organization's advantage.

LEARNING THE LANGUAGE OF BUSINESS

Match each of the following key terms with the appropriate definition.

A. bureaucracy
B. centralized authority
C. competitive benchmarking
D. continuous improvement
E. core competencies
F. cross-functional teams
G. decentralized authority
H. departmentalization
I. downsizing
J. economy of scale
K. extranet
L. formal organization
M. hierarchy
N. informal organization
O. intranets
P. inverted organization

Q. line organization
R. line personnel
S. matrix organization
T. networking
U. organizational (or corporate) culture
V. organizational design
W. outsourcing
X. real time
Y. reengineering
Z. restructuring
AA. span of control
BB. staff personnel
CC. total quality management (TQM)
DD. transparency
EE. virtual corporation

____ 1. The rethinking and radical redesign of organizational processes to achieve dramatic improvements in critical measures of performance.

____ 2. Widely shared values within an organization that provide coherence and cooperation to achieve common goals.

____ 3. Assigning various functions, such as accounting and legal work, to outside organizations.

____ 4. The optimum number of subordinates a manager should supervise.

____ 5. Satisfying customers by building in and ensuring quality from all departments in an organization.

____ 6. The structure that details lines of responsibility, authority, and position. It is the structure that is shown on organizational charts.

____ 7. Functions that the organization can do as well or better than anyone else in the world.

____ 8. The system of relationships and lines of authority that develops spontaneously as employees meet and form power centers. It is the human side of the organization and does not show on any formal charts.

____ 9. A system with layers of authority, where top managers make decisions, middle managers develop procedures for implementing decisions, and workers and supervisors do the work. Responsibility is clearly defined.

____ 10. Organization in which specialists from different parts of the organization are brought together to work on specific projects but still remain part of a traditional line and staff structure.

Lesson 12 Page 122

____ 11. The establishment of manageable groups of people who have clear responsibilities and who know how to accomplish the objectives of the organization.

____ 12. Procedures designed to insure and inspire constant creative interaction and problem solving.

____ 13. Dividing tasks into homogeneous departments such as manufacturing and marketing.

____ 14. Organization that has contact people at the top and the chief executive officer at the bottom of the organization chart.

____ 15. Organization with several levels of managers, who set rules and regulations and oversee all decisions.

____ 16. Groups of employees from different departments who work together on a semi-permanent basis (as opposed to the temporary teams established in matrix-style organizations).

____ 17. Rating an organization's practices, processes, and products against the world's best.

____ 18. Employees who perform functions that assist line personnel in achieving their goals.

____ 19. Delegating decision-making authority to lower-level managers who are more familiar with local conditions.

____ 20. Redesigning organizations to make them more productive.

____ 21. Linking organizations with communications technology in order for them to work together on common objectives.

____ 22. Maintaining decision-making authority with the top level of management at its headquarters.

____ 23. Employees who perform functions that contribute directly to the primary goals of the organization.

____ 24. An extended Internet that connects suppliers, customers, and other organizations via secure Web sites.

____ 25. A company-wide network, closed to public access, that uses Internet-type technology.

____ 26. A temporary, networked organization made up of replaceable firms that join the network and leave it as needed.

____ 27. The situation in which companies can produce goods more inexpensively if they can purchase the raw materials in bulk; the average cost of goods goes down as production levels increase.

____ 28. The present moment or the actual time in which something takes place; data sent over the Internet to various organizational partners as they are developed or collected are said to be available in this.

____ 29. The process of eliminating managerial and nonmanagerial positions.

_____ 30. An organization that has direct two-way lines of responsibility, authority, and communication running from the top to the bottom of the organization, with all the people reporting to only one supervisor.

_____ 31. A concept that describes a company being so open to other companies working with it that the once solid barriers between them become "see through" and electronic information is shared as if the companies were one.

SELF-TEST

1. John has just taken a job in the marketing department with the Shelling Company. After just a few days on the job, John has learned that the company has many layers of management, and seems to have a rule to cover almost every situation. He has also discovered that most of the other employees in his department have spent their entire career specializing in marketing. These conditions suggest that Shelling Company is a(n):
   A) cross-functional organization.
   B) decentralized organization.
   C) oligopolistic organization.
   D) bureaucratic organization.

2. Mike prepared a paper for his class about organizational styles used in business. He found that one reason the traditional bureaucratic style is not used as much as it once was is because:
   A) business organizations are much larger than they once were.
   B) restructuring has not produced the increased efficiency that was expected.
   C) the chain of command clearly identifies areas of responsibility.
   D) today's workforce is better educated and seeks involvement in their jobs.

3. Campbell is a middle manager for a bureaucratic organization. According to Max Weber's views on bureaucratic organizations, Campbell's function within the organization is to:
   A) make key operating decisions.
   B) evaluate the daily performance of first-line employees.
   C) ensure the organization achieves esprit de corps.
   D) develop the rules and procedures needed to implement the decisions of top management.

4. Criminex Industries produces a variety of anti-crime and safety products such as burglar alarms, smoke detectors, surveillance cameras, and special kinds of locks. Criminex sells some of its products to households, some to business firms, and even some to state and local government agencies. They have found that each group requires a different marketing approach. Criminex would probably benefit if it departmentalized according to:
   A) function.
   B) process.
   C) customer type.
   D) economies of scale.

5. As the head of the marketing department at a medium sized corporation, Jodelle works with subordinates on a variety of complex and challenging projects. Jodelle has found that she must spend a significant amount of time each week with each subordinate to provide advice and support. Jodelle probably has a(n):
   A) wide span of control.
   B) narrow span of control.
   C) unlimited span of control.
   D) functional span of control.

6. The 1st Infantry Division is based in Fort Riley, Kansas. Its organization provides for direct two-way lines of responsibility, authority, and communication running from the top to the bottom. Each person in the division reports to only one superior. The 1st Infantry Division is clearly an example of a(n):
   A) matrix organization.
   B) functional organization.
   C) line organization.
   D) service organization.

7. Eileen is employed by the personnel department of a corporation with several hundred employees. Her main function is to advise and assist managers in other departments, such as marketing and production, when they make staffing decisions. Eileen's position would be classified as a(n) _____ position.
   A) staff
   B) line
   C) first-line
   D) secondary

8. When a firm assigns various functions, such as accounting or legal work, to other organizations rather than performing these functions for itself, it is engaging in:
   A) distributive sharing.
   B) outsourcing.
   C) outplacement.
   D) cross-functionalizing.

9. Heather works as a sales representative for the Westerly Company. She really enjoys working for Westerly, because the company treats her and other sales representatives as highly valued employees. Sales reps at Westerly are given a lot of freedom and flexibility when they deal with customers. While there are only a few layers of management at Westerly, Heather has found that these managers try their best to support and assist her efforts. Based on Heather's experience, it appears that Westerly is a(n):
   A) bureaucratic organization.
   B) inverted organization.
   C) tall organization.
   D) casual organization.

10. Carlos is the person to see in the welding department if you are a new employee. He is not in management, but is the person that most of the others in the department look to for advice and assistance. Carlos is an important member of the firm's:
    A) supervisory management.
    B) participatory control.
    C) informal organization.
    D) closet cabinet.

ANSWER KEY

LEARNING THE LANGUAGE OF BUSINESS

1. Y
2. U
3. W
4. AA
5. CC
6. L
7. E
8. N
9. M
10. S
11. V
12. D
13. H
14. P
15. A
16. F
17. C
18. BB
19. G
20. Z
21. T
22. B
23. R
24. K
25. O
26. EE
27. J
28. X
29. I
30. Q
31. DD

SELF-TEST

Answer	Page #
1. D	Page: 236-237
2. D	Page: 235-236
3. D	Page: 236
4. C	Page: 242
5. B	Page: 239-240
6. C	Page: 245
7. A	Page: 245-246
8. B	Page: 254
9. B	Page: 252-253
10. C	Page: 255-256

LESSON 13

MANAGING HUMAN RESOURCES

ASSIGNMENTS

1. Review the Learning Goals and read the Lesson Overview for this lesson.

2. Read Chapter 11 pp. 326-357 in *Understanding Business,* 6th edition by Nickels, McHugh, and McHugh.

3. Watch the video *Managing Human Resources.*

4. Review the textbook material.

5. Match the key terms with the correct definitions in the Learning the Language of Business exercise.

6. Take the Self-Test.

7. Use the Answer Key to check your answers and review when necessary.

LEARNING GOALS

After you watch the video, read the textbook, and study this lesson, you should be able to:

1. Explain the importance of human resource management and describe current issues in managing human resources.

2. Summarize the six steps in planning human resources.

3. Describe methods that companies use to recruit new employees and explain some of the issues that make recruitment challenging.

4. Outline the six steps in selecting employees.

5. Illustrate the use of various types of employee training and development methods.

6. Trace the six steps in appraising employee performance.

7. Summarize the objectives of employee compensation programs, and describe various pay systems and fringe benefits.

8. Explain scheduling plans managers use to adjust to workers' needs.

9. Describe the ways employees can move through a company: promotion, reassignment, termination, and retirement.

10. Illustrate the effects of legislation on human resource management

LESSON NOTES

The PROFILE at the beginning of this chapter focuses on Diane Charness of Flextime Staffing Inc. Diane built a business based upon matching the needs of workers with the needs of employers. Many people today are looking for flexible employment, while many employers are looking for temporary employees, thus, the advent of the contingent worker. Today fewer workers expect to work at one company for their entire careers. The specific job you take is becoming less important than the skills you build over time. Employment for a contingent worker is an opportunity to build skills and experience. Employers also like the idea of "test driving" an employee. Both the needs of the worker and the employer are met with contingent workers.

I. WORKING WITH PEOPLE IS JUST THE BEGINNING

   A. **HUMAN RESOURCE MANAGEMENT** is the process of evaluating human resource needs, finding people to fill those needs, and optimizing this important resource by providing the right incentives and job environment, all with the goal of meeting the objectives of the organization.

   B. DEVELOPING THE ULTIMATE RESOURCE
      1. There is a major shift from traditional manufacturing industries to service industries and high-tech industries that require more technical job skills.
      2. A major problem is retraining workers for new, more challenging jobs.
      3. Employees are the ultimate resource.
         a. This resource has always been plentiful, so there was little need to nurture and develop it.
         b. Qualified labor is scarcer today.
      4. Historically, most firms assigned the job of recruiting, selecting, training, motivating, and firing people to functional departments.
      5. Today's human resource departments go beyond the clerical functions of the old personnel departments.
         a. The role of the human resource management is a function of all managers, not just one department's.
         b. Most human resource functions are shared between the human resource manager and other managers.

   C. THE HUMAN RESOURCE CHALLENGE
      1. Changes in the labor force have created problems in the human resource area.
      2. Some of the problems discussed in the text include:
         a. Shortages in people trained to work in high tech areas.
         b. Abundance of skilled and unskilled workers in obsolete fields who need retraining.
         c. Growing number of undereducated workers.
         d. A shift in age composition in the work force, including many older workers.
         e. A complex set of laws and regulations.
         f. An increasing number of single parent and two-income families.
         g. Shifts in employee attitudes toward work.
         h. Continued downsizing.
         i. More competition overseas.
         j. Increased demand for benefits tailored to the individual.
         k. Growing concern over health issues, elder care, childcare, etc.
         l. A decrease in the sense of employee loyalty.

II. DETERMINING YOUR HUMAN RESOURCE NEEDS

A. There are six steps in the human resource planning process.
1. Preparing forecasts of future human resource needs.
2. Preparing a human resource inventory.
3. Preparing a job analysis.
    a. A **JOB ANALYSIS** is a study of what is done by employees who fill various job titles.
    b. The results of the job analysis are two written statements:
        1) A **JOB DESCRIPTION** specifies the objectives of the job, the type of work to be done, the duties, and the relationship of the job to other functions.
        2) **JOB SPECIFICATIONS** specify the minimum qualifications required of a worker to fill specific jobs.
4. Assessing future demand – human resource managers who are proactive anticipate future needs of their organizations.
5. Assessing future supply in a shifting labor market.
6. Establishing a strategic plan that addresses recruiting, scheduling, and other functions.

III. RECRUITING EMPLOYEES FROM A DIVERSE POPULATION

A. **RECRUITMENT** is the set of activities used to obtain a sufficient number of the right people at the right time to select those who best meet the needs of the organization.

B. Recruiting is difficult for several reasons:
1. People with the necessary skills are not available, and must be hired and then trained.
2. The emphasis on corporate culture and teamwork makes it important to hire skilled people who also fit in with the culture.
3. Some organizations have policies or regulations that make recruitment more restrictive.

C. Human resource managers turn to many sources for assistance.
1. Internal sources include hiring from within the firm and employee recommendations.
    a. Internal sources are less expensive.
    b. Hiring from within helps maintain employee morale.
2. However, it isn't always possible to find qualified workers within the company, so human resource managers must use external recruitment sources.

IV. SELECTING EMPLOYEES WHO WILL BE PRODUCTIVE

A. **SELECTION** is the process of gathering information to decide who should be hired, under legal guidelines, for the best interest of the individual and the organization.

B. There six steps in the selection process:
1. Completion of an application form.
2. Conduct initial and follow-up interviews.
    a. A member of the human resource department staff often screens applicants in a first interview.
    b. Potential employees are then interviewed by the manager who will supervise the new employee.
3. Give employment tests.
    a. Although testing has been severely criticized, organizations continue to use tests to measure basic competencies.

        b. It is important that the test be directly related to the job.
    4. Conduct background investigations to help weed out candidates least likely to succeed and identify those most likely to succeed.
    5. Obtain the results of physical exams.
        a. Medical tests cannot be given just to screen out individuals.
        b. Preemployment testing to detect drug or alcohol abuse or AIDS screening is controversial.
        c. Eighty percent of U.S. companies now test their employees and applicants for drug use.
    6. Trial periods allow organizations to hire an employee conditionally.

C. HIRING CONTINGENT WORKERS
    1. Sometimes it is more cost-effective to hire contingent workers when a company has a varying need for employees.
    2. **CONTINGENT WORKERS** are workers who do not have the expectation of regular, full-time employment.
    3. Temporary staffing is a $40 billion industry.
    4. Managers see using temporary workers as a way of weeding out people and finding good hires.

V. TRAINING AND DEVELOPING EMPLOYEES FOR OPTIMUM RESULTS

A. **TRAINING AND DEVELOPMENT** involves all attempts to improve performance by increasing an employee's ability to perform.
    1. Training is short-term skills oriented; development is long-term career oriented.
    2. The process of creating training and development programs includes:
        a. Assessing the needs of the organization and the skills of the employees to determine training needs.
        b. Designing training activities to meet the identified needs.
        c. Evaluating the effectiveness of the training.

B. Common training and development activities include:
    1. **EMPLOYEE ORIENTATION** programs range from formal programs to informal programs which acquaint the new employee with the organization and its policies and procedures.
    2. ON-THE-JOB TRAINING
        a. In an **ON-THE-JOB TRAINING** program, employees immediately start their tasks. They learn by doing or watching others.
        b. This type of training is easy and effective for learning low skill, repetitive jobs, but can be disastrous if used in areas demanding more knowledge and expertise.
    3. Apprentice programs
        a. **APPRENTICESHIP PROGRAMS** involve a period of time when a learner works alongside a skilled worker to learn the skills and procedures of a craft.
        b. Many skilled crafts require a new worker to serve several years as an apprentice.
        c. There may be more but shorter apprenticeship programs in the future, as jobs require more intense training.
    4. **OFF-THE-JOB TRAINING** consists of internal and external programs to develop skills and to foster personal development that occurs away from the workplace (conferences, workshops, etc).
    5. On-line-training consists of training programs in which employees "attend" classes via the Internet.
    6. **VESTIBULE TRAINING** takes place in schools where equipment is used, which is similar to that used on the job (i.e. computer school).

7. **JOB SIMULATION** is the use of equipment that duplicates the job conditions and tasks so that an employee can learn without endangering himself or the company's expensive equipment (pilots, astronauts, etc).

C. MANAGEMENT DEVELOPMENT
1. Managers need special training; they must learn communication, listening skills, planning, human relation skills, time management, and empathy.
2. **MANAGEMENT DEVELOPMENT** is the process of training and educating employees to become good managers and then developing managerial skills over time.
3. Management development programs include several of the following:
   a. On-the-job coaching by a senior manager.
   b. Understudy positions as assistants who participate in planning and other managerial functions.
   c. Job rotation, to expose managers to different functions of the organization.
   d. Off-the-job courses and training expose managers to the latest concepts and create a sense of camaraderie.

D. NETWORKING
1. **NETWORKING** is the process of establishing and maintaining contacts with key managers in one's own organization and in other organizations and using those contacts to weave strong relationships that serve as informal development systems.
2. **MENTORS** are corporate managers who supervise, coach, and guide selected lower-level employees by introducing them to the right people and just acting as their organizational sponsors.

E. DIVERSITY IN MANAGEMENT DEVELOPMENT
1. Since most older managers are male, women often have more difficulty finding mentors and entering the network.
2. Men only clubs were declared illegal, allowing women access to areas where contacts are made.
3. African-American managers also are learning the benefits of networking.
4. Principles to develop female and minority managers:
   a. Grooming women and minorities for management positions is the key to long-term profitability.
   b. The best women and minorities will become harder to attract and retain.
   c. More women and minorities means that businesses can serve female and minority customers better.

VI. APPRAISING EMPLOYEE PERFORMANCE TO GET OPTIMUM RESULTS

A. A **PERFORMANCE APPRAISAL** is an evaluation of the performance level of employees against established standards to make decisions about promotions, compensation, additional training, or firing.

B. The six steps of performance appraisals are:
1. Establishing performance standards.
2. Communicating those standards.
3. Evaluating performance.
4. Discussing results with employees.
5. Taking corrective action.
6. Using the results to make decisions.

C. The latest form of performance appraisal is the 360-degree review because it uses feedback from all directions in the organization: up, down, and all around.

VII. COMPENSATING EMPLOYEES: ATTRACTING AND KEEPING THE BEST

A. Compensation is one of the main marketing tools used to attract qualified employees.
   1. The long-term success of a firm may depend on how well it can control employee costs.
   2. The primary cost of service operations is the cost of labor.
   3. Manufacturing firms have asked employees to take reductions in wages to make the firm more competitive.
   4. Compensation and benefit packages are being given special attention.

B. The objectives of compensation and benefit programs include:
   1. Attracting qualified workers.
   2. Providing productivity incentives.
   3. Keeping valued employees.
   4. Maintaining a competitive edge by increasing productivity.
   5. Providing financial security.

C. PAY SYSTEMS
   1. Pay systems normally include the following:
      a. Salary systems are fixed compensation programs (managers).
      b. Hourly wage or day-work (blue-collar and clerical workers).
      c. Piecework means that employees are paid according to the number of items they produce (manufacturing).
      d. Commission (salespeople).
      e. Bonus plans are earned for accomplishing or surpassing certain objectives (executives, salespeople).
      f. Profit sharing is giving employees some share of profits over their normal pay.
      g. Stock option plans give employees the right to purchase stock at a specific price.
   2. Many companies use the Hay System, based on job tiers each of which has a strict pay range.
   3. Another system begins with base pay and gives all employees the same percent merit raise.

D. COMPENSATING TEAMS
   1. Compensating teams is a complex issue.
   2. Some studies have shown that team-based pay programs may not be effective.
   3. Skill-based pay is related to the growth of both the individual and the team.
      a. Base pay is raised when team members learn and apply new skills.
      b. The skill-based pay system is complex, and it is difficult to correlate skill acquisition to bottom-line gains.
   4. In gain-sharing systems, bonuses are based on improvements over a performance baseline.
   5. It is also important to reward individual team players.

E. FRINGE BENEFITS
   1. **FRINGE BENEFITS** include vacation pay, pension plans, and health plans that provide additional compensation to employees.
      a. In recent years benefit programs grew faster than wages.
      b. Many employees want more fringe benefits instead of more salary to avoid higher taxes.
   2. Fringe benefits can include everything from paid vacations to childcare programs, use of recreational facilities, and more.
   3. Some companies offer **CAFETERIA-STYLE FRINGE BENEFITS** from which employees can choose the benefits they want based on their personal needs.

4. Because of the cost of administering benefit programs, many companies are contracting with outside companies (outsourcing) to run their benefit plans.

VIII. SCHEDULING EMPLOYEES TO MEET ORGANIZATIONAL AND EMPLOYEE NEEDS

A. Managers and workers are demanding more flexibility and responsiveness from their jobs.

B. **FLEXTIME PLANS** allow employees some freedom in choosing their own hours.
   1. Most flextime plans include a period known as **CORE TIME** in which all employees are expected to be at work.
   2. There are some disadvantages of flextime plans.
      a. It does not work in assembly-line processes or for shift work.
      b. Managers often have to work longer days in order to supervise employees.
      c. Flextime makes communication more difficult.
      d. Some employees could abuse the system.

C. A **COMPRESSED WORKWEEK** allows employees to concentrate their work hours in a fewer number of days rather than working five days a week.
   1. There are advantages for employees in working only four days.
   2. But some employees get tired working such long hours, and productivity could decline.

D. HOME-BASED AND OTHER MOBILE WORK
   1. Nearly 57% of U.S. workers now work at least several days each month from their homes.
   2. To be successful, a home-based worker must have the discipline to stay focused on the work.
   3. Telecommuting can be a cost saver for employers.

E. **JOB SHARING** plans are plans that allow two employees to share the same job.
   1. Job sharing lets parents work part-time while their children are in school.
   2. Benefits include:
      a. Employment opportunities for those who cannot or prefer not to work full-time.
      b. A high level of enthusiasm and productivity.
      c. Reduced absenteeism and tardiness.
      d. Ability to schedule people into peak demand periods.
   3. Disadvantages: having to hire, train, motivate, and supervise twice as many people.
   4. Most firms have found the benefits outweigh the disadvantages.

IX. MOVING EMPLOYEES UP, OVER, AND OUT

A. Employees don't always stay in the position they were initially hired to fill.

B. PROMOTING AND REASSIGNING EMPLOYEES.
   1. Promotions are cost-effective ways to improve employee morale.
   2. Due to the prevalence of flatter corporate structures, it is more common today for workers to transfer over to a new position than to move up to one.

C. TERMINATING EMPLOYEES
   1. Downsizing and restructuring, increasing customer demands for greater value and the relentless pressure of global competition and shifts in technology have human resource managers struggling to manage layoffs and firings.

2. The cost of terminating employees is so high that managers choose to use temporary employees or outsource certain functions.
3. Employment at will
   a. Employment at will meant that managers had as much freedom to fire workers, as workers had to leave voluntarily.
   b. Most states now have written employment laws that limit the at will doctrine to protect employees from wrongful firing.

D. RETIRING EMPLOYEES
   1. Another tool used to downsize companies is to offer early retirement benefits to entice older workers to resign.
   2. The advantage of offering early retirement benefits rather than laying off employees is that early retirement offers increase the morale of the surviving employees.
   3. Retiring senior workers increases promotion opportunities for younger employees.

E. LOSING EMPLOYEES
   1. Despite all the company's efforts some good people still leave the organization.
      a. Exit interviews are very useful in finding out why employees leave.

X. LAWS AFFECTING HUMAN RESOURCE MANAGEMENT

A. Legislation has made hiring, promoting, firing, and managing employee relations complex and subject to legal complications.

B. One of the most important laws ever passed by Congress was the Civil Rights Act of 1964.
   1. Title VII of the Act prohibits discrimination in hiring, firing, compensation, apprenticeships, training, terms, conditions, or privileges of employment based on race, religion, creed, sex, or national origin (age was added later).
   2. Specific language in the law often made its enforcement difficult.

C. The Equal Employment Opportunity Act (EEOA) was added as an amendment to Title VII in 1972.
   1. It strengthened the EEOC which issues guidelines for administering equal employment opportunity.
   2. Congress gave the EEOC broad powers, making it a formidable regulatory force.

D. AFFIRMATIVE ACTION
   1. **AFFIRMATIVE ACTION** is a set of activities designed to increase opportunities for minorities and women.
   2. The EEOC enforces affirmative action, which is designed to right past wrongs made against women and minorities.
   3. This has led to problems including **REVERSE DISCRIMINATION**, the feeling of unfairness unprotected groups have when protected groups are given preference.

E. The Civil Rights Act of 1991 expanded the remedies available to victims of discrimination by amending Title VII of the Civil Rights Act of 1964.

F. LAWS PROTECTING THE DISABLED AND OLDER EMPLOYEES
   1. The Vocational Rehabilitation Act (1973).
      a. The Act extended the same protection given to minorities and women to people with disabilities.
      b. Businesses cannot discriminate against people with disabilities on the basis of their physical or mental handicap.
   2. The Americans with Disabilities Act of 1990 (ADA) requires that disabled applicants be given the same consideration for employment as people without disabilities.

        a. It requires that businesses make " reasonable accommodations" for people with disabilities.
        b. Most companies are having more trouble making cultural changes than structural changes to be accommodating.
    3. In 1997, the EEOC issued new guidelines for the ADA that tells employers how they are to treat workers and applicants with mental disabilities.
    4. The Age Discrimination in Employment Act protects older employees.
        a. It outlawed mandatory retirement before age 70.
        b. Many companies are voluntarily phasing out mandatory retirement after age 70.

G. EFFECTS OF LEGISLATION
    1. Legislation affects all areas of human resource management.
    2. In summary:
        a. Employers must be sensitive to the legal rights of their employees.
        b. Legislation affects all areas of human resource management.
        c. It is sometimes legal to go beyond providing equal rights for minorities and women to provide special employment to correct discrimination in the past.
        d. New court cases and legislation continuously change human resource management; it is important to keep current.

LEARNING THE LANGUAGE OF BUSINESS

Match each of the following key terms with the appropriate definition.

A. affirmative action
B. apprenticeship programs
C. cafeteria-style fringe benefits
D. compressed workweek
E. contingent workers
F. core time
G. employee orientation
H. flextime plan
I. fringe benefits
J. human resource management
K. job analysis
L. job description
M. job sharing
N. job simulation
O. job specifications
P. management development
Q. mentor
R. networking
S. off-the-job training
T. on-the-job training
U. performance appraisal
V. recruitment
W. reverse discrimination
X. selection
Y. training and development
Z. vestibule training

____ 1. All attempts to improve employee performance by increasing an employee's ability to perform through learning.

____ 2. Training program in which the employee immediately begins his or her tasks and learns by doing, or watches others for a while and then imitates them, all right at the workplace.

____ 3. Training conducted out of the workplace where employees are given instructions on equipment similar to that used on the job.

____ 4. The feeling of unfairness unprotected groups may have when protected groups are given preference in hiring and promoting.

____ 5. The process of training and educating employees to become good managers and then developing managerial skills over time.

____ 6. Internal and external programs to develop a variety of skills and foster personal development away from the workplace.

____ 7. Work schedule that gives employees some freedom to adjust when they work, as long as they work the required number of hours.

_____ 8. The process of establishing and maintaining contacts with key managers in one's own organization and in other organizations and using those contacts to weave strong relationships that serve as informal development systems.

_____ 9. The set of legal activities used to obtain a sufficient number of the right people at the right time to select those who best meet the needs of the organization.

_____ 10. The process of gathering information to decide who should be hired, under legal guidelines, for the best interests of the individual and the organization.

_____ 11. Work schedule that involves same number of hours per week in fewer days.

_____ 12. Employment activities designed to "right past wrongs" endured by females and minorities.

_____ 13. Written summary of the qualifications required of workers to do a particular job.

_____ 14. Benefits such as sick-leave pay, vacation pay, pension plans, and health plans that represent additional compensation to employees.

_____ 15. The activity that introduces new employees to the organization, to fellow employees, to their immediate supervisors, and to the policies, practices, and objectives of the firm.

_____ 16. Fringe benefits plan, which allows employees to choose the benefits, they want up to a certain dollar amount.

_____ 17. An arrangement whereby two or more part-time employees share one full-time job.

_____ 18. An evaluation of the performance level of employees against standards to make decisions about promotions, compensation, additional training, or firing.

_____ 19. The period when all employees are present in a flextime system.

_____ 20. A study of what is done by employees who fill various job titles.

_____ 21. Training involving a new worker working alongside a master technician to learn the skills and procedures of a job.

_____ 22. A training method that uses equipment that duplicates job conditions and tasks so that trainees can learn skills before attempting them on the job.

_____ 23. The process of evaluating human resource needs, finding people to fill those needs, and getting the best work from each employee by providing the right incentives and job enrichment, all with the goal of meeting the objectives of the organization.

_____ 24. A summary of the objectives of a job, the type of work, the responsibilities of the job, the necessary skills, the working conditions, and the relationship of the job to other functions.

_____ 25. An experienced employee who supervises, coaches, and guides lower level employees by introducing them to the right people and groups and generally being their organizational sponsors.

_____ 26. Workers who do not have the expectation of regular, full-time employment.

SELF-TEST

1. When Carl Remmick lost his job as a highly skilled craftsman at a metal working shop, he searched for a good job for several months before finally accepting a position as a maintenance worker at a local community college. He is happy to have a job, but frustrated by the fact that he had to settle for a job that did not take full advantage of his skills. Carl is a(n):
   A) structurally unemployed worker.
   B) semi-employed worker.
   C) underemployed worker.
   D) quasi-employed worker.

2. Steve Patterson is gathering information about the names, ages, education, specialized skills, and capabilities of all of his firm's employees. The information Steve is acquiring suggests he is working on a(n):
   A) performance evaluation.
   B) human resource inventory.
   C) job description.
   D) Gantt Chart.

3. Which of the following is the most important advantage of using internal sources to hire from within? Hiring from within:
   A) eliminates the need to meet affirmative action regulations.
   B) ensures that the best qualified person gets the job.
   C) helps maintain employee morale.
   D) allows the firm to effectively use the "employment at will" strategy.

4. Betty Roosevelt is a human resource manager with Avondale Industries. Her current assignment is to revise and update Avondale's employment testing procedures. Betty should:
   A) design tests that are directly related to an applicant's ability to perform the job.
   B) are so difficult that only a small fraction of qualified workers can pass them.
   C) measure general aptitudes rather than ability to do the job.
   D) inform her superiors that such tests are now illegal.

5. Reggie Barnes is a member of the electricians' union and is classified as a journeyman. This means that Reggie:
   A) is still working to learn the most basic skills needed to be an electrician.
   B) wants to work on a part-time basis.
   C) has completed his apprenticeship program.
   D) is currently unemployed.

6. Benny Joplin is a manager at the Rookerton Metal Works. He has just been evaluated using a new process that provides feedback about his performance not only from his superiors but also from his subordinates and other managers at his level. This type of evaluation is known as a(n):
   A) organization-wide appraisal.
   B) 360 degree review.
   C) circular analysis.
   D) multilevel assessment.

7. Howie Van Zant recently earned his license to sell real estate in Indiana, and has interviewed with several agencies in an attempt of find a job. All have told him that his income will be based on a percentage of his real estate sales for the month. Howie will be paid:
A) a monthly salary.
B) a piece rate.
C) on a commission basis.
D) through a profit sharing plan.

8. A major characteristic of a compressed workweek is that:
A) workers receive the same pay for fewer hours of work.
B) the pace of work is increased so that workers perform the same amount of work in fewer hours.
C) employees work fewer days each week, but work more hours each workday.
D) two or more part-time workers are hired to fill each full-time position.

9. The Krandall Corporation wants to reduce its labor force, but is concerned about the impact downsizing will have on its remaining employees. One policy that might allow Krandall to reduce its labor force without adversely affecting morale is to:
A) develop an affirmative action plan.
B) offer early retirement benefits.
C) implement a job-sharing program.
D) make more extensive use of job rotation.

10. Evan McConnell is angry and upset because he was passed over for a promotion even though he believes he was the most qualified candidate. He heard through the company grapevine the promotion went to a female because the firm was afraid of possible action by the EEOC if they did not select a female. What Evan is experiencing is known as:
A) reverse discrimination.
B) double indemnity.
C) de facto discrimination.
D) compensatory discrimination.

ANSWER KEY

LEARNING THE LANGUAGE OF BUSINESS

1. Y
2. T
3. Z
4. W
5. P
6. S
7. H
8. R
9. V
10. X
11. D
12. A
13. O
14. I
15. G
16. C
17. M
18. U
19. F
20. K
21. B
22. N
23. J
24. L
25. Q
26. E

SELF-TEST

Answer	Page #
1. C	Page: 330
2. B	Page: 331
3. C	Page: 333-334
4. A	Page: 336
5. C	Page: 339
6. B	Page: 343
7. C	Page: 345
8. C	Page: 348
9. B	Page: 351
10. A	Page: 352-353

LESSON 14

MANAGING THE WORK ENVIRONMENT

ASSIGNMENTS

1. Review the Learning Goals and read the Lesson Overview for this lesson.

2. Read Chapter 10 pp. 294-322 and Chapter 12 pp. 375-386 in *Understanding Business*, 6th edition by Nickels, McHugh, and McHugh.

3. Watch the video *Managing the Work Environment.*

4. Review the textbook material.

5. Match the key terms with the correct definitions in the Learning the Language of Business exercise.

6. Take the Self-Test.

7. Use the Answer Key to check your answers and review when necessary.

LEARNING GOALS

After you watch the video, read the textbook, and study this lesson, you should be able to:

1. Explain Taylor's scientific management.

2. Describe the Hawthorne studies and relate their significance to human-based management.

3. Identify the levels of Maslow's hierarchy of needs and relate their importance to employee motivation.

4. Differentiate among Theory X, Theory Y, and Theory Z.

5. Distinguish between motivators and hygiene factors identified by Herzberg.

6. Explain how job enrichment affects employee motivation and performance.

7. Identify the steps involved in implementing a management by objectives (MBO) program.

8. Explain the key factors involved in expectancy theory.

9. Examine the key principles of equity theory.

10. Explain how open communication builds teamwork, and describe how managers are likely to motivate teams in the future.

11. Explain some of the controversial employee-management issues such as executive compensation; comparable worth; child care and elder care; AIDS testing, drug testing, and violence in the workplace; and employee stock ownership plans (ESOPs).

LESSON NOTES

The PROFILE at the beginning of this chapter focuses on Herb Kelleher of Southwest Airlines. The company now ranks as the 4th largest airline in the nation. Analysts were concerned due to Kelleher's health problems, but they believe his corporate culture is so ingrained in Southwest Airlines that it will continue as will the airline's success.

I. THE IMPORTANCE OF MOTIVATION

   A. People are motivated by a variety of things.
      1. An **INTRINSIC REWARD** is the good feeling you have when you have done a good job.
      2. An **EXTRINSIC REWARD** is something given to you by someone else as recognition for good work, this includes pay increases, praise, and promotions.
      3. Motivation, the drive to satisfy a need, ultimately comes from within an individual.
      4. The most important person to motivate is you.
      5. The job of a manager is to find each worker's commitment, encourage it, and focus it on some common goal.

   B. EARLY MANAGEMENT STUDIES (TAYLOR)
      1. Frederick Taylor is known as, The Father of Scientific Management.
         a. His book, The Principles of Scientific Management was published in 1911.
         b. Taylor's goal was to increase productivity.
         c. The way to improve productivity was to scientifically study the most efficient way to do things then teach people those methods, this was called **SCIENTIFIC MANAGEMENT**.
         d. Three elements of his approach were time, methods, and rules of work.
         e. **TIME-MOTION STUDIES** break down the tasks needed to do a job and measure the time needed to do each task.
      2. H. L. Gantt, one of Taylor's followers, developed Gantt Charts by which managers plotted the work of employees a day in advance.
      3. Frank and Lillian Gilbreth used Taylor's ideas in the **PRINCIPLE OF MOTION ECONOMY** breaking down every job into a series of motions (therbligs) and then analyzing each motion to make it more efficient.
      4. Scientific management viewed people as machines that needed to be properly programmed.
         a. There was little concern for the psychological or human aspects of work.
         b. Much emphasis in some companies is still placed on conformity to work rules rather than on creativity, flexibility, and responsiveness.

   C. THE HAWTHORNE STUDIES (MAYO)
      1. Elton Mayo conducted the Hawthorne Studies, at the Western Electric Company's Hawthorne plant in Cicero, Illinois.
         a. Begun in 1927, the studies ended six years later.
         b. The purpose of the studies was to determine the best lighting for optimum productivity.
         c. The productivity of the experimental group increased compared to the control group whether the lighting was bright or dim.
      2. A second series of studies were conducted to see if other factors contributed to increased production.
         a. Productivity increased during each of the 13 experimental periods.
         b. When conditions were returned to their original status (before the studies were started), productivity continued to go up. Why?
      3. Mayo hypothesized that human or psychological factors caused the increases:

a. The workers in the test room thought of themselves as a social group.
   b. The workers were involved in the planning of the experiments.
   c. The workers enjoyed the special atmosphere and additional pay for the increased productivity.
4. The term **HAWTHORNE EFFECT** refers to the tendency for people to behave differently when they know they're being studied.
   a. The Hawthorne studies' results encouraged researchers to study human motivation and the managerial styles that lead to more productivity.
   b. Mayo's findings led to new assumptions about employees.
   c. Money was found to be a relatively low motivator.

II. MOTIVATION AND MASLOW'S HIERARCHY OF NEEDS

A. Abraham Maslow believed that motivation arises from need.
   1. An individual is motivated to satisfy unmet needs.
   2. Satisfied needs no longer motivate.

B. Maslow placed needs on a hierarchy of importance, referred to as **MASLOW"S HIERARCHY OF NEEDS**.
   1. Physiological needs are basic survival needs including the need to drink, eat, and be sheltered from heat and cold.
   2. Safety needs are the need to feel secure at work and at home.
   3. Social needs are the need to feel loved, accepted, and part of the group.
   4. Self-esteem needs are the need for recognition and acknowledgment from others, as well as self-respect and a sense of status.
   5. Self-actualization needs are the need to develop to your fullest potential.

C. When one need is satisfied, another, higher-level need emerges.
   1. The satisfied need is no longer a motivator.
   2. Lower-level needs, however, can pop up at any time and take attention away from higher-level needs.

D. APPLYING MASLOW'S THEORY
   1. The text relates how Andrew Grove, former president of Intel, used Maslow's concepts to motivate employees in his firm.
   2. Once one understands the need level of employees, it is easier to design programs that will trigger self-motivation.

III. MCGREGOR'S THEORY X AND THEORY Y

A. Douglas McGregor categorized managers by their attitudes, which lead to different managerial styles: Theory X and Theory Y.

B. THEORY X
   1. The assumptions of Theory X management are:
      a. The average person dislikes work and will avoid it if possible.
      b. Because of this dislike, the average person must be forced, controlled, directed, or threatened with punishment to be motivated to put forth the effort to achieve the organization's goals.
      c. The average worker prefers to be directed, wishes to avoid responsibility, has relatively little ambition, and wants security.
      d. Primary motivators are fear and money.
   2. The consequence of such attitudes is a manager who is always busy.

        a. Motivation is more likely to take the form of punishment for bad work rather than reward for good work.
        b. Those were the assumptions behind Taylor's scientific management.

  C. THEORY Y
    1. Theory Y makes entirely different assumptions about people:
       a. Most people like work; it is as natural as play or rest.
       b. Most people naturally work toward goals to which he or she is committed.
       c. The depth of a person's commitment to goals depends on the perceived rewards for achieving them.
       d. Under certain conditions, most people not only accept but also seek responsibility.
       e. People are capable of using a high degree of imagination, creativity, and cleverness to solve problems.
       f. In industry, the average person's intellectual potential is only partially realized.
       g. People are motivated by a variety of rewards. Each worker is stimulated by a reward unique to that worker (time off, money, recognition, etc.)
    2. Theory Y emphasizes a relaxed managerial atmosphere in which workers are free to set objectives and be flexible.
    3. Empowerment is a key technique in meeting these objectives. To be a real motivator, empowerment requires management to:
       a. Find out what people think the problems in the organization are.
       b. Let them design the solutions.
       c. Get out of the way and let them put those solutions into action.
    4. The trend in many U.S. businesses is toward Theory Y management.

IV. OUCHI'S THEORY Z

  A. Another reason for a more flexible managerial style is to meet competition from foreign firms.
    1. In the 1980s Japanese companies seemed to be outperforming U.S. companies.
    2. Out of William Ouchi's study of the Japanese system evolved a concept called Theory Z, which contains the following items:
       a. Long-term employment.
       b. Collective decision-making.
       c. Individual responsibility for the outcomes of decisions.
       d. Slow evaluation and promotion.
       e. Moderately specialized career paths.
       f. Holistic concern for employees.

V. HERZBERG'S MOTIVATING FACTORS

  A. Theories X, Y, and Z are concerned with management styles.
    1. Another theorist looked at what managers can do with the job itself to motivate employees.
    2. Herzberg was concerned with the content of work rather than style of management.

  B. Frederick Herzberg surveyed workers to find out how they would rank job-related factors. The results were:
    1. Sense of achievement.
    2. Earned recognition.
    3. Interest in the work itself.
    4. Opportunity for growth.
    5. Opportunity for advancement.
    6. Importance of responsibility.

7. Peer and group relationships.
8. Pay.
9. Supervisor's fairness.
10. Company policies and rules.
11. Status.
12. Job security.
13. Supervisor's friendliness.
14. Working conditions.

C. Herzberg noted that the highest ranking factors dealt with job content.
 1. He referred to these as **MOTIVATORS** since they gave employees a great deal of satisfaction.
 2. They include the work itself, achievement, and responsibility.

D. The remaining factors had to do with the job environment.
 1. They could cause dissatisfaction if they were missing but were not necessarily motivating if they increased.
 2. These **HYGIENE FACTORS** included working conditions and salary.

E. APPLYING HERZBERG'S THEORIES
 1. The text offers several current examples of Herzberg's theories in action.
 2. Further surveys support Herzberg's finding that the number one motivator is not money, but a sense of achievement and recognition.
 3. There is a good deal of similarity in Maslow's hierarchy and Herzberg's two-factor theory.

VI. JOB ENRICHMENT

A. **JOB ENRICHMENT** is a motivational strategy that emphasizes motivating the worker through the job itself.

B. The five characteristics of work believed to be important in affecting motivation and performance are:
 1. Skill variety, the extent to which a job demands different skills of the person.
 2. Task identity, the degree to which the job requires doing a task with a visible outcome from beginning to end.
 3. Task significance, the degree to which the job has a substantial impact on the lives of others in the company.
 4. Autonomy, the degree of freedom, independence, and discretion in scheduling work and determining procedures.
 5. Feedback, the amount of direct, clear information received about job performance.

C. OTHER JOB DESIGNS
 1. **JOB SIMPLIFICATION** produces task efficiency by breaking down the job into simple steps, which is sometimes necessary with people learning new skills.
 2. **JOB ENLARGEMENT** combines a series of tasks into one assignment that is more challenging and motivating.
 3. **JOB ROTATION** makes work more interesting by moving employees from one job to another.

VII. GOAL-SETTING THEORY AND MANAGEMENT BY OBJECTIVES

A. **GOAL-SETTING THEORY** is based on setting specific, attainable goals.

1. This will lead to high motivation and performance if the goals are accepted, accompanied by feedback, and facilitated by organizational conditions.
2. Peter Drucker developed such a system in the 1960s called **MANAGEMENT BY OBJECTIVES (MBO).**

B. Management by objectives (MBO) is an example of goal-setting.
   1. Management by Objectives was developed to help employees motivate themselves.
   2. MBO is a system of goal setting and implementation that involves a cycle of discussion, review, and evaluation of objectives among all levels of management and employees.
   3. There are six steps in the MBO process.
   4. Some critics see MBO as being out of date and inconsistent with contemporary management thought.

C. Management by objectives is most effective in relatively stable situations.
   1. It is important to understand the difference between helping and coaching subordinates.
   2. Helping is working with the subordinate, even doing part of the work if necessary.
   3. Coaching means acting as a resource, teaching, guiding, recommending, but not helping by doing the task.
   4. Problems can arise when management uses MBO as a strategy for forcing managers to commit to goals that are not mutually agreed upon.

VIII. MEETING EMPLOYEE EXPECTATIONS: EXPECTANCY THEORY

A. According to Victor Vroom's **EXPECTANCY THEORY**, employee expectations can affect an individual's motivation.
   1. The amount of effort employees exert on a specific task depends on their expectations of the outcome.
   2. Expectation varies from individual to individual.

B. Five steps to improve employee performance:
   1. Determine what rewards are valued by employees.
   2. Determine the employee's desired performance standard.
   3. Ensure performance standards are attainable.
   4. Guarantee rewards are tied to performance.
   5. Be certain rewards are considered adequate.

IX. TREATING EMPLOYEES FAIRLY: EQUITY THEORY

A. The basic principle of **EQUITY THEORY** is that workers try to maintain equity between inputs and outputs compared to people in similar positions.

B. When workers do perceive inequity, they will try to reestablish equitable exchanges.
   1. They can reduce or increase their efforts or rationalize the situation.
   2. In the workplace, inequity leads to lower productivity, reduced quality, increased absenteeism, and voluntary resignation.

C. Equity judgements are based on perceptions, and are therefore subject to errors in perception.
   1. Organizations can try to deal with this by keeping salaries secret.
   2. However, the best remedy, in general, is clear and frequent communication.

X. BUILDING TEAMWORK THROUGH OPEN COMMUNICATION

    A. In companies with successful management and motivation, open communication and self-managed teams are key elements.
        1. Communication must flow freely throughout the organization when teams are empowered to make decisions.

    B. Procedures for encouraging open communication include:
        1. Creating an organizational culture that rewards listening; creating facilities for dialogues; and showing others that talking with superiors counts.
        2. Training supervisors and managers in listening skills.
        3. Removing barriers to open communication (separate washrooms, parking lots, etc).
        4. Providing ways to facilitate communication (company athletic teams, picnics, etc).

    C. APPLYING OPEN COMMUNICATION IN SELF-MANAGED TEAMS
        1. The text offers several examples of communication among members of self-managed teams in organizations like Ford Motor Company.
        2. For companies to implement such groups, managers must re-invent work.

    D. CHANGING ORGANIZATIONS IS NOT EASY
        1. Many managers were trained under a different system.
            a. Many are used to telling people what to do rather than consulting them.
        2. Employees often have a difficult time changing as well, and some have trouble getting involved in participative management.

    E. A MODEL FOR THE FUTURE: EMPLOYEE EMPOWERMENT
        1. The text tells the stories of Miller Brewing Company and Mary Kay Cosmetics as examples of companies that successfully created efficient and effective teams.
        2. Understanding what motivates employees is the key to success in goods-producing companies such as Miller Brewing Company and service-based firms such as Mary Kay Cosmetics.
        3. The lessons learned from these companies include:
            a. The future growth of industry depends on a motivated, productive work force.
            b. Workers themselves internally generate motivation.
            c. The first step in any motivational program is to establish open communications.

XI. MOTIVATION IN THE FUTURE

    A. Motivating employees
        1. Employees are not alike; different employees respond to different managerial and motivational styles.
        2. Tomorrow's managers will not be able to use any one formula for all employees.
        3. They will need to work with each employee as an individual and fit the motivational effort to that individual.
        4. Different cultures experience motivational approaches differently.

    B. Generation X
        1. People born between 1965 and 1980 are "Gen Xers."
        2. Gen Xers respond to different motivational methods.
        3. Rather than focus on job security, Gen Xers focus on career security.
        4. In their search for opportunities they are willing to change jobs.
        5. Gen X managers will motivate people by:

a. Understanding that there is more to life than work.
   b. Focusing on results not hours of work.
   c. Thinking in broader terms.
   d. Providing positive feedback.

XII. CONTROVERSIAL EMPLOYEE-MANAGEMENT ISSUES

   A. EXECUTIVE COMPENSATION
      1. Today the government, boards of directors, and stockholders have argued that executive compensation is getting out of line.
      2. In the past, executive compensation was determined by the firm's profitability or increase in stock price.
         a. Today, many executives receive stock options, the ability to buy the company stock at a set price at a later date.
         b. The assumption is that the CEO will raise the price of the firm's stock, but often executive pay continues to soar, even when the company does poorly.
      3. Peter Drucker has suggested that CEOs should not earn much more than 20 times as much as the company's lowest-paid employee.
         a. Some companies followed his advice, but many have not.
         b. Today the average chief executive makes 475 times the pay of a typical American factory worker.
      4. The imbalance between starting pay and top pay is less for European and Japanese executives.

   B. COMPARABLE WORTH
      1. Women make up a larger percentage of the workforce, up from 15% in 1890 to 50% in 2000.
      2. **COMPARABLE WORTH** is the demand for equal pay for jobs requiring similar levels of education, training, and skills.
         a. Keep in mind that this is a different concept than equal pay for equal work, which means that equal wages should be paid to men and women who do the same job.
         b. The issue of comparable worth centers on comparing the value of jobs.
      3. Women earn approximately 74% of what men earn.
         a. One reason for the disparity is that many women try to work as well as care for their families and fall off the career track.
         b. Other women opt for more flexible jobs that pay less.

   C. SEXUAL HARASSMENT
      1. **SEXUAL HARASSMENT** refers to unwelcome sexual advances, requests for sexual favors, and other conduct of a sexual nature (verbal or physical).
      2. Both men and women are covered under the Civil Rights Act of 1991 that governs sexual harassment.
      3. Sexual harassment becomes illegal when:
         a. An employee's submission to such conduct is made either explicitly or implicitly a term or condition of employment.
         b. An employee's submission to or rejection of such conduct is used as the basis for employment decisions affecting the worker's status.
         c. The conduct unreasonably interferes with a worker's job performance or creates an intimidating, hostile, or offensive working environment
      4. Managers and workers are now much more sensitive to comments and behavior of a sexual nature.
      5. In 1996 the U.S. Supreme Court broadened the scope of what can be considered a hostile work environment.

Lesson 14

6. One of the major problems is that workers and managers often know a policy concerning sexual harassment exists, but they have no idea what it says.

D. CHILD CARE
1. Child care remains an important issue.
2. The need for child care is obvious.
   a. A sizable percentage of the over 50 million working women are likely to become pregnant during their working years.
   b. So who is going to provide child care? Who will pay for it?
3. Many companies are now providing child care for their employees.
4. Working parents have made it clear that safe, affordable child-care is an issue on which they will not compromise.

E. ELDER CARE
1. By 2005, 40% of U.S. workers will be aged 40 to 58.
   a. These workers will not be concerned with child care.
   b. Instead, they will be faced with the responsibility, for caring for older parents and other relatives.
2. Some predict that this will have a greater impact on the workplace than child care.

F. AIDS TESTING, DRUG TESTING, AND VIOLENCE IN THE WORKPLACE
1. AIDS
   a. AIDS is a leading cause of death for Americans between the ages of 25 and 44.
   b. Mandatory testing for the AIDS antibody is one of the more controversial employee-management issues.
   c. Preemployment medical testing cannot be used to intentionally screen out potential employees.
      1) If used at all they must be given to everyone.
      2) Many firms have gone beyond pre-employment testing and suggested that all employees should be tested.
2. Drug testing
   a. Some companies feel that alcohol and drug abuse is an even more serious workplace issue.
   b. Over 80% of major companies now test workers and job applicants for substance abuse.
3. Violence in the workplace
   a. Employers are also struggling with a growing trend of violence in the workplace.
   b. Many executives don't take workplace violence seriously and believe it is primarily media hype.
   c. Other organizations recognize the threat and hire managers with strong interpersonal skills to deal with growing employee violence.

G. EMPLOYEE STOCK OWNERSHIP PLANS (ESOPs)
1. **EMPLOYEE STOCK OWNERSHIP PLANS (ESOPs)** are plans that allow employees to buy part or total ownership of the company in which they work.
   a. Louis O. Kelso started the idea for ESOPs about 50 years ago when he helped the employees of a newspaper buy their company.
   b. Since then, the idea of employees taking over ownership of their companies has gained much favor.
   c. ESOPs have had mixed results.
2. Benefits of ESOPs
   a. There are about 11,500 businesses with ESOPs today.
   b. Giving employees a share in the profits of the firm motivates them to enhance their involvement in the firm and increases morale.
   c. Productivity also seems to rise.
3. Problems with ESOPs:

       a. ESOPs can be used to refinance a company with workers' money without giving them more participation or job security.
       b. In about 85% of the companies with ESOPs, employees do not have voting rights.
4. Companies with healthy employee-management relations have a better chance to compete.
5. Managers must constantly be aware of emerging issues that affect employee-management relations.

LEARNING THE LANGUAGE OF BUSINESS

Match each of the following key terms with the appropriate definition.

A. comparable worth
B. employee stock ownership plans (ESOPs)
C. equity theory
D. expectancy theory
E. extrinsic reward
F. goal-setting theory
G. Hawthorne effect
H. hygiene factors
I. intrinsic reward
J. job enlargement
K. job enrichment
L. job rotation
M. job simplification
N. management by objectives (MBO)
O. Maslow's hierarchy of needs
P. motivators
Q. principle of motion economy
R. scientific management
S. sexual harassment
T. time-motion studies

_____ 1. Something given to you by someone else as recognition for good work.

_____ 2. The good feeling you have when you have done a job well.

_____ 3. A system of goal setting and implementation that involves a cycle of discussion, review, and evaluation of objectives among top and middle-level managers, supervisors, and employees.

_____ 4. Theory that every job can be broken down into a series of elementary motions.

_____ 5. The concept that people in jobs that require similar levels of education, training, or skills should receive equal pay.

_____ 6. Victor Vroom's theory that the amounts of effort employees exert on a specific task depends on the expectations of the outcome.

_____ 7. Job enrichment strategy involving combining a series of tasks into one assignment that is more challenging and interesting.

_____ 8. Job enrichment strategy involving moving employees from one job to another.

_____ 9. Theory of motivation that places different types of human needs in order of importance, from basic physiological needs to safety, social, and esteem needs to self actualization needs.

_____ 10. Studies of the tasks performed to complete a job and the time needed to do each task.

_____ 11. Theory that employees try to maintain equity among inputs and outputs compared to others in similar positions.

_____ 12. Factors that cause dissatisfaction if they are missing but do not motivate if they are increased.

____ 13. A motivational strategy that emphasizes motivating the worker through the job itself.

____ 14. Unwelcome sexual advances, requests for sexual favors, and other conduct of a sexual nature (verbal or physical).

____ 15. Plans whereby employees can buy part or total ownership of the firm where they work.

____ 16. The tendency for people to behave differently when they know they are being studied.

____ 17. Process of producing task efficiency by breaking down the job into simple steps and assigning people to each of those steps.

____ 18. Factors that provide satisfaction and motivate people to work.

____ 19 The study of workers to find the most efficient way of doing things and then teaching people those techniques.

____ 20. Theory that setting specific, attainable goals can motivate workers and improve performance if the goals are accepted, are accompanied by feedback, and are facilitated by organizational conditions.

SELF-TEST

1. Frederick Taylor thought that the best way to improve productivity was to:
   A) make jobs more interesting and challenging.
   B) establish open two-way communications among all of the organization's workers and managers.
   C) guarantee long-term employment to all workers.
   D) scientifically determine the best method of doing each job, then teach those methods to workers.

2. Dr. Mo T. Vadar, a professor of psychology at a respected university, is planning a study of the factors that affect the motivation of workers. Dr. Vadar is concerned that the results of his experiments may be misleading because workers in an experimental group tend to behave differently when they know they are being studied. This concern shows that Dr. Vadar is aware of the:
   A) Hawthorne effect.
   B) Taylor effect.
   C) potential confusion between correlation and causation.
   D) Heisenberg principle.

3. John is an employee of a major corporation. For the past five years his performance ratings have been very good, but his pay increases have been few and far between. John is finding it increasingly difficult to pay his rent and utility bills. His boss should be aware of John's unmet:
   A) esteem needs.
   B) self-actualization needs.
   C) social needs.
   D) physiological needs.

4. Gerald believes that most of his subordinates dislike work and would avoid it if possible. He also believes that his workers have little, if any, ambition, and that the only way to motivate them is by using threats and punishment. Gerald's views are consistent with:
   A) Theory B management.
   B) Theory X management.
   C) Theory Y management.
   D) Theory Z management.

5. Herzberg's research identified several factors, which could cause workers to become dissatisfied if they were missing, but did not motivate workers if they were increased. Herzberg called these factors:
   A) retro-motivators.
   B) inverted motivators.
   C) hygiene factors.
   D) negative reinforcers.

6. Which of the following practices is most consistent with the views of Frederick Taylor?
   A) job enlargement.
   B) job simplification.
   C) job enrichment.
   D) job rotation.

7. The fundamental purpose of MBO is to:
   A) give top management discretion in setting long-term goals and objectives.
   B) make better use of staff managers by giving them control over various line departments.
   C) involve all members of the organization in goal setting and implementation.
   D) reduce the amount of time managers must spend communicating with subordinates.

8. According to the equity theory, which of the following statement is most accurate?
   A) The best way to motivate workers is to give everyone the same reward.
   B) Workers perceptions of fairness will affect their willingness to perform.
   C) Workers generally do a good job of estimating their contributions to a firm.
   D) In the United States, workers tend to focus on their own situation and pay little attention to the efforts and rewards of other workers.

9. Working conditions recently have changed at the Bariol Corporation. Managers and employees now answer their own phones, and even top managers are addressed by their first name. The company even eliminated executive wash rooms and parking spaces. Bariol implemented all of these changes in an effort to help workers motivate themselves by creating team spirit within the company. Bariol's efforts are consistent with an attempt to:
   A) improve motivation through open communication.
   B) fully implement the scientific management approach developed by Taylor.
   C) establish a pure Type J approach to management.
   D) ensure the maintenance factors were satisfactory.

10. Typron Enterprises has launched a program to evaluate the relative levels of skills, education and training needed to perform various jobs. Based on the results of this evaluation, the firm intends to adjust pay scales so that jobs requiring similar levels of skills and abilities will receive similar pay. Typron's program is an attempt to deal with the issue of:
    A) comparable worth.
    B) affirmative action.
    C) reverse discrimination.
    D) equal employment opportunities.

ANSWER KEY

LEARNING THE LANGUAGE OF BUSINESS

1. E
2. I
3. N
4. Q
5. A
6. D
7. J
8. L
9. O
10. T
11. C
12. H
13. K
14. S
15. B
16. G
17. M
18. P
19. R
20. F

SELF-TEST

Answer	Page #
1. D	Page: 297
2. A	Page: 300
3. D	Page: 300
4. B	Page: 303
5. C	Page: 307
6. B	Page: 309
7. C	Page: 311
8. B	Page: 313
9. A	Page: 314
10. A	Page: 377

LESSON 15

HANDLING LABOR RELATIONS

ASSIGNMENTS

1. Review the Learning Goals and read the Lesson Overview for this lesson.

2. Read Chapter 12 pp. 360-374 in *Understanding Business,* 6th edition by Nickels, McHugh, and McHugh.

3. Watch the video *Handling Labor Relations.*

4. Review the textbook material.

5. Match the key terms with the correct definitions in the Learning the Language of Business exercise.

6. Take the Self-Test.

7. Use the Answer Key to check your answers and review when necessary.

LEARNING GOALS

After you watch the video, read the textbook, and study this lesson, you should be able to:

1. Trace the history of organized labor in the United States and discuss the major legislation affecting labor unions.

2. Outline the objectives of labor unions.

3. Describe the tactics used by labor and management during conflicts and discuss the role of unions in the future.

LESSON NOTES

The PROFILE at the beginning of this chapter focuses on Don Fehr, the Executive Director of the Major league Baseball Players' Association. He has critics and supporters, but the players he represents are among his most enthusiastic supporters. He has been able to negotiate a minimum salary of $200,000 for the nine month work season, as well as other important things. There are still many controversies present in baseball's labor future; the high ticket prices due to salaries and the big payroll teams acquiring all the talent, are a couple of the critical issues.

I. EMPLOYEE-MANAGEMENT ISSUES

   A. The relationship of employees and their managers has always been filled with discussions on certain issues.
      1. The text discusses several of the key employee-management issues.
      2. These issues must be worked out through open discussion, goodwill, and compromise.

   B. The discussion of employee-management relations begins with unions.
      1. **UNIONS** are employee organizations that have as their main goal the representation of members in employee-management bargaining over job-related issues.
      2. Historically, employees turned to unions to gain specific rights and benefits.
      3. However, in the 1990s, unions failed to regain their previous power.

II. LABOR UNIONS FROM DIFFERENT PERSPECTIVES

   A. One's opinion concerning the need for unions usually depends upon one's position in the workplace.

   B. The one thing about unions that most people do agree on is the reason unions were started in the first place.
      1. The industrial revolution moved workers out of the field and into the factories.

   C. THE EARLY HISTORY OF ORGANIZED LABOR
      1. As early as 1792, the Cordwainers (shoemakers) met to discuss labor issues in Philadelphia.
         a. The cordwainers were a **CRAFT UNION**, that is, an organization of skilled workers in a specific trade.
         b. Usually a craft union met to deal with a specific problem and then disbanded.
      2. The Industrial Revolution changed the economic structure of the U.S.
         a. Factory conditions were deplorable, and the hours were long (the average work week was 60 hours, but 80 hours was not unusual).
         b. There was a need for an organization that would attack long-term problems such as child labor and subsistence wages.
      3. The first national labor organization was The **KNIGHTS OF LABOR** formed by Uriah Smith Stephens in 1869.
         a. It included employers as well as workers.
         b. The Knights of Labor was short-lived.
      4. The **AMERICAN FEDERATION OF LABOR (AFL)** was formed under the leadership of Samuel Gompers.
         a. The AFL was an organization of craft unions.
         b. An unauthorized committee in the AFL began to organize workers in **INDUSTRIAL UNIONS**, that is, organizations of unskilled workers.
      5. When the AFL rejected these unions, John Lewis, president of the United Mine Workers Union, formed a new, rival organization.

Lesson 15

a. The **CONGRESS OF INDUSTRIAL ORGANIZATIONS (CIO)** soon rivaled the AFL in membership.
b. The AFL and CIO volleyed for leadership of the labor movement until the two organizations merged in 1955 under the leadership of George Meany.
c. The AFL-CIO now has 68 national and international labor unions.

III. LABOR LEGISLATION AND COLLECTIVE BARGAINING

A. The growth and influence of organized labor in the U.S. has depended on two major factors: the law and public opinion.

B. The National Labor Relations Act (Wagner Act) gave employees the right to form or join unions.
   1. **COLLECTIVE BARGAINING** is the process whereby union representatives sit down with management and work out a mutually agreed-upon contract for the workers.
   2. The Warner Act also established the National Labor Relations Board (NLRB), to oversee labor-management relations.
   3. **CERTIFICATION** is the process of a union becoming recognized by the NLRB as the bargaining agent for a group of employees.
   4. **DECERTIFICATION** is the process that takes away the union's rights.

C. OBJECTIVES OF ORGANIZED LABOR
   1. Union objectives change according to the needs of the workers.
      a. In the 1970s the primary objective of labor unions was additional pay and benefits.
      b. Throughout the 1980s, objectives shifted to job security and union recognition.
      c. The 1990s also focused on job security, complicated by the issue of global competition.
   2. The **NEGOTIATED LABOR-MANAGEMENT AGREEMENT (Labor Contract)** sets the tone and clarifies the terms and conditions under which management and labor agree to function over a specific period of time.
   3. Common types of labor-management agreements:
      a. A **UNION SECURITY CLAUSE** stipulates that employees who reap benefits from a union must either join or pay union dues.
      b. A **CLOSED-SHOP AGREEMENT** specified that workers had to be members of a union before being hired for a job.
      c. Under the **UNION SHOP AGREEMENT**, workers do not have to be members of a union to be hired, but must agree to join.
      d. Under the **AGENCY SHOP AGREEMENT**, employers may hire nonunion workers who are not required to joint the union, but must pay a union fee.
   4. Twenty-one states have passed **RIGHT-TO-WORK LAWS** which give workers the right to have the option to join a union, if one exists, or to not join.
      a. In a right-to-work state, workers are required to work under the **OPEN SHOP AGREEMENT** and have the option to join or not join a union.
      b. If they choose not to join a union they cannot be forced to pay a union fee.

D. RESOLVING LABOR-MANAGEMENT DISAGREEMENTS
   1. Labor and management do not always agree concerning the interpretation of the labor-management agreement.
   2. If such a disagreement cannot be resolved, a grievance may be filed.
   3. A **GRIEVANCE** is a charge by employees that management is not abiding by the terms of the negotiated labor agreement.
   4. **SHOP STEWARDS** are union officials who represent employee interests on a daily basis, they negotiate the majority of grievances.

E. MEDIATION AND ARBITRATION
1. The **BARGAINING ZONE** is the range of options between the initial and final offers that each party will consider.
2. If negotiations don't result in an alternative within this bargaining zone, mediation may be necessary.
3. **MEDIATION** is the use of a third party, called a mediator, to encourage both sides to continue negotiating.
4. The mediator makes suggestions for settling the dispute.
5. **ARBITRATION** is the agreement to bring in an impartial third party to render a binding decision.

IV. TACTICS USED IN LABOR-MANAGEMENT CONFLICTS

A. Both sides may use specific tactics if labor and management reach an impasse in collective bargaining.

B. UNION TACTICS
1. A **STRIKE** means that workers refuse to go to work.
   a. Strikers may also picket, or walk around outside the firm carrying signs and talking with the public about the issues.
   b. The public often realizes how important a worker is when he or she goes on strike.
   c. Often police, teachers, or others engage in sick-outs or the blue flu when union members don't strike but refuse to come to work due to illness.
   d. Employees of the federal government can organize unions but are denied the right to strike.
   e. Under the provisions of the Taft-Hartley Act, the President can ask for a cooling-off period to prevent a strike in a critical industry.
   f. During a **COOLING-OFF PERIOD**, workers return to their jobs while the union and management continue negotiations.
2. Primary and secondary boycotts
   a. A **PRIMARY BOYCOTT** is when organized labor encourages its membership not to buy the product(s) of a firm involved in a labor dispute.
   b. A **SECONDARY BOYCOTT** is an attempt by labor to convince others to stop doing business with a firm that is the target of the primary boycott.
   c. Labor unions can legally authorize primary boycotts, but the Taft-Hartley Act prohibits the use of secondary boycotts.

C. MANAGEMENT TACTICS
1. A **YELLOW-DOG CONTRACT** (outlawed by the Norris-LaGuardia Act) required employees to agree as a condition of employment not to join a union.
2. A **LOCKOUT** (rarely used today) puts pressure on unions by temporarily closing the business and denying employment to the workers.
3. Management most often uses injunctions and strikebreakers.
4. An **INJUNCTION** is a court order directing someone to do something or refrain from doing something.
5. The use of **STRIKEBREAKERS**, workers who are hired to do the jobs of striking employees, has been a source of hostility in labor relations.

D. THE FUTURE OF UNIONS AND LABOR-MANAGEMENT RELATIONS
1. Several new labor-management issues have emerged.
2. Many unions have granted concessions or **GIVEBACKS**, where members give back previous gains.
3. The unions' share of nonfarm workers has declined from its peak in 1945 (35.5% to 13.9% today).

4. In order for U.S. firms to remain competitive with foreign firms, unions are likely to assume a role in maintaining competitiveness.
5. In exchange for cooperating with management, unions may receive improved job security, profit sharing, or higher wages.

LEARNING THE LANGUAGE OF BUSINESS

Match each of the following key terms with the appropriate definition.

A. agency shop agreement
B. American Federation of Labor (AFL)
C. arbitration
D. bargaining zone
E. certification
F. closed-shop agreement
G. collective bargaining
H. Congress of Industrial Organizations (CIO)
I. cooling-off period
J. craft union
K. decertification
L. giveback
M. grievance
N. industrial union
O. injunction
P. Knights of Labor
Q. lockout
R. mediation
S. negotiated labor-management agreement (labor contract)
T. open shop agreement
U. primary boycott
V. right-to-work laws
W. secondary boycott
X. shop stewards
Y. strike
Z. strikebreakers
AA. unions
BB. union security clause
CC. union shop agreement
DD. yellow-dog contracts

_____ 1. An attempt by labor to convince others to stop doing business with a firm that is the subject of a primary boycott.

_____ 2. A management tool for putting pressure on unions by closing the business.

_____ 3. Employee organizations that have the main goal of representing members in employee-management bargaining about job-related issues.

_____ 4. Agreement in right-to-work states which gives workers the option to join or not join a union, if one exists in their workplace.

_____ 5. Range of options between the initial and final offer that each party will consider before a union will strike or before management will close a plant.

_____ 6. An organization of craft unions that championed bread-and-butter labor issues.

_____ 7. Union strategy of workers refusing to go to work in order to further their objectives after an impasse in collective bargaining.

_____ 8. The use of a third party, called a mediator, to encourage both parties to continue negotiating.

_____ 9. A court order directing someone to do something or refrain from doing something.

_____ 10. Legislation which gives workers the right, under an open shop, to join or not join a union if it is present.

_____ 11. Provision in a negotiated labor-management agreement, which stipulates that employees who benefit from a union must either join or pay dues to the union.

_____ 12. A contract agreement whereby employees agreed not to join a union as a condition of employment (outlawed by the Norris-La Guardia Act).

Lesson 15

____ 13. Clause in labor-management agreement, which says workers do not have to be members of a union to be hired, but must agree to join the union within a prescribed period.

____ 14. Clause in labor-management agreement that specified that workers had to be members of a union before being hired.

____ 15. Clause in labor-management agreement that says employers may hire nonunion workers who are not required to join the union but must pay a union fee.

____ 16. Union encouragement of members not to buy products of a firm involved in a labor dispute.

____ 17. Process by which workers take away a union's right to represent them.

____ 18. Period during which workers return to their jobs while the union and management continue negotiations.

____ 19. Labor officials who work permanently in an organization and represent employee interests on a daily basis

____ 20. Settlement which sets the tone and clarifies the terms under which management and labor agree to function over a period of time.

____ 21. Process of a union's becoming recognized by the NLRB as the bargaining agent for a group of employees.

____ 22. The agreement to bring in an impartial third party (an arbitrator) to render a binding decision in a labor dispute.

____ 23. Labor organization of skilled specialists in a particular craft or trade.

____ 24. A charge by employees that management is not abiding by the terms of the negotiated labor agreement.

____ 25. Workers hired to do the jobs of striking workers until the labor dispute is resolved.

____ 26. Union organization of unskilled workers which broke away from the AFL in 1935 and rejoined it in 1955.

____ 27. Labor organizations of unskilled workers in mass-production-related industries such as automobiles and mining.

____ 28. The first national labor union (1869).

____ 29. A concession made by unions to help employers remain competitive and save jobs.

____ 30. The process whereby union and management representatives reach a negotiated labor- management agreement.

SELF-TEST

1. The Wagner Act is best described as a(n):
   A) pro-management law.
   B) pro-union law.
   C) anti-communism law.
   D) anti-capitalism.

2. The law designed to guarantee the rights of individual union members in dealing with their union was the:
   A) Wagner Act.
   B) Landrum-Griffin Act.
   C) Norris-LaGuardia Act.
   D) Taft-Hartley Act.

3. Geraldo works on the assembly line for a major automobile manufacturer. He was hired for the job without any specific training or skill. Geraldo joined a union with other assembly line workers who perform a variety of jobs that do not require a highly specialized skill. Geraldo belongs to a(n):
   A) industrial union.
   B) craft union.
   C) assembly union.
   D) traditional union.

4. In a union shop:
   A) workers must join the union within a stipulated time period (usually 30, 60, or 90 days) in order to keep their jobs.
   B) workers must belong to the union before the company can hire them.
   C) workers who do not join the union must pay a union fee.
   D) workers are required to sign yellow-dog contracts.

5. Union shops are illegal in the state of North Carolina. This means that North Carolina:
   A) is violating federal law.
   B) has passed a right-to-work law.
   C) allows firms to use yellow-dog contracts.
   D) is taking advantage of a loophole in the National Labor Relations Act.

6. Akiko was recently hired at Kreighouser Industries as a maintenance repairperson. She was informed she would have to join the union at the company within 30 days of her starting date. Apparently, Kreighouser operates under a(n):
   A) open shop agreement.
   B) closed shop agreement.
   C) union shop agreement.
   D) agency shop agreement.

7. In the late 1930s management at Bodenger Industries agreed to hire only those workers who were already members of the Steelworkers Union. This type of labor agreement is referred to as a(n):
   A) closed shop.
   B) open shop.
   C) union shop.
   D) restricted shop.

8. In the future, unions are likely to:
   A) die out completely in the United States.
   B) take a more hard-line approach to achieving their objectives.
   C) focus on maintaining strength in their traditional strongholds.
   D) put more emphasis on attracting women, foreign born and professional workers into unions.

9. The Fague Grocery Store chain stocks the products of Vegi-Delite Food Company at all of their supermarkets. The Teamsters Union is currently involved in a labor dispute with Vegi-Delite. The union has already encouraged its members and the general public not to buy Vegi-Delite products. Now it is threatening Fague with the possibility of a boycott if it continues to carry the Vegi-Delite line. The union is threatening Fague with a(n):
   A) primary boycott.
   B) secondary boycott.
   C) jurisdictional boycott.
   D) informational boycott.

10. A labor dispute between the AFL-CIO and Gainesville Brewery is into its eighth month. The AFL-CIO has called on its membership and the general public to refuse to purchase Gainesville products. The AFL-CIO is calling for a:
    A) general boycott.
    B) secondary boycott.
    C) primary boycott.
    D) public boycott.

ANSWER KEY

LEARNING THE LANGUAGE OF BUSINESS

1. W
2. Q
3. AA
4. T
5. D
6. B
7. Y
8. R
9. O
10. V
11. BB
12. DD
13. CC
14. F
15. A
16. U
17. K
18. I
19. X
20. S
21. E
22. C
23. J
24. M
25. Z
26. H
27. N
28. P
29. L
30. G

SELF-TEST

Answer		Page #
1.	B	Page: 365
2.	B	Page: 365
3.	A	Page: 364
4.	A	Page: 368
5.	B	Page: 368
6.	C	Page: 368
7.	A	Page: 368
8.	D	Page: 373
9.	B	Page: 373
10.	C	Page: 373

LESSON 16

MARKETING PRODUCTS

ASSIGNMENTS

1. Review the Learning Goals and read the Lesson Overview for this lesson.

2. Read Chapter 13 pp. 394-423 in Understanding Business, 6th edition by Nickels, McHugh, and McHugh.

3. Watch the video Marketing Products.

4. Review the textbook material.

5. Match the key terms with the correct definitions in the Learning the Language of Business exercise.

6. Take the Self-Test.

7. Use the Answer Key to check your answers and review when necessary.

LEARNING GOALS

After you watch the video, read the textbook, and study this lesson, you should be able to:

1. Explain the marketing concept.

2. Given an example of how to use the four Ps of marketing.

3. Describe the marketing research process, and tell how marketers use environmental scanning to learn about the changing marketing environment.

4. Explain the various ways of segmenting the consumer market.

5. List several ways in which the business-to-business market differs from the consumer market.

6. Show how the marketing concept has been adapted to fit today's modern markets.

7. Describe the latest marketing strategies, such as stakeholder marketing and customer relationship management.

LESSON NOTES

The PROFILE in this chapter focuses on Robert L. Johnson of BET Holdings, Inc. He pioneered African American television entertainment by making his entrepreneurial vision of a network, become reality. He believed that the African American segment of the market was not being given the attention that it deserved. His plan was quickly funded and achieved tremendous success. The power of market segmentation was the key to BETs success, reaching about 35 million African Americans.

I. A BRIEF HISTORY OF MARKETING

   A. THE MARKETING CONCEPT
      1. The returning service men and women after WWII created a tremendous market.
         a. Businesses scrambled to capture their share.
         b. Businesses knew they needed to respond to consumers needs.
      2. The **MARKETING CONCEPT** emphasizes:
         a. A consumer orientation.
         b. A service orientation, which means the training of employees from all departments in customer service.
         c. A profit orientation.
      3. During the 1980s businesses began to more aggressively apply the marketing concept.
      4. In the 1990s, they extended the concept by adopting the concepts of **CUSTOMER RELATIONSHIP MANAGEMENT (CRM).**

   B. DEFINING MARKETING AS MEETING CUSTOMER NEEDS
      1. **MARKETING** is the process of determining customer wants and needs and then providing customers with goods and services that meet or exceed their expectations.
      2. Find a need and fill it, is a simpler description of the marketing process.

   C. NONPROFIT ORGANIZATIONS USE MARKETING TOO
      1. Marketing is a crucial part of almost all organizations, profit and nonprofit.
      2. Charities, churches, politicians, states, and many other organizations all use marketing.

II. MARKETING MANAGEMENT AND THE MARKETING MIX

   A. **MARKETING MANAGEMENT** is the process of planning and executing the conception, pricing, promotion, and distribution of ideas, goods, and services to create mutually beneficial exchanges.
      1. A mutually beneficial exchange means that both parties to the exchange believe they have received good value for their efforts.
      2. Managing the marketing process involves the four factors:
         a. Designing a want-satisfying product.
         b. Setting a price for the product.
         c. Distributing the product to a place where people will buy it.
         d. Promoting the product.
      3. These four factors have become known as the four Ps of marketing or the **MARKETING MIX**.
      4. The environment of marketing is rapidly changing, so marketers must make changes faster.

   B. APPLYING THE MARKETING PROCESS
      1. The first step is to find a need.

2. Research customer wants and needs to find a need that has not yet been fulfilled.

C. DESIGNING A PRODUCT TO MEET NEEDS
1. The next step is to develop a product to fill that need.
2. A **PRODUCT** is any physical good, service, or idea that satisfies a want or need.
3. Concept testing involves developing an accurate description of your product and asking people whether or not the concept appeals to them.
4. Prototypes are samples of the product that you take to consumers to test their reactions.
5. **TEST MARKETING** is the process of testing products among potential users.
6. Outsourcing is the allocation of production and other functions to outside firms.
7. Once the product is made, you have to design a package, and think up a brand name for the product. A **BRAND NAME** is a word, letter or group of words or letters that differentiates a good or service from others.

D. SETTING AN APPROPRIATE PRICE
1. Set a price that is appropriate, that is it should be competitive and cover all the applicable costs.

E. GETTING THE PRODUCT TO THE RIGHT PLACE
1. Once the product is manufactured, you have to choose how to get it to the consumer.
2. You may want to sell your product through organizations that specialize in distributing them, these are called middlemen.

F. DEVELOPING AN EFFECTIVE PROMOTIONAL STRATEGY
1. **PROMOTION** consists of all the techniques sellers use to motivate people to buy products or services.
2. Relationship building with customers includes responding to any suggestions they may make to improve the product or the marketing of the product.
3. Marketing is an ongoing process.

III. PROVIDING MARKETERS WITH INFORMATION

A. **MARKETING RESEARCH** is the analysis of markets to determine opportunities and challenges.
1. One goal is to determine exactly what consumers want and need.
2. Businesses need information to compete effectively, and marketing research is the activity that gathers that information.

B. THE MARKETING RESEARCH PROCESS
1. Step 1: Define the problem and determine the present situation.
2. Step 2: Collect data.
   a. Research can be quite expensive, so some trade-off must be made between information needs and the cost.
   b. Secondary data are sources of information that have been published previously (journals, books, etc.), and are usually cheaper.
   c. Usually secondary research doesn't provide all the necessary information, so marketers must do their own studies.
   d. Primary data are facts and figures not previously published that you gather for a specific purpose.
      1) Telephone surveys, online surveys, mail surveys, and personal interviews are the most common methods of gathering survey information.
      2) A **FOCUS GROUP** consists of a small group of people who meet under the direction of a discussion leader to communicate their opinions about an organization or its product.

3. Step 3: analyze the research data.
4. Step 4: choose the best solutions.
   a. Researchers present alternative strategies and make recommendations as to which strategy may be best, and why.
   b. Consumers are becoming more demanding for ethical behavior from companies.

C. THE MARKETING ENVIRONMENT
   1. Marketing managers must be aware of their surrounding environment when making decisions involving the marketing mix.
      a. **ENVIRONMENTAL SCANNING** is the process of identifying the factors that can affect marketing success.
      b. The factors include:
         1) Global factors – such as the Internet and global marketing.
         2) Technological factors – the Internet and the growth of consumer databases.
         3) Social factors – population growth and demographic changes.
         4) Competitive factors – watch the dynamic competitive market.
         5) Economic factors – adapt to changes.

D. RECOGNIZING DIFFERENT MARKETS: CONSUMER AND BUSINESS-TO-BUSINESS
   1. There are two major markets:
      a. The **CONSUMER MARKET** consists of all the individuals who want goods and services for personal consumption or use.
      b. The **BUSINESS-TO-BUSINESS (B2B) MARKET** consists of all the individuals and organizations that want goods and services to produce other goods and services.
      c. The buyer's reason for buying and the end use of the product determine whether it is considered a consumer product or an industrial product.

IV. THE CONSUMER MARKET

A. Marketers must learn to select different consumer groups to develop products and services specially tailored to their needs.

B. Dividing the market
   1. The process of dividing the total market into several groups (segments) that have similar characteristics is called **MARKET SEGMENTATION**.
   2. **TARGET MARKETING** is the process by which an organization decides which groups (market segments) it can serve profitably.

C. SEGMENTING THE CONSUMER MARKET
   1. There are several ways to segment the market.
      a. **GEOGRAPHIC SEGMENTATION** divides the market by geographic areas.
      b. **DEMOGRAPHIC SEGMENTATION** divides the market by age, income and education level.
      c. **PHYCHOGRAPHIC SEGMENTATION** divides the market by user group's values, attitudes and interests.
      d. **BENEFIT SEGMENTATION** divides the market by determining which benefits of a product to talk about.
      e. **VOLUME SEGMENTATION** divides the market by its volume of use.

D. REACHING SMALLER MARKET SEGMENTS
   1. **NICHE MARKETING** is the process of finding small, but profitable market segments and designing custom-made products for those groups.
   2. **ONE-TO-ONE MARKETING** means developing a unique mix of goods and services for each individual customer.

3. This is easier to do in B2B markets, but mass customization is making it possible in consumer markets.

E. MOVING AWAY FROM MASS MARKETING TOWARD RELATIONSHIP MARKETING
1. **MASS MARKETING** means developing products and promotions that are designed to please large groups of people.
   a. The mass marketer tries to sell products to as many people as possible.
   b. That means using mass media, such as TV, radio, and newspapers.
2. Relationship marketing is more concerned with retaining old customers than creating new ones.
3. **RELATIONSHIP MARKETING** moves away from mass production toward custom-made goods and services.
4. The latest in technology enables sellers to work with buyers to determine their individual wants and needs and to develop goods and services specifically designed for those individuals.
   a. One-way messages in mass media give way to a personal dialogue among participants.

F. FORMING COMMUNITIES OF BUYERS
1. A database can be established so that every contact with consumers results in more information about them.
2. Over time, the seller knows more and more about consumers.
3. Many companies have established Web sites where customers can provide their input and talk to other customers.
4. An important next step in relationship marketing is to establish a community of customers.

G. THE CONSUMER DECISION-MAKING PROCESS
1. Studying consumer behavior centers on the consumer decision-making process:
   a. Problem recognition.
   b. Information search.
   c. Evaluate alternatives.
   d. Make purchase decision.
   e. Postpurchase evaluation.
2. Marketing researchers investigate consumer thought processes and behavior at each stage.
3. Consumer behavior is influenced by:
   a. Learning involves changes in an individual's behavior resulting from previous experiences.
   b. Reference group is the group that an individual uses as a reference point in forming beliefs, attitudes, or behavior.
   c. Culture is the set of values, attitudes, and ways of doing things that are transmitted from one generation to another.
   d. Subculture is the set of values, attitudes, and ways of doing things that result from belonging to a certain group with which one identifies.
   e. Cognitive dissonance means that after the purchase, consumers may have doubts about whether they got the best product at the best price.

V. THE BUSINESS-TO-BUSINESS MARKET
1. The marketing of goods and services to manufacturers, institutions, commercial operations, and the government is called business-to-business B2B marketing.
2. Several factors make B2B marketing different.
   a. There are relatively few B2B customers compared to consumers.
   b. Though few in number, B2B customers are very large.
   c. B2B markets tend to be concentrated in certain areas of the country.

  f. B2B buyers are generally more rational in their purchase decisions.
  g. B2B sales tend to be direct.
  h. B2B markets emphasize personal selling.

VI. UPDATING THE MARKETING CONCEPT

 A. Updating all of the elements of the marketing concepts.

 B. FROM A CONSUMER ORIENTATION TO DELIGHTING CUSTOMERS AND STAKEHOLDERS
  1. Today, the goal of some total quality firms is to totally delight customers by providing goods and services that exactly meet their requirements or exceed their expectations.
   a. Most firms haven't yet reached this goal.
   b. Businesses have learned that employees won't provide first-class goods and services to customers unless they receive first-class treatment themselves.
   c. Marketers must work with others in the organization to make sure employees are pleased.

 C. FROM AN ORGANIZATIONAL SERVICE ORIENTATION TO UNITING ORGANIZATIONS
  1. Competitive benchmarking is used to compare a company to the best.
  2. Manufacturers can't delight customers alone; they need close relationships with suppliers and dealers.

 D. MAINTAINING A PROFIT ORIENTATION
  1. Marketing managers must make sure that everyone in the organization understands that the purpose behind pleasing customers and unitizing organizations is to ensure a profit for the firm.
  2. Using that profit the organization can then satisfy other stakeholders of the firm.

VII. ESTABLISHING RELATIONSHIPS WITH ALL STAKEHOLDERS

 A. Balancing the wants and needs of all the firm's stakeholders is a huge challenge for marketing.
  1. **STAKEHOLDER MARKETING** is establishing and maintaining mutually beneficial exchange relationships with all the stakeholders of the organization.
  2. Many companies have responded to the environmental movement by introducing **GREEN PRODUCTS**, those whose production, use, and disposal doesn't damage the environment.

 B. CUSTOMER RELATIONSHIP MANAGEMENT
  1. The 80/20 rule states that 80% of your business will come from 20% of your customers.
  2. Some businesses have found it more profitable to focus on existing profitable customers then to get new ones.
  3. Today's computer software is helping those in consumer relationship management provide more efficient service.

 C. YOUR PROSPECTS IN MARKETING
  1. Marketing careers include jobs in retailing, marketing research, product management, selling, advertising, and sales promotion.
  2. Other areas include public relations, transportation, storage, and international distribution.

LEARNING THE LANGUAGE OF BUSINESS

Match each of the following key terms with the appropriate definition.

A. Benefit segmentation
B. brand name
C. business-to-business (B2B) market
D. consumer market
E. customer relationship management
F. demographic segmentation
G. environmental scanning
H. focus group
I. geographic segmentation
J. green product
K. market segmentation
L. marketing
M. marketing concept
N. marketing management
O. marketing mix
P. marketing research
Q. mass marketing
R. niche marketing
S. one-to-one marketing
T. product
U. promotion
V. psychographic segmentation
W. relationship marketing
X. stakeholder marketing
Y. target marketing
Z. test marketing
AA. volume segmentation

_____ 1. All the individuals and organizations that want goods and services to use in producing other goods and services.

_____ 2. Any physical good, service, or idea that satisfies a want or need.

_____ 3. All individuals or households who want goods and services for personal consumption or use.

_____ 4. Developing a unique mix of goods and services for each individual customer.

_____ 5. Refers to a three-part business philosophy: (1) a consumer orientation, (2) training of all employees in customer service, and (3) a profit orientation.

_____ 6. The process used both to determine what consumer and industrial clients want and need and to select the most effective way to satisfy those wants and needs.

_____ 7. All the techniques that sellers use to motivate people to buy goods or services.

_____ 8. The process of dividing the total market into several groups that have similar characteristics.

_____ 9. The process of finding very small, but profitable market segments and designing custom-made products for those groups.

_____ 10. The process by which an organization decides which market segments to serve.

_____ 11. The process of determining customer wants and needs and then providing customers with goods and services that meet or exceed their expectations.

_____ 12. A small group of people who meet under the direction of a discussion leader to communicate their feelings concerning an organization, its products, or other important issues.

_____ 13. Establishing and maintaining mutually beneficial exchange relationships with customers and all the other stakeholders of the organization.

____ 14. Developing products and promotions that are designed to please large groups of people.

____ 15. The ingredients that go into a marketing program: product, price, place, and promotion.

____ 16. A product whose production, use, and disposal doesn't damage the environment.

____ 17. The process of planning and executing the conception, pricing, promotion, and distribution of ideas, goods, and services to create mutually beneficial exchanges.

____ 18. The process of testing products among potential users.

____ 19. A word, letter, or group of words or letters that differentiates the goods and services of a seller from those of competitors.

____ 20. The process of dividing the market by determining which benefits of a product to talk about.

____ 21. Learning as much as possible about customers and doing everything you can to satisfy them or delight them with goods and services over time.

____ 22. The process of dividing the market by age, income, and education level.

____ 23. The process of identifying the factors that can affect marketing success.

____ 24. The process of dividing the market by geographic areas.

____ 25. The process of dividing the market by using groups' values, attitudes, and interests.

____ 26. Establishing and maintaining mutually beneficial exchange relationships over time with all the stakeholders of the organization.

____ 27. The process of dividing the market by usage.

SELF-TEST

1. Which of the following statements is most consistent with today's views on marketing?
   A) "There's a sucker born every minute."
   B) "Where there's a will, there's a way."
   C) "Waste not, want not."
   D) "Find a need and fill it."

2. A comparison of the marketing concept and customer relationship management indicates that:
   A) the two concepts are identical.
   B) customer relationship management attempts to improve profits by keeping quality high while the marketing concept attempts to improve profits by a careful design of the promotional mix.
   C) customer relationship management turns the marketing concept upside down. The marketing concept emphasized that marketing was the most important function performed by a firm, but customer relationship management views marketing to be the least important function.
   D) customer relationship management extends the marketing concept by calling for the firm to learn more about its customers so that it not only satisfies them, but also pleases and delights them with goods and services over time.

3. Keith Collins has just been hired as a marketing manager for a textbook publishing company. His primary responsibilities are likely to be concerned with:
   A) establishing inventory control methods.
   B) making certain production schedules are met.
   C) planning and executing the conception, pricing, promotion and distribution of his firm's products.
   D) preparing job descriptions and job specifications for sales representatives.

4. Jorge Martinez is a marketing manager for Belltown Financial Services. He has been looking at a variety of factors, such as technological, social and economic trends and competitive conditions, in an effort to identify factors that could be vital to Belltown's future marketing success. Jorge's efforts are an example of:
   A) target marketing.
   B) concept testing.
   C) relationship marketing.
   D) environmental scanning.

5. Marketing manager Jan Draper has just finished reviewing a great deal of data her department has gathered through a variety of telephone interviews, mail surveys and focus groups. Jan is disappointed because the research results strongly suggest that a product idea she helped develop is unlikely to be popular with customers. Jan should:
   A) go full steam ahead with the proposed product because the opinions of experienced marketing managers often turn out to be more accurate than marketing research.
   B) accept the research results and reevaluate the proposed product.
   C) continue developing the product, but try to find ways to reduce production costs.
   D) put the product on temporary hold, throw out the results of the research, and design and conduct new surveys and questionnaires.

6. Southern Sun is a maker of clothing for active people. It focuses its marketing efforts on people who enjoy strenuous outdoor activities such as running and mountain climbing. For example, the firm advertises heavily in magazines for runners. This approach suggests that Southern Sun is using _____ factors to segment its market.
   A) demographic
   B) kinesthetic
   C) geographic
   D) psychographic

7. Cool People Publications has identified African-American teenage girls as a specific group of consumers they believe they could serve profitably. The efforts of Cool People to direct its efforts toward this specific group is an example of:
   A) mass marketing.
   B) target marketing.
   C) prime marketing.
   D) focus group marketing.

8. Marketing manager Hideki Suzuki has just been transferred from a position in his firm where he dealt with the consumer market, to a position that deals with buyers in the business-to-business market. Which of the following statements correctly identifies a key difference Hideki is likely to observe between consumer markets and business-to-business markets?
   A) In consumer markets the key is to discover new needs and fill them, while in the business-to-business market marketers must efficiently fill needs they already know about.
   B) Relationship marketing tends to be much more important in consumer markets than in business-to-business markets.
   C) Buyers in the business-to-business markets tend to be more rational than buyers in consumer markets.
   D) Business-to-business marketers make greater use of marketing intermediaries such as wholesalers and retailers than do consumer markets.

9. Which of the following statements best summarizes the purpose behind the marketing process? The purpose of marketing is to:
   A) convince customers to buy whatever the firm is trying to sell.
   B) attain the largest possible share of the overall market.
   C) do whatever it takes to satisfy the consumer, even if the welfare of the other stakeholders is adversely affected.
   D) ensure a profit for the firm so that the organization can satisfy its stakeholders.

10. Abigail Simpson is a marketing manager who believes that her firm should try to balance the needs of its customers with those of the firm's employees, stockholders, suppliers, dealers, and members of the community. Abigail's views are:
    A) inconsistent with current marketing views which emphasize that the customer's needs always come first.
    B) an example of theory X management.
    C) most closely linked to the views of scientific management.
    D) consistent with the concept of stakeholder marketing.

ANSWER KEY

LEARNING THE LANGUAGE OF BUSINESS

1. C
2. T
3. D
4. S
5. M
6. P
7. U
8. K
9. R
10. Y
11. L
12. H
13. W
14. Q
15. O
16. J
17. N
18. Z
19. B
20. A
21. E
22. F
23. G
24. I
25. V
26. X
27. AA

SELF-TEST

Answer	Page #
1. D	Page: 397
2. D	Page: 396
3. C	Page: 397
4. D	Page: 407
5. B	Page: 405-406
6. D	Page: 412
7. B	Page: 410-411
8. C	Page: 417
9. D	Page: 418
10. D	Page: 419

LESSON 17

DEFINING PRODUCTS

ASSIGNMENTS

1. Review the Learning Goals and read the Lesson Overview for this lesson.

2. Read Chapter 14 pp. 426-445 in Understanding Business, 6th edition by Nickels, McHugh, and McHugh.

3. Watch the video Defining Products.

4. Review the textbook material.

5. Match the key terms with the correct definitions in the Learning the Language of Business exercise.

6. Take the Self-Test.

7. Use the Answer Key to check your answers and review when necessary.

LEARNING GOALS

After you watch the video, read the textbook, and study this lesson, you should be able to:

1. Explain the concept of a package value.

2. Describe the various kinds of consumer and industrial goods.

3. List and describe the six functions of packaging.

4. Give examples of a brand, a brand name, and a trademark, and explain the concepts of brand equity and loyalty.

5. Explain the role of brand managers and the six steps of the new-product development process.

6. Identify and describe the stages of the product life cycle, and describe marketing strategies at each stage.

LESSON NOTES

The PROFILE at the beginning of this chapter focuses on Jack Greenberg of McDonald's. When Greenberg came to McDonald's from Ernst & Young he used his accounting background and analyze the McDonald's product mix. It had been nearly twenty years since their last successful new product. Greenberg decided that discussions with customers would yield the answers to their product mix problem. Several changes were implemented, the "Made for You," approach, new faster custom-made food equipment, new chicken offerings, a focus on quality and individual franchisee product innovations. McDonald's has begun a campaign to move "outside the arches" with new nonhamburger restaurants, new product development and pricing strategies.

I. PRODUCT DEVELOPMENT AND THE VALUE PACKAGE

 A. **VALUE** is providing good quality at a fair price. When customers evaluate products or services they want the benefits to exceed the costs.
   1. To satisfy consumers, marketers must learn to listen better and to adapt constantly to changing market demands.
   2. This chapter explores two key parts of the marketing mix: product and price.
   3. Customer wants and needs must be constantly monitored because these needs change over time.
   4. Product development is a key activity in any business.
   5. Marketers must create excitement and demand for their products.

 B. DEVELOPING A VALUE PACKAGE
   1. A **VALUE PACKAGE** (total product offer) consists of everything that consumers evaluate when deciding whether or not to buy something.
      a. The basic product may be a physical good or service.
      b. The text lists such intangibles as: price, package, store surroundings, image created by advertising, guarantee, reputation of the producer, brand name, service, buyers' past experience, speed of delivery and accessibility of the marketer.
      c. When people buy a product, they evaluate and compare value packages using all these dimensions.
   2. The value package as perceived by the consumer is much more than the product itself.
      a. Often a high price indicates exceptional quality.
      b. A guarantee of satisfaction can increase the product's value in the mind of consumers.
      c. An organization can also use low price to create an attractive value package.

 C. PRODUCT LINES AND THE PRODUCT MIX
   1. Companies usually sell several different, but complementary, products.
   2. A **PRODUCT LINE** is a group of products that are physically similar or are intended for a similar market.
   3. A **PRODUCT MIX** is the combination of product lines offered by a manufacturer.
   4. Service providers also have product lines and product mixes.

II. PRODUCT DIFFERENTIATION

 A. **PRODUCT DIFFERENTIATION** is the creation of real product differences or perceptions that make one product seem superior to others.
   1. Actual product differences are sometimes quite small, so marketers must create a unique, attractive image.
   2. Different products call for different marketing strategies.

3. Small businesses can often win market share with creative product differentiation.

B. MARKETING DIFFERENT CLASSES OF CONSUMER GOODS AND SERVICES
1. **CONVENIENCE GOODS AND SERVICES** are products that the consumer wants to purchase frequently and with a minimum of effort.
   a. Location, brand awareness, and image are important for marketers.
   b. Examples: candy, snacks, and banking.
   c. Best marketing strategy: make them readily available, the Internet has done this for some service industries.
2. **SHOPPING GOODS AND SERVICES** are those products that the consumer buys only after comparing value, quality, and price from a variety of sellers.
   a. Shopping goods and services are sold largely through shopping centers where consumers can shop around.
   b. Examples: clothes, shoes, and appliances.
   c. Best marketing strategy: good price and quality.
3. **SPECIALTY GOODS AND SERVICES** are products that have a special attraction to consumers, who are willing to go out of their way to obtain them.
   a. These products are often marketed through specialty magazines.
4. **UNSOUGHT GOODS AND SERVICES** are goods and services that consumers are unaware of, haven't necessarily thought of buying, or find that they need to solve an unexpected problem.
   a. Example: emergency car-towing services.
5. The marketing task varies depending on the kind of product or service.
6. The individual consumer determines whether or not a good or service falls into a particular class.

C. MARKETING INDUSTRIAL GOODS AND SERVICES
1. **INDUSTRIAL GOODS** are products used in the production of other products.
2. The buyer's intended use of the product is what determines whether it is a consumer or an industrial product.
   a. Installations – major capital equipment.
   b. Capital items – products that last a long time and cost a lot.
   c. Accessory equipment – capital items that don't last as long.

III. PACKAGING CHANGES THE PRODUCT

A. Packaging can be very important in the customers' evaluation of the value package.
1. It can change and improve its basic product (salt.)
2. Packaging changes the product by changing its visibility, usefulness, or attractiveness.
3. Packaging can also help make a product more attractive to retailers (UPCs on packages make inventory easier).

B. THE GROWING IMPORTANCE OF PACKAGING
1. Today the package carries more of the promotional burden than in the past.
2. Packaging must do the following:
   a. Protect the goods inside, stand up under handling and storage, be tamperproof, and easy to open.
   b. Attract the buyer's attention.
   c. Describe the contents and give information about the contents.
   d. Explain the benefits of the goods inside.
   e. Provide information on warranties, warnings, and other consumer matters.
   f. Give some indication of price, value, and uses.

IV. BRANDIND AND BRAND EQUITY

   A. A **BRAND** is a name, symbol, or design that identifies the goods or services of one seller and distinguishes them from those of competitors.
      1. Brand name is that part of the brand consisting of a word, letter, or group of words or letters comprising a name that differentiates the goods or services of a seller from those of competitors.
      2. A **TRADEMARK** is a brand that has been given exclusive legal protection for both the brand name and the pictorial design.
      3. Most people choose the brand name product even when they say there's no difference.

   B. BRAND CATEGORIES
      1. **MANUFACTURERS' BRAND NAMES** are the brand names of manufacturers.
      2. **KNOCKOFF BRANDS** are illegal copies of national brand name goods.
      3. **DEALER (PRIVATE) BRANDS** are products that do not carry the manufacturer's name, but carry the name of a distributor or retailer instead.
      4. Many manufacturers fear having their brand names become generic names.
         a. A **GENERIC NAME** is the name for a product category.
         b. Names such as nylon, escalator, and zipper became so popular that they lost their brand status and became generic.
         c. Companies that are working hard to protect their brand names today include Xerox and Styrofoam.
      5. **GENERIC GOODS** are nonbranded products that usually sell at a sizable discount compared to national brands.
         a. They have very basic packaging and are backed with little or no advertising.
         b. Consumers today are buying more generic products because their quality has improved.

   C. GENERATING BRAND EQUITY AND LOYALTY
      1. **BRAND EQUITY** is a combination of factors including awareness, loyalty, perceived quality, the feeling and images, and any other emotion people associate with a brand name.
      2. **BRAND LOYALTY** is the degree to which customers are satisfied, like the brand, and are committed to further purchases.
      3. **BRAND AWARENESS** means that your product is the first recalled when a product category is mentioned.
      4. Perceived quality is an important part of brand equity.
         a. A product that's perceived as better quality can be priced accordingly.
         b. Quality factors include, price, appearance, and reputation.
         c. Brand preference means that consumers prefer one brand to another.
      5. Brand name manufacturers have to develop new products even faster and hold off the challenge of competitors.

   D. CREATING BRAND ASSOCIATIONS
      1. **BRAND ASSOCIATION** is the linking of a brand to other favorable images.

V. BRAND MANAGEMENT

   A. A **BRAND MANAGER** has direct responsibility for one brand or one product line, including all the elements of the marketing mix.

   B. NEW -PRODUCT SUCCESS
      1. Chances that a new product will fail are high, as high as 86%.
      2. A leading cause of failure is a product not delivering what it promised.

3. Other reasons for failure include poor positioning, not enough difference from competitors, and poor packaging.

C. THE NEW-PRODUCT DEVELOPMENT PROCESS
   1. Idea generation
   2. Screening
   3. Product analysis
   4. Development
   5. Testing
   6. Commercialization (bringing the product to market)

D. GENERATING NEW-PRODUCT IDEAS
   1. The largest percentage of new consumer product ideas (38%) come from studying the competition, but copying slows the flow of new ideas.
   2. The largest percentages of new industrial product ideas come from company sources other than research and development.
   3. Since more than a third of all new ideas for industrial products come from users, managers should listen to their suppliers and customers.

E. PRODUCT SCREENING
   1. **PRODUCT SCREENING** reduces the number of new-product ideas being worked on at any time.
   2. It takes about seven ideas to generate one commercial product.

F. PRODUCT ANALYSIS
   1. This is done after screening; it is a matter of making cost estimates and sales forecasts to determine profitability.
   2. Products that don't meet the established criteria are withdrawn from further consideration.

G. PRODUCT DEVELOPMENT AND TESTING
   1. A product idea can be developed into many different product concepts.
   2. **CONCEPT TESTING** involves taking a product idea to consumers to get their reactions.

H. COMMERCIALIZATION
   1. The text uses the example of the long struggle for the inventor of zippers to gain consumer acceptance of the product.
   2. The marketing effort must include **COMMERCIALIZATION**:
      a. Promoting the product to distributors and retailers.
      b. Developing strong advertising and sales campaigns.
   3. Today new products are getting more rapid exposure to global markets by being promoted on the Internet.

I. THE INTERNATIONAL CHALLENGE
   1. The key to success is to bring out new high-quality products faster than your competitors.
   2. Other countries, particularly Japan, are known for their rapid development processes.
   3. To stay competitive in world markets, U.S. businesses must develop a new product development process.
      a. This requires continuous, incremental improvements in function, cost, and quality.
      b. Cost-sensitive design and new process technologies are also crucial.
   4. Successful new-product development is an interactive process between customers and marketers.

5. The focus shifts from internal product development processes to external customer responsiveness.

VI. THE PRODUCT LIFE CYCLE

   A. The **PRODUCT LIFE CYCLE** is a theoretical model of what happens to a product class over time.
      1. Not all products follow the life cycle, and some brands may act differently.
      2. Knowing what stage in the cycle a product is in helps marketing managers to decide when strategic changes are needed.

   B. EXAMPLE OF THE PRODUCT LIFE CYCLE
      1. The text uses the example of the introduction of instant coffee.

   C. THE IMPORTANCE OF THE PRODUCT LIFE CYCLE
      1. Different stages in the product life cycle call for different marketing strategies.
      2. Each stage calls for multiple marketing mix changes.

LEARNING THE LANGUAGE OF BUSINESS

Match each of the following key terms with the appropriate definition.

A. brand
B. brand association
C. brand awareness
D. brand equity
E. brand loyalty
F. brand manager
G. commercialization
H. concept testing
I. convenience goods and services
J. dealer (private) brands
K. generic goods
L. generic name
M. industrial goods
N. knockoff brands
O. manufacturers' brand names
P. product analysis
Q. product differentiation
R. product life cycle
S. product line
T. product mix
U. product screening
V. shopping goods and services
W. specialty goods and services
X. trademark
Y. unsought goods and services
Z. value
AA. value package

_____ 1. Products that the consumer buys only after comparing quality and price from a variety of sellers.

_____ 2. A manager who is directly responsible for one product line or one brand.

_____ 3. Products that have a special attraction to consumers who are willing to go out of their way to obtain them.

_____ 4. Taking a product idea to consumers to test their reaction.

_____ 5. The degree to which customers are satisfied, like the brand, and are committed to further purchases.

_____ 6. Products that consumers are unaware of , haven't necessarily thought of buying, or find that they need to solve an unexpected problem.

_____ 7. The attempt to create product perceptions in the minds of consumers so that one product seems superior to others.

_____ 8. The first product recalled when a product category is mentioned.

_____ 9. The name of a product category.

Lesson 17 Page 186

____ 10. A group of products that are physically similar or are intended for a similar market.

____ 11. The combination of product lines offered by a manufacturer.

____ 12. Illegal copies of national brand-name goods such as Polo shirts or Rolex watches.

____ 13. Brand that has been given exclusive legal protection for both the brand name and the pictorial design.

____ 14. Products used in the production of other products.

____ 15. Products that the consumer wants to purchase frequently and with a minimum of effort.

____ 16. Nonbranded products that usually sell at a sizable discount from national or private brands, have very basic packaging, and are backed with little or no advertising.

____ 17. The four-stage theoretical depiction of the process from birth to death of a product class: introduction, growth, maturity, and decline.

____ 18. A name, symbol, or design (or combination of these) that identifies the goods or services of one seller or group of sellers and distinguishes them from those of competitors.

____ 19. Combination of factors such as awareness, loyalty, perceived quality, the feeling and images and any other emotion people associate with a brand name.

____ 20. The linking of a brand to other, favorable images.

____ 21. Everything that consumers evaluate when deciding whether or not to buy something.

____ 22. Products that don't carry the manufacturers' name but carry a retailer or distributor's name instead.

____ 23. The brand names of manufacturers that distribute products nationally.

____ 24. A process designed to reduce the number of new product ideas being worked on at any one time.

____ 25. Promoting a product to distributors and retailers to get a wide distribution and generate and maintain interest in the product.

____ 26. Making cost estimates and sales forecasts to get an idea about the profitability of new product lines.

____ 27. Providing good quality goods and services at a fair price.

SELF-TEST

1. A group of products offered by a firm that are physically similar or are intended for a similar market are referred to as a(n):
   A) product matrix.
   B) product line.
   C) product mix.
   D) value package.

2. Heavenly Taste Confectioners uses the same ingredients as most other producers of chocolate candies. In fact, taste test suggest that the candy itself, while quite good, isn't much better than other well-known brand chocolate. However, the company wraps its candies in expensive looking foil and places them in very attractive boxes. It promotes its products in advertisements as "the ultimate in chocolate experience." Heavenly Taste charges a much higher price than most competitors, but sales continue to grow. This success indicates that:
   A) consumers often behave in an irrational manner.
   B) there is more to the value package than the physical product.
   C) consumers seldom consider price when making a buying decision for goods such as chocolate.
   D) chocolate is best classified as a convenience good.

3. _____ are products that the consumer buys only after comparing quality and price from a variety of sellers.
   A) Shopping goods.
   B) Specialty goods.
   C) Convenience goods.
   D) Unsought goods.

4. Entice-mint Breath Mints is a new brand of breath fresheners. The company realizes that product location is very important since consumers desire to buy this type product with a minimum of effort. Entice-mint mints are in the category of:
   A) shopping goods and services.
   B) specialty goods and services.
   C) convenience goods and services.
   D) industrial goods and services.

5. Attracting attention, describing contents, explaining benefits, and indicating uses for a product are all functions of:
   A) target marketing.
   B) Universal Product Codes.
   C) packaging.
   D) trademarks.

6. The Pillsbury Doughboy is an example of a:
   A) patent.
   B) trademark.
   C) private brand.
   D) generic label.

7. Sears sells batteries under its own Diehard brand name even though another company actually produces these batteries. This is an example of a:
   A) knockoff brand.
   B) generic brand.
   C) dealer (private) brand.
   D) loyalty brand.

8. The greatest source of ideas for new consumer products is:
   A) consumer suggestions.
   B) supplier suggestions.
   C) research and development.
   D) analysis of the competition.

9. "If you create a better mouse trap, the world will beat a path to your door." This statement ignores the need for which step in the new-product development process?
   A) Commercialization
   B) Screening
   C) Idea generation
   D) Development

10. Which stage of the product life cycle tends to be characterized by rapidly rising sales, very high profit levels, and a growing number of competitors?
    A) Growth
    B) Maturity
    C) Saturation
    D) Decline

ANSWER KEY

LEARNING THE LANGUAGE OF BUSINESS

1. V
2. F
3. W
4. H
5. E
6. Y
7. Q
8. C
9. L
10. S
11. T
12. N
13. X
14. M
15. I
16. K
17. R
18. A
19. D
20. B
21. AA
22. J
23. O
24. U
25. G
26. P
27. Z

SELF-TEST

Answer	Page #
1. B	Page: 430
2. B	Page: 428-429
3. A	Page: 432
4. C	Page: 431
5. C	Page: 435-436
6. B	Page: 436
7. C	Page: 437
8. D	Page: 439 and 441
9. A	Page: 441-442
10. A	Page: 444-445

LESSON 18

MANAGING OPERATIONS

ASSIGNMENTS

1. Review the Learning Goals and read the Lesson Overview for this lesson.

2. Read Chapter 9 pp. 262-287 in Understanding Business, 6th edition by Nickels, McHugh, and McHugh.

3. Watch the video Managing Operations.

4. Review the textbook material.

5. Match the key terms with the correct definitions in the Learning the Language of Business exercise.

6. Take the Self-Test.

7. Use the Answer Key to check your answers and review when necessary.

LEARNING GOALS

After you watch the video, read the textbook, and study this lesson, you should be able to:

1. Define operations management.

2. Describe the operations management functions that are involved in both the manufacturing and service sectors.

3. Discuss the problem of measuring productivity in the service sector, and tell how new technology is leading to productivity gains in service companies.

4. Explain process planning and the various manufacturing processes being used today.

5. Describe the seven new manufacturing techniques that have made U.S. companies more productive: just-in-time inventory control, Internet purchasing, flextime manufacturing, lean manufacturing, mass customization, competing in time, and computer-aided design and manufacturing.

6. Explain the use of PERT and Gantt charts.

LESSON NOTES

The PROFILE at the beginning of this chapter focuses on Demetria Giannisis founder of the Chicago Manufacturing Center. The CMC is a manufacturing consulting organization with over 1000 clients. When a client needs help CMC assembles a team to investigate the situation and find solutions. Finding ways to improve operations can significantly effect profits for manufacturing and service organizations.

I. AMERICA'S EVOLVING MANUFACTURING AND SERVICES BASE

   A. A new era in the industrial revolution.
      1. American manufacturers implemented a number of things in the 1970s and 1980s to regain a competitive lead.
      2. Competition from foreign manufacturers forced U.S. companies to alter their production techniques and managerial styles.
      3. To regain a competitive edge, American manufacturers have implemented:
         a. A customer focus.
         b. Cost savings through site selection.
         c. Total quality management.
         d. Computer-integrated manufacturing and other modern practices.
         e. A reliance on the Internet to unit companies.
      4. What are the merits of moving production facilities to foreign countries?
      5. Will the replacement of workers with robots and machinery work?
      6. Should we be protecting American manufacturers through quotas and other restrictions of free trade?
      7. Tomorrow's college graduates will face tremendous challenges (and career opportunities) in redesigning and rebuilding America's manufacturing base.

   B. FROM PRODUCTION TO OPERATIONS MANAGEMENT
      1. Production and operations management is all the activity managers do to create goods and services.
      2. **PRODUCTION** is the creation of finished goods and services using the factors of production: land, labor (machinery), capital, entrepreneurship, and information.
      8. The concepts that apply to service organizations apply generally to manufacturing organizations as well.
      9. **OPERATIONS MANAGEMENT** is a specialized area in management that converts or transforms resources into goods and services.

   C. MANUFACTURERS TURN TO SERVICES AND A CUSTOMER ORIENTATION FOR PROFIT
      1. For the last decade most U.S. manufacturers have had slow profit growth.
      2. U.S. companies have spent a lot of money on productivity and quality initiatives.
      3. They have expanded operations management by moving closer to the customer.

II. OPERATIONS MANAGEMENT FUNCTIONS

   A. FACILITIES LOCATION
      1. The process of selecting a geographic location for a company's operations is called **FACILITY LOCATION**.
         a. Easy customer access might be important.
         b. The Internet allows customers to shop from home.
      2. There are several key issues when choosing a location for a manufacturing facility.
         a. Availability of inexpensive labor.
         b. Availability of skilled laborers.
         c. Inexpensive resources.

        d. Reducing the time to market.
        e. Access to transportation.
   3. Locating a business close to the markets.
        a. Foreign factories are used to get close to the international markets.
        b. Near transportation facilities.
        c. Quality of life in the area.
        d. Does the local community support the business?
        e. Schools and other infrastructure elements.
   4. Facilities location in the future.
        a. Locations in the future will have flexibility due to technology.

B. FACILITY LAYOUT
   1. The physical arrangement of the resources employed in the production process is the **FACILITY LAYOUT**.
   2. Arrange things for the best possible production.
   3. Layout depends upon the process used.
   4. Service layout is customer oriented.
   5. Manufacturing plant layout focuses on cost saving.
   6. Many companies are changing from assembly lines to modular layouts that employ teams of workers.

C. Operations management and the Internet.
   1. Today, many firms outsource production.
   2. Due to communication technology operations management is becoming interfirm, with firms working on coordinating with each other.
   3. Most major manufacturing companies are developing Internet focused strategies.

D. QUALITY CONTROL
   1. **QUALITY CONTROL** is the measurement of products and services against set standards.
        a. Earlier, quality control was often done at the end of the production line by a quality control department.
        b. Quality now means satisfying customers by building in and ensuring quality from product planning to production, purchasing, sales, and service.
        c. Emphasis is placed on customer satisfaction.
   2. Total quality management programs begin by analyzing the consumer to see what quality standards need to be established.
   3. Quality is then designed into products, and every product must meet those standards.
   4. The Malcolm Baldrige National Quality Awards established in 1987, created a set of standards for overall company quality.
        a. It focuses on seven key areas:
            1) leadership
            2) strategic planning
            3) customer and market focus
            4) information and analysis
            5) human resource focus
            6) process planning and
            7) business results.
   5. ISO 9000 and 14000 standards are global measures of quality.
        a. **ISO 9000** is also referred to as quality management and assurance standards.
   6. **ISO 14000** is a collection of the best practices for managing an organization's impact on the environment.
   7. Certification in ISO 9000 and 14000 would indicate a world-class management system, in both quality and environmental standards.

III. OPERATIONS MANAGEMENT IN THE SERVICE SECTOR

   A. Creating a good experience
      1. Operations management in the service sector focuses on creating a good experience for those who use the service.
      2. Operations management in the service sector delights customers by anticipating their needs.

   B. MEASURING QUALITY IN THE SERVICE SECTOR
      1. The greatest productivity problem in the U.S. is within the service sector.
      2. The latest technology must be used in the service sector to increase productivity.
         a. In the 1970s and 1980s productivity increases in the service sector were almost zero.
         b. Over 70% of jobs in the U.S. are in the service sector.
      3. Evidence seems to indicate that productivity has actually grown in the service sector, but no good means of measuring it exists.
         a. Quality increases are hard to measure.
      4. Some gains come from new technology.
         a. Drive-up windows at fast food restaurants are now using wireless microphones.
         b. Laser scanners at the grocery store checkout increases speed.

   C. SERVICES GO INTERACTIVE
      1. The service industry has always taken advantage of new technology to increase customer satisfaction.
      2. Now interactive computer networks are revolutionizing services.
      3. As computers and modems get faster, the Internet may take over much of traditional retailing.

IV. OPERATIONS MANAGEMENT IN THE MANUFACTURING SECTOR

   A. Production uses basic inputs to produce outputs.
      1. **FORM UTILITY** is the value added by the creation of finished goods and services using raw materials, components, and other inputs.

   B. PROCESS PLANNING
      1. **PROCESS PLANNING** involves the choosing of the best methods for converting resources into useful goods and services.
      2. Andrew S. Grove, chief executive officer of Intel, defines the three basic requirements of production:
         a. To build and deliver products in response to the demands of the customer at a scheduled delivery time.
         b. To provide an acceptable level of quality.
         c. To provide everything at the lowest possible cost.
      3. There are several types of production processes.
         a. **PROCESS MANUFACTURING** is an activity that physically or chemically changes material.
         b. An **ASSEMBLY PROCESS** is one in which components are put together to constitute a new entity.
      4. Continuous versus intermittent processes
         a. A **CONTINUOUS PROCESS** is one in which long production runs turn out finished goods over time.
         b. An **INTERMITTENT PROCESS** is an operation where the production run is short and the machines are changed frequently to produce different products.
         c. Today, most new manufacturers use intermittent processes.

C. MATERIALS REQUIREMENT PLANNING
   1. **MATERIALS REQUIREMENT PLANNING (MRP)** is a computer-based operations management system that uses sales forecasts to make sure the needed parts and materials are available at the right place and the right time.
      a. MRP was most popular with companies that made products with a lot of different parts.
   2. MRP II is an advanced version of MRP that involves more than materials planning.
   3. **ENTERPRISE RESOURCE PLANING (ERP)** is a computer-based production and operations system that links multiple firms into one, integrated production unit.
      a. The software enables the monitoring of quality and customer satisfaction as it's happening.
      b. ERP is better than MRP or MRP II because it monitors processes in multiple firms at the same time.
      c. Eventually, such programs will link suppliers, manufacturers, and retailers in a completely integrated manufacturing and distribution system.

V. MODERN PRODUCTION TECHNIQUES

   A. The goal of manufacturing and process management is to provide high-quality goods and services instantaneously in response to customer demand.
      1. Traditional organizations were not designed to be so responsive, but to make a limited variety of products at a low cost.
      2. They used **MASS PRODUCTION** processing which meant making large quantities of a limited variety of goods.
      3. Over the years, low cost often came at the expense of quality and flexibility.
      4. Such inefficiencies made U.S. companies subject to foreign competition.
      5. As a result of this competition, companies today must make a wide variety of high-quality custom-designed products at a very low cost.

   B. JUST-IN-TIME INVENTORY CONTROL
      1. One major cost of production is holding parts in warehouses.
      2. **JUST-IN-TIME (JIT) INVENTORY CONTROL** is a system which arranges for delivery of the smallest possible quantities at the latest possible time to keep inventory as low as possible.
         a. Suppliers deliver their products just in time to go on the assembly line; a minimum of inventory is kept.
         b. Using enterprise requirement planning (ERP) or similar system, the manufacturer determines what parts and supplies will be needed.
         c. Efficiency is maintained by having the supplier linked by computer to the producer,
      3. ERP and JIT systems make sure: the right materials are at the right place at the right time at the cheapest cost to meet customer needs.

   C. INTERNET PURCHASING
      1. **PURCHASING** is the function in the firm that searches for quality material resources, finds the best suppliers, and negotiates the best price for quality goods and services.
      2. In the past, manufacturers tended to deal with many different suppliers.
      3. Today, they rely more heavily on one or two; the relationship between suppliers and manufacturers is now much closer.
      4. The Internet allows manufacturers to contact dozens of Internet-based purchasing services and find the best supplies at the best prices.
         a. A buying and selling marketplace is created online.

   D. FLEXIBLE MANUFACTURING
      1. **FLEXIBLE MANUFACTURING** is the design of machines to do multiple tasks so that they can produce a variety of products.

E. LEAN MANUFACTURING
1. **LEAN MANUFACTURING** is the production of goods using less of everything compared to mass production: less human effort, less manufacturing space, less investment in tools, and less engineering time to develop a new product in half the time.
2. A company can become lean by continuously increasing the capacity to produce, with higher quality results using fewer resources.
3. GM redesigned its production processes, abandoning the assembly line, to make the Saturn automobile.
   a. The most dramatic change was to switch to modular construction.
   b. GM also expanded the use of robots. A **ROBOT** is a computer-controlled machine capable of performing many tasks requiring the use of materials and tools.
   c. Robots usually are fast, efficient, and accurate, but there is still a need for creative workers.

F. MASS CUSTOMIZATION
1. **MASS CUSTOMIZATION** means tailoring products and services to meet the needs of individual customers.
2. Mass customization is also coming to services.

G. COMPETING IN TIME
1. **COMPETING IN TIME** means getting your product to market before your competitors.

H. COMPUTER-AIDED DESIGN AND MANUFACTURING
1. **COMPUTER-AIDED DESIGN (CAD)** is the integration of computers into the design of products.
2. **COMPUTER-AIDED MANUFACTURING (CAM)** is the integration of computers into the manufacturing of products.
3. CAD/CAM, the combining of computer-aided design with computer-aided manufacturing, which made it possible to custom-design products for small markets.
4. Computer-aided design has doubled the productivity in many firms.
   a. In the past computer-aided design machines couldn't talk to computer-aided manufacturing machines.
   b. Recently software programs have been designed to unite CAD with CAM creating **COMPUTER-INTEGRATED MANUFACTURING (CIM).**

VI. CONTROL PROCEDURES: PERT AND GANTT CHARTS

A. An important function of a production manager is to be sure that products are manufactured and delivered on time, on budget, and to specifications.
   1. **PROGRAM EVALUATION AND REVIEW TECHNIQUE (PERT)** is a method for analyzing the tasks involved in completing a given project, estimating the time needed to complete each task, and identifying the minimum time needed to complete the total project.
   2. The steps involved in using PERT include:
      a. Analyzing tasks that need to be done and sequencing the tasks.
      b. Estimating the time needed to complete each task.
      c. Drawing a PERT network illustrating the information from steps a and b.
      d. Identifying the **CRITICAL PATH**, the sequence of tasks that takes the longest time to complete.
      e. This path is referred to as the critical path, because a delay in the time needed to complete this path would cause the project or production run to be late.

3. A PERT network can be made up of thousands of events over many months, and is usually done by computer.
4. The **GANTT CHART** is a bar graph that clearly shows what projects are being worked on and how much has been completed at any given time.
   a. Using a Gantt-like computer program, a manager can trace the production process minute by minute.

VII. PREPARING FOR THE FUTURE
   A. What's ahead?
      1. The new era in manufacturing and service sectors will require special training to manage the new high-tech workers.
      2. Universities are adding courses in manufacturing management and robotics to help prepare students.
      3. There will be more emphasis on participative management and the design of attractive work environments.

LEARNING THE LANGUAGE OF BUSINESS

Match each of the following key terms with the appropriate definition.

A. assembly process
B. competing in time
C. computer-aided design (CAD)
D. computer-aided manufacturing (CAM)
E. computer-integrated manufacturing (CIM)
F. continuous process
G. critical path
H. enterprise resource planning (ERP)
I. facility location
J. facility layout
K. flexible manufacturing
L. form utility
M. Gantt chart
N. Intermittent process
O. ISO 9000
P. ISO 14000
Q. Just-in-time (JIT) inventory control
R. lean manufacturing
S. mass customization
T. mass production
U. materials requirement planning (MRP)
V. operations management
W. process planning
X. process manufacturing
Y. production
Z. program evaluation and review technique (PERT)
AA. purchasing
BB. quality control
CC. robot

_____ 1. The creation of finished goods and services using the factors of production: land, labor, capital, entrepreneurship, and information.

_____ 2. A collection of the best practices for managing an organizations impact on the environment.

_____ 3. The process of selecting a geographic location for a company's operations.

_____ 4. Production processes which physically or chemically changes materials.

_____ 5. The value added by the creation of finished goods and services using raw materials, components, and other inputs.

_____ 6. The sequence of tasks that takes the longest time to complete.

_____ 7. The production of goods using less of everything compared to mass production: half the human effort, half the manufacturing space, half the investment in tools, and half the engineering time to develop a new product in half the time.

_____ 8. Bar graph showing production managers what projects are being worked on and what stage they are in on a continuous basis.

____ 9. A method of analyzing the tasks involved in completing a given project, estimating the time needed to complete each task, and identifying the minimum time needed to complete the total project.

____ 10. Production process that puts together components.

____ 11. The use of computers in the design of products.

____ 12. The use of computers in the manufacturing of products.

____ 13. Designing machines to do multiple tasks so they can produce a variety of products.

____ 14. The uniting of computer-aided design with computer-aided manufacturing.

____ 15. Tailoring products to meet the needs of individual customers.

____ 16. Computer-based production and operations system that links multiple firms into one, integrated production unit.

____ 17. A computer-controlled machine capable of performing many tasks.

____ 18. The measurement of products and services against set standards.

____ 19. The function in the firm that searches for quality material resources, finds the best suppliers, and negotiates the best price for goods and services.

____ 20. A production process in which long production runs turn out finished goods over time.

____ 21. A specialized area in management that converts or transforms resources into goods and services.

____ 22. A computer-based production management system that uses sales forecasts to make sure that the needed parts and materials are available at the right time and place.

____ 23. The common name given to quality management and assurance standards.

____ 24. Be as fast or faster than competition in responding to customer wants and needs and getting quality goods and services to them.

____ 25. Choosing the best means for turning resources into useful goods and services.

____ 26. A production process in which the production run is short and the machines are changed frequently to make different products.

____ 27. The physical arrangement of resources in the production process.

____ 28. A production process in which a minimum of inventory is kept on the premises and parts, suppliers, and other needs are delivered just-in-time to go on the assembly lines.

____ 29. The process of making a large number of a limited variety of products at a very low cost.

Lesson 18   Page 199

SELF-TEST

1. Sit Rite Furniture Company uses labor and machinery to transform wood, plastic, metal and cloth into comfortable chairs, sofas, and love seats. This process creates:
   A) form utility.
   B) place utility.
   C) use facility.
   D) intangible productivity.

2. A firm that has been classified as meeting both ISO 9000 and ISO 14000 standards has demonstrated:
   A) world-class management of both quality and environmental standards.
   B) sound financial and manufacturing practices.
   C) ethical treatment of both customers and employees.
   D) that its recruitment and training programs for employees protect and promote basic human rights.

3. Wild Bill's Cap Emporium says no order is too big or too small! The company offers to produce hats and caps according to customers' requests. Wild Bill's must be using a(n):
   A) analytic system.
   B) just-in-time system.
   C) intermittent process.
   D) continuous process.

4. Cooltreet, Inc., combines sugar, cream, eggs, and flavorings, then churns and cools the resulting mixture to a very low temperature until it freezes, creating ice cream. The method Cooltreet is using is an example of:
   A) an analytic production system.
   B) process manufacturing.
   C) an assembly process.
   D) a symbiotic process.

5. A just-in-time inventory system usually reduces costs for:
   A) both the producer and its suppliers.
   B) suppliers, but not the producer.
   C) the producer, but not its suppliers.
   D) neither the supplier nor the producer.

6. Edwin Rivera is a production manager who believes his firm uses more of virtually all types of resources than is necessary to produce its products. He would like to find a way to cut back on labor, and reduce the firm's investment in tools and space as well. It seems that Edwin would like to adopt:
   A) mass production.
   B) marginal cost management.
   C) lean manufacturing.
   D) the maximum production method.

7. HandZone, a manufacturer of high quality gloves and a variety of fashion accessories, already has both computer-aided design and computer-aided manufacturing. Unfortunately, the two systems cannot communicate with each other. David Fosnough, a production manager at HandZone, has heard about some software that allows CAD and CAM to work together, and wants to learn more about it. David is interested in:
   A) linear programming software.
   B) holistic internalization of operations.
   C) computer integrated manufacturing.
   D) complex systems integration.

8. Both PERT diagrams and Gantt charts are useful to managers concerned with:
   A) calculating the rate of profit earned in a particular market.
   B) making sure that projects are completed on time.
   C) estimating the cost of completing a project.
   D) establishing formal lines of authority and responsibility within an organization.

9. A PERT network consists of activities linked by arrows. Suppose two of the activities on the network are labeled "A" and "B". An arrow from "A" to "B" indicates that:
   A) the same resources used to complete "A" can also be used to complete "B".
   B) "A" and "B" can be completed at the same time.
   C) "A" takes longer to complete than "B".
   D) "A" must be completed before "B" can begin.

10. Recent trends in the service sector suggest that:
    A) the Internet is unlikely to become a major force in retailing because most customers are unwilling to buy and sell goods electronically.
    B) services can only improve productivity by reducing the quality of the service they provide.
    C) technological change is less likely to boost productivity in services than in manufacturing.
    D) services are using computer networks to become increasingly interactive.

ANSWER KEY

LEARNING THE LANGUAGE OF BUSINESS

1. Y
2. P
3. I
4. X
5. L
6. G
7. R
8. M
9. Z
10. A
11. C
12. D
13. K
14. E
15. S
16. H
17. CC
18. BB
19. AA
20. F
21. V
22. U
23. O
24. B
25. W
26. N
27. J
28. Q
29. T

SELF-TEST

	Answer	Page #
1.	A	Page: 275
2.	A	Page: 272
3.	C	Page: 276
4.	B	Page: 275
5.	C	Page: 279
6.	C	Page: 280-281
7.	C	Page: 282
8.	B	Page: 282-283
9.	D	Page: 282-283
10.	D	Page: 274-275

LESSON 19

PRICING PRODUCTS

ASSIGNMENTS

1. Review the Learning Goals and read the Lesson Overview for this lesson.

2. Read Chapter 14 pp. 445-454 in Understanding Business, 6th edition by Nickels, McHugh, and McHugh.

3. Watch the video Pricing Products.

4. Review the textbook material.

5. Match the key terms with the correct definitions in the Learning the Language of Business exercise.

6. Take the Self-Test.

7. Use the Answer Key to check your answers and review when necessary.

LEARNING GOALS

After you watch the video, read the textbook, and study this lesson, you should be able to:

1. Give examples of various pricing objectives and strategies.

2. Explain why nonpricing strategies are growing in importance.

LESSON NOTES

I. COMPETITIVE PRICING

   A. Price is a critical ingredient when consumers evaluate products.

   B. PRICING OBJECTIVES
1. When setting a pricing strategy, the firm may have several objectives in mind.
2. A firm must formulate price objectives clearly before developing an overall pricing objective.
3. Popular pricing strategies include:
   a. Achieving a target return on investment or profit.
   b. Building traffic.
   c. Achieving greater market share.
   d. Increasing sales.
   e. Creating an image.
   f. Furthering social objectives.
4. A company's short-term pricing objectives may differ from its long-term objectives.
5. Pricing objectives are influenced by other marketing decisions regarding product design, packaging, branding, distribution, and promotion.

   C. COST-BASED PRICING
1. Producers often use cost as a primary basis for setting price.
2. In the long run, the market not the producer determines what the price will be.
3. **TARGET COSTING** is designing a product so that it satisfies customers and meets the profit margin desired by the firm.

   D. VALUE PRICING
1. **VALUE PRICING** means that marketers are providing consumers with brand name goods and services at fair prices.
2. The way to offer value prices and not go broke is to redesign products from the bottom up and to cut costs wherever possible.
3. Small businesses can often capture a healthy share of the market by offering a great price at the inception.

   E. VALUE PRICING IN THE SERVICE SECTOR
1. Service industries are adopting many of the same pricing tactics as goods-producing firms.
   a. Service firms begin by cutting costs as much as possible.
   b. Those services that aren't important to customers are cut.
2. With both goods and services, the idea is to give the consumer value.

   F. BREAK-EVEN ANALYSIS
1. **BREAK-EVEN ANALYSIS** is the process used to determine profitability at various levels of sales.
2. The break-even point (BEP) is the point where revenues from sales equal all costs.
3. BEP is calculated: $$\frac{\text{total fixed cost (FC)}}{\text{price of one unit minus variable cost (VC) of one unit}}$$
4. **TOTAL FIXED COSTS** are costs that remain the same no matter how many products are sold.
5. **VARIABLE COSTS** are costs that change according to the level of production.

G. PRICING STRATEGIES
1. A **SKIMMING PRICE STRATEGY** is one in which the product is priced high to make optimum profit while there is little competition.
2. A **PENETRATION STRATEGY** is one in which a product is priced low to attract more customers and discourage competitors.
3. Retailers use several different pricing strategies.
   a. **EVERYDAY LOW PRICING (EDLP)** sets prices below the competitors' and doesn't use special sales.
   b. **HIGH-LOW PRICING STRATEGY** sets prices that are higher the EDLP stores, but then uses special sales to lower prices below the competition.

H. HOW MARKET FORCES AFFECT PRICING
1. Ultimately, price is determined by supply and demand in the marketplace.
   a. Different consumers may be willing to pay different prices.
   b. Marketers sometimes price on the basis of consumer demand, called demand-oriented pricing, rather than cost or other calculations.
2. **PRICE LEADERSHIP** is the procedure by which all the competitors in an industry follow the pricing practices of one or more dominant firms.
3. Competition-oriented pricing is a strategy based on what all the other competitors are doing.
4. Marketers now face a new pricing problem: customers can compare prices of many goods and services on the Internet.

II. NONPRICE COMPETITION

A. Marketers often compete on product attributes other than price.
   1. Many smaller organizations promote the services that accompany basic products rather than price in order to compete with bigger firms.

B. NONPRICE STRATEGIES
   1. Marketers emphasize nonprice differences because prices are so easy to match.
   2. Other strategies for avoiding price wars include:
      a. Add value.
      b. Educate consumers.
      c. Establish relationships.

LEARNING THE LANGUAGE OF BUSINESS

Match each of the following key terms with the appropriate definition.

A. break-even analysis
B. every day low pricing (EDLP)
C. high-low pricing strategy
D. penetration strategy
E. price leadership
F. skimming price strategy
G. target costing
H. total fixed costs
I. value pricing
J. variable costs

____ 1. When marketers provide consumers with brand name goods and services at fair prices.

____ 2. Method of pricing by which a product is priced low to attract more customers and discourage competitors.

____ 3. Method of pricing by which the product is priced high to make optimum profit while there is little competition.

____ 4. The process used to determine profitability at various levels of sales.

____ 5. The procedure by which all competitors in an industry follow the pricing practices of one or more dominant firms.

____ 6. All the expenses that remain the same no matter how many products are sold.

____ 7. Costs that change according to the level of production.

____ 8. Setting prices that are higher than EDLP stores, but having special sales to sell below the EDLP stores.

____ 9. Designing a product so that it satisfies customers and meets the profit margins described by the firm.

____ 10. Setting prices lower than competitors' and not using special sales.

SELF TEST

1. Value pricing involves marketers providing:
   A) consumers with brand name goods and services at fair prices.
   B) consumers with an item price a few cents under a whole, round price to make the product appear less expensive.
   C) a high profit margin is exchanged for additional services.
   D) consumers with generic goods at reasonable prices.

2. The strategy of setting prices at uneven amounts that are slightly below an even or whole number of dollars is called:
   A) penetration pricing.
   B) adaptive pricing.
   C) odd pricing.
   D) target pricing.

3. A pricing strategy of charging a low price in order to attract a great number of customers and discourage competitors is referred to as a:
   A) penetration strategy.
   B) odd pricing strategy.
   C) skimming strategy.
   D) price lining strategy.

4. A pricing strategy that sets prices based on what all the rival firms are doing is called:
   A) competition-oriented pricing.
   B) wholesale-demand pricing.
   C) odd-line pricing.
   D) centralized pricing.

5. Phil asks you to calculate the breakeven point for his firm. You respond that you will need the following information:
   A) the values for all assets and liabilities.
   B) total fixed costs, selling price, and variable costs per unit.
   C) net income, operating expenses, and asset values.
   D) the current market values for all assets and owners' equity.

6. In determining prices, it is important to remember that:
   A) price must always be linked to cost of production.
   B) instincts and past history are the best guides in determining price.
   C) regardless of the strategy used by a firm, ultimately the price of a good reflects its supply and demand.
   D) firms seldom have much freedom in setting prices because they must follow government guidelines.

7. The strategy of first determining what the market is willing to pay, then subtracting a desired profit margin to determine a desired cost of production is called:
   A) cost-based pricing.
   B) target costing.
   C) penetration pricing.
   D) skimming pricing.

8. Costs that are incurred no matter how many units of a product are produced or sold are called:
   A) overhead costs.
   B) markup costs.
   C) fixed costs.
   D) variable costs.

9. What does a breakeven quantity of 100 units mean?
   A) The firm must sell 100 units to maximize its profits.
   B) Fixed costs plus variable costs equals 100 units.
   C) By producing 100 units, the firm can ensure that variable costs completely cancel our fixed costs..
   D) If the firm sells 100 units, its revenues will equal total costs.

10. Many products are promoted by emphasizing the benefits of using the product, rather than keeping the price lower than that of the competitive goods. This emphasis on product images and benefits illustrates:
    A) a penetration strategy.
    B) nonprice competition.
    C) the follow-the-leader strategy.
    D) the price-led strategy.

ANSWER KEY

LEARNING THE LANGUAGE OF BUSINESS

1. I
2. D
3. F
4. A
5. E
6. H
7. J
8. C
9. G
10. B

SELF-TEST

	Answer	Page #
1.	A	Page: 446
2.	C	Page: 449
3.	A	Page: 448
4.	A	Page: 450
5.	B	Page: 447
6.	C	Page: 450
7.	B	Page: 446
8.	C	Page: 447
9.	D	Page: 447-448
10.	B	Page: 450-451

LESSON 20

PROMOTING PRODUCTS

ASSIGNMENTS

1. Review the Learning Goals and read the Lesson Overview for this lesson.

2. Read Chapter 16 pp. 488-513 in Understanding Business, 6th edition by Nickels, McHugh, and McHugh.

3. Watch the video Promoting Products.

4. Review the textbook material.

5. Match the key terms with the correct definitions in the Learning the Language of Business exercise.

6. Take the Self-Test.

7. Use the Answer Key to check your answers and review when necessary.

LEARNING GOALS

After you watch the video, read the textbook, and study this lesson, you should be able to:

1. Define promotion and list the four traditional tools that make up the promotion mix.

2. Define advertising and describe the advantages and disadvantages of various advertising media, including the Internet.

3. Illustrate the seven steps of the selling process and discuss the role of a consultative salesperson.

4. Describe the role of the public relations department and how publicity fits in that role.

5. Explain the importance of sales promotion and word of mouth as promotional tools.

6. Describe integrated marketing communication and the role of interactive communications within it.

LESSON NOTES

The PROFILE in this chapter focuses on Tina Damron of Coordinated Resources Inc. Tina sells office furniture. In the past she used her personality to personally sell products. Today she uses her laptop to show three-dimensional images of furniture and cubicles. Tina uses a Website called UpShot.com which tracks customers and provides leads and information on prospects. Her customers place orders online, which has cut delivery time from five weeks down to five days. As a single mother she enjoys the flexibility that being able to use the Internet and working from home allows her. The role of a salesperson is changing; it is evolving from a personal seller to becoming more of a consultant and problem solver. Changes in technology have had a dramatic effect on all the areas of promotion, not just selling.

I. CONSTANT CHANGE AND THE PROMOTION MIX

  A. The promotional mix
   1. **PROMOTION** is an attempt by marketers to persuade others to participate in an exchange with them.
   2. Marketers use such promotional tools as advertising, personal selling, word-of-mouth, public relations, and sales promotion.
   3. The **PROMOTION MIX** is the combination of promotional tools marketers use to promote their products or services.
   4. **INTEGRATED MARKETING COMMUNICATION (IMC)** is a technique that combines all the promotional tools into one comprehensive and unified promotional strategy.

  B. HOW CONSTANT CHANGE IS AFFECTING PROMOTION
   1. Promotion has been affected by rapid change in the business environment.
   2. The Internet is changing the whole approach to working with customers.
      a. Now working with, instead of promoting to.
      b. Relationship building requires that customers be listened to.
   3. **INTERACTIVE PROMOTION** changes the promotion process from a monologue to a dialogue.

II. ADVERTISING: PERSUASIVE COMMUNICATION

  A. **ADVERTISING** is paid nonpersonal communication through various media by organizations and individuals that are in some way identified in the advertising message.

  B. Importance of advertising
   1. The total ad volume exceeds $215 billion yearly.
      a. The number one advertising medium in terms of total dollars spent is TV with 23% of total expenditures.
      b. Previously the number one media, newspapers are now number two, with 21% of the total.
      c. Internet advertising has been growing at about 85% per year, but still only accounts for 2% of total expenditures.
   2. The public benefits from advertising in the following ways:
      a. Advertising is informative.
      b. Advertising provides us with free TV and radio programs, because advertisers cover most of the production costs.
   3. TV has many advantages to national advertisers, but it is expensive.
      a. However, there are few ways to reach as many people with such impact.

b. Marketers must choose which media can best be used to reach the audience they desire.

C. THE GROWING USE OF INFOMERCIALS
1. **INFOMERCIALS** are TV programs devoted exclusively to promoting goods and services.
2. They are so successful because they show the product in great detail.
3. Some products, such as workout tapes, are hard to sell without showing people testimonials.

D. ADVERTISING AND PROMOTION ON THE INTERNET
1. Advertising on the Internet is a relatively new phenomenon.
2. The benefits of the Internet become apparent once a customer visits the Web.
   a. Internet advertising brings customers and companies together.
3. Once potential customers see what information is available, they can go online with sellers to get additional information.
4. New technology will allow customers to examine goods with online video.

E. GLOBAL ADVERTISING
1. Global advertising and marketing refers to developing products and promotional strategies that can be used worldwide.
2. Promotion targeted at specific countries is more successful since each country has its own culture, language, and buying habits.
3. Because of cultural differences, promotional efforts designed specifically for individual countries may work best.
4. Even in the U.S., selected groups are large enough and different enough to call for specially designed promotions.

III. PERSONAL SELLING: PROVIDING PERSONAL ATTENTION

A. **PERSONAL SELLING** is the face-to-face presentation and promotion of products and services plus searching out prospects and providing follow-up service.
1. Effective selling today is more than persuading others to buy; it is helping them to satisfy their wants and needs.
2. Nearly 10% of the total labor force is employed in personal selling.
3. The average cost of a single sales call to a potential B2B buyer is about $400.

B. STEPS IN THE SELLING PROCESS
1. Prospect and qualify
   a. **PROSPECTING** involves researching potential buyers and choosing those most likely to buy.
   b. **PROSPECTS** are people with the means to buy a product, the authority to buy and the willingness to listen to a sales message.
   c. **QUALIFY** means making sure that prospects have the need for a product, the authority to buy, and the willingness to listen to a sales message.
2. Preapproach
   a. Before making a sales call, do further research.
   b. Sales people should learn as much as possible about customers and their wants and needs.
3. Approach
   a. You don't have a second chance to make a first impression.
   b. Try to give an impression of friendly professionalism, to create rapport, and to build credibility, and start a relationship.

4. Make presentation
   a. The idea is to match the benefits of your value package to the client's needs.
5. Answer objections
   a. A salesperson should anticipate potential objections and determine proper responses.
   b. Questions should be viewed as opportunities for creating better relationships.
6. Close sale
   a. You have to ask for the sale to finalize the sales process.
   b. **CLOSING TECHNIQUES** include getting a series of small commitments and then asking for the order and showing the client where to sign.
7. Follow up
   a. Selling is more than simply sales; it is a matter of establishing relationships.
   b. Follow-up includes handling customer complaints, making sure that the customer's questions are answered, and supplying what the customer wants.
8. The selling process varies somewhat among different goods and services, but the general idea is the same.
   a. Companies today provide many high-tech aids to help salespeople.
   b. Salespeople often have laptop computers connected to databases to track orders or get product information.

C. USING TECHNOLOGY TO PRACTICE CONSULTATIVE SELLING
   1. Technology allows us to have information throughout the supply chain.
   2. Many B2B buyers purchase goods over the Internet.
   3. A **CONSULTATIVE SALESPERSON** begins by analyzing customer needs and then comes up with solutions to those needs.
   4. Salespeople in retail stores will also see dramatic changes in the way they do things.
   5. The B2B salesperson will become more like a consultant, but there will always be a need for salespeople who direct people to goods.

IV. PUBLIC RELATIONS: BUILDING RELATIONSHIPS WITH ALL PUBLICS

A. Public relations
   1. **PUBLIC RELATIONS (PR)** is the management function that evaluates public attitudes, identifies the policies and procedures of an individual or an organization with the public interest, and executes a program of action to earn public understanding and acceptance.
   2. A good public relations program has three steps:
      a. Listen to the public.
      b. Develop policies and procedures in the public interest.
      c. Inform people of the fact that you're being responsive to their needs.
   3. The public relations department has responsibility for maintaining close relationships with the media, community leaders, government officials, and other stakeholders.

B. PUBLICITY: THE TALKING ARM OF PR
   1. **PUBLICITY** is any information about an individual, a product, or an organization that is distributed to the public through the media, and that is not paid for, or controlled by, the seller.
   2. Advantages of publicity include:
      a. It's free.
      b. It reaches people who do not read advertising messages.
      c. It can be placed in a prominent place (like the front page of the newspaper).
      d. A story in the newspaper is treated as news, and news is more believable than advertising.
   3. Disadvantages of publicity include:
      a. You have no control over how, when, or if the media will use the story.

  b. Media does not have to publish it.
  c. The story can be altered.
  d. There is such a thing as bad publicity.
  e. Stories are not likely to be repeated; advertising can be repeated as often as needed.
 4. To see that publicity is handled well by the media, establish a friendly relationship with the media and cooperate with them.

V. SALES PROMOTION: GETTING A GOOD DEAL

 A. Sales promotion
  1. **SALES PROMOTION** is the promotional tool that stimulates consumer purchasing and dealer interest by means of short-term activities.
   a. Sales promotion programs are designed to supplement personal selling, advertising, and public relations by creating enthusiasm.
  2. Internal sales promotion (within company):
   a. Sales training.
   b. Sales aids such as flip charts, portable audiovisual displays, and movies.
   c. Trade shows.
  3. External sales promotion (outside company, including distributors and dealers):
   a. It is important to get distributors and dealers involved so they too are enthusiastic.
   b. Techniques include samples, displays, contests, etc.
   c. Trade shows are important because buyers are able to see products from many different sellers.
   d. Virtual trade shows, trade shows on the Internet, enable buyers to see many products without leaving the office.
  4. The next step is to promote to final customers.
   a. Sales promotion is an ongoing effort to maintain enthusiasm.
 B. SAMPLING IS A POWERFUL SALES PROMOTION TOOL
  1. **SAMPLING**, letting consumers have a small sample of the product free, is a quick, effective way of demonstrating a product's superiority at the time consumers are making a purchase decision.

 C. WORD OF MOUTH
  1. **WORD-OF-MOUTH PROMOTION** is one of the most effective promotional tools.
   a. It encourages people to tell other people about products they have enjoyed.
  2. Anything that encourages people to talk favorably about an organization is effective word of mouth.
   a. Clever commercials and samples can generate word of mouth.

 D. VIRAL MARKETING AND OTHER WORD-OF-MOUTH STRATEGIES
  1. **VIRAL MARKETING** is a term used to describe everything from paying people to say positive things on the Internet to setting-up multilevel sales schemes whereby customers get commissions for directing friends to specific websites.
   a. An effective strategy for spreading word of mouth is to send testimonials to current customers.
   b. These are effective in confirming customers' belief that they chose the right company.
   c. However, negative word of mouth can be very destructive to a firm.
   d. Upset customers are now getting on the Internet and publishing their complaints.

E. OTHER WAYS THAT NEW TECHNOLOGIES ARE AFFECTING PROMOTION
1. When people purchase goods over the Internet firms gather information on the purchaser.
2. They are then able to design things to meet the specific needs of those customers.
3. Customers can have a continuous connection to the Internet.
   a. Video files can be sent to customers.

VI. MANAGING THE PROMOTION MIX: PUTTING IT ALL TOGETHER
A. Each target group calls for a separate promotion mix.
1. Large, homogenous groups of consumers are most efficiently reached through advertising.
2. Large organizations are best reached through personal selling.
3. Sales promotion motivates people to buy now rather than later.
4. Publicity adds support to the other efforts and can create a good impression.
5. Word-of-mouth is often the most powerful promotional tool.

B. PROMOTION STRATEGIES
1. **PUSH STRATEGY** involves the producer using promotional tools to convince wholesalers and retailers to stock and sell merchandise.
2. **PULL STRATEGY** involves heavy advertising and sales promotion efforts directed toward consumers so they will request the products from retailers.
3. A third strategy is to make promotion part of supply chain management.
   a. The idea would be to develop a value package to appeal to everyone: manufacturers, distributors, retailers, and consumers.

C. CREATING AN INTEGRATED MARKETING COMMUNICATION (IMC) SYSTEM
1. An integrated marketing communication system (IMC) is a formal mechanism for uniting all the promotional efforts in an organization to make it more responsive to its customers and other stakeholders.
   a. In the past, advertising was created by ad agencies, public relations by PR firms, and so forth, with little coordination.
   b. To implement an IMC system, you start with customers and stakeholders and their information needs.
   c. All messages must be consistent and coordinated.

D. BUILDING INTERACTIVE MARKETING PROGRAMS
1. An **INTERACTIVE MARKETING PROGRAM** is a system where consumers can access company information on their own and supply information about themselves in an ongoing dialogue. The basic steps in implementing such programs are:
   a. Gather data about the target groups in a database.
      1) An information database is critical to any successful program.
      2) A company can gather such data from sales transactions, letters, e-mail, and companies that specialize in gathering such data.
   a. Respond quickly to customer and other stakeholder information by adjusting company policies and by designing wanted products.
      1) A responsive firm adapts to changing wants and needs quickly.
   b. Make it possible for customers to access information that they need to make a purchase.

LEARNING THE LANGUAGE OF BUSINESS

Match each of the following key terms with the appropriate definition.

A. advertising
B. closing techniques
C. consultative salesperson
D. infomercials
E. integrated marketing communication (IMC) system
F. interactive marketing program
G. interactive promotion
H. personal selling
I. promotion
J. promotion mix
K. prospects
L. prospecting
M. public relations (PR)
N. publicity
O. pull strategy
P. push strategy
Q. qualify
R. sales promotion
S. sampling
T. viral marketing
U. word-of-mouth promotion

_____ 1. The promotional tool that stimulates consumer purchasing and dealer interest by means of short-term activities (displays, shows and exhibitions, contests, etc.).

_____ 2. The combination of tools marketers use to promote their products or services.

_____ 3. Any information about an individual, a product, or an organization that is distributed to the public through the media, that is not paid for, or controlled by, the sponsor.

_____ 4. The management function that evaluates public attitudes, develops policies and procedures consistent with the public interest, and takes steps to earn public understanding and acceptance.

_____ 5. The face-to-face presentation and promotion of products and services.

_____ 6. Researching potential buyers and choosing those most likely to buy.

_____ 7. Consumers talking about products they have liked or disliked.

_____ 8. TV programs that are devoted exclusively to promoting goods and services.

_____ 9. A formal mechanism for uniting all the promotional efforts in an organization to make it more responsive to its customers and other stakeholders.

_____ 10. Use of promotional tools to motivate consumers to request products from stores.

_____ 11. Use of promotional tools to convince wholesalers and retailers to stock and sell merchandise.

Lesson 20 Page 216

_____ 12. A system in which customers can access company information on their own and supply information about themselves in an organized dialogue.

_____ 13. Ways to conclude a sale by getting commitments, asking for the order and obtaining a signature.

_____ 14. An attempt by marketers to inform people about products to persuade them to participate in an exchange.

_____ 15. Paid, nonpersonal communication through various media by organizations and individuals that are in some way identified in the advertising message.

_____ 16. In the selling process, to make sure the person has a need, and the authority to buy, and a willingness to listen to a sales message.

_____ 17. Changing the promotion process from a monologue to a dialogue in which a mutually beneficial relationship occurs between buyer and seller.

_____ 18. A promotional tool in which a company lets customers have a small portion of a product for no charge.

_____ 19. People with the means to buy a product, the authority to buy, and the willingness to listen to a sales message.

_____ 20. The term used to describe everything from paying people to say positive things on the Internet to setting-up multilevel selling schemes whereby consumers get commissions for directing friends to specific websites.

_____ 21. A salesperson that begins by analyzing customer needs and then comes up with solutions to those needs.

SELF-TEST

1. Nightbrite Services has found the best way of promoting its company is to use heavy advertising and personal selling, with small doses of sales promotions. These components make up Nightbrite's:
   A) marketing mix.
   B) promotional mix.
   C) communication network.
   D) transfer marketing.

2. A(n) _____ begins by analyzing customer needs and then comes up with solutions to meet those needs.
   A) integrated marketer.
   B) full service intermediary
   C) consultative salesperson
   D) public relations specialist

3. A careful look at the personal selling process clearly indicates that selling is:
   A) a mater of establishing relationships.
   B) getting a name on a contract.
   C) about 90% luck and 10% skill.
   D) giving way to computers in responding to customer needs.

4. Lenny has just finished writing a news release about a new product that his firm has developed. He intends to send it to all of the local radio stations as well as the newspapers in several nearby towns and cities, in hopes that some of them will find the information newsworthy and run a story about the product. Lenny's efforts indicate that he is involved in:
   A) public relations.
   B) institutional advertising.
   C) secondary advertising.
   D) interactive advertising.

5. Chip Off The Old Block is a new chocolate chip cookie created by the Arizona Cookie Company. To generate interest for this new product, the company sent a free package of six cookies to selected homes along with a 50-cent coupon. Arizona Cookie is making use of:
   A) trade advertising.
   B) retail publicity.
   C) sales promotions.
   D) public relations.

6. The best advertising medium for reaching a specific target market is:
   A) radio.
   B) newspapers.
   C) television.
   D) direct mail.

7. The evidence supports the theory that promotional efforts specifically designed for individual countries are:
   A) usually less successful than a global promotional strategy.
   B) usually more successful than a global promotional strategy.
   C) generally less expensive than a global promotional strategy.
   D) likely to succeed only if the product is also produced in each individual country.

8. CarGo uses its Web page to reach car parts stores and car owners and tell them of the benefits of using their long lasting sparkplugs. CarGo seems to use the Internet:
   A) for its push strategy.
   B) for its pull strategy.
   C) for both its push and pull strategies.
   D) for its stretch strategy.

9. _____ is the term now used to describe such tactics as paying people to say good things about a product on the Internet or setting up multilevel selling schemes that reward people for directing their friends to a company's Website.
   A) Virtual inducement
   B) Inter-tie-ins
   C) Viral marketing
   D) Pseudo-marketing

10. The Missouri Department of Travel and Tourism promotes tourism in the state by sending travel agents and bus companies information regarding the many attractions that the state has to offer. The hope is that by stimulating interest in tour and travel agents, they will encourage their customers to include Missouri in their travel plans. This is an example of a _____ promotional strategy.
    A) push
    B) pull
    C) systems
    D) regional

ANSWER KEY

LEARNING THE LANGUAGE OF BUSINESS

1. R
2. J
3. N
4. M
5. H
6. L
7. U
8. D
9. E
10. O
11. P
12. F
13. B
14. I
15. A
16. Q
17. G
18. S
19. K
20. T
21. C

SELF-TEST

Answer	Page #
1. B	Page: 490
2. C	Page: 501
3. A	Page: 498-500
4. A	Page: 502
5. C	Page: 505-506
6. D	Page: 493
7. B	Page: 496-497
8. C	Page: 509-510
9. C	Page: 507
10. A	Page: 509

LESSON 21

DISTRIBUTING PRODUCTS

ASSIGNMENTS

1. Review the Learning Goals and read the Lesson Overview for this lesson.

2. Read Chapter 15 pp. 458-484 in Understanding Business, 6th edition by Nickels, McHugh, and McHugh.

3. Watch the video Distributing Products.

4. Review the textbook material.

5. Match the key terms with the correct definitions in the Learning the Language of Business exercise.

6. Take the Self-Test.

7. Use the Answer Key to check your answers and review when necessary.

LEARNING GOALS

After you watch the video, read the textbook, and study this lesson, you should be able to:

1. Explain the concept of marketing channels and the value of marketing intermediaries.

2. Give examples of how intermediaries perform the six utilities.

3. Describe the various wholesale organizations in the distribution system.

4. Explain the ways in which retailers compete and the distribution strategies they use.

5. Explain the various kind of nonstore retailing.

6. Discuss how a manufacturer can get wholesalers and retailers in a channel system to cooperate by the formation of systems.

7. Describe some supply chain management problems and how they are solved.

8. Review the various distribution modes and their benefits and how they tie in with the materials handling and storage.

LESSON NOTES

The PROFILE at the beginning of this chapter focuses on Randall Larrimore of United Stationers. When he took over the firm in 1994 they weren't doing well due to the misfortune of thousands of small stationary stores who were unable to compete with the superstores and went out of business. Larrimore decided to use the latest supply chain concepts to improve his firm's position. The system for distributing goods has changed over the last decade or so. The advent of online retailers has altered the way customers buy and the way manufacturers sell. The Internet has changed the way goods are distributed. Larrimore was able to use the changes to benefit United Stationers and their customers.

I. THE IMPORTANCE OF CHANNELS OF DISTRIBUTION

   A. Distribution
      1. **MARKETING INTERMEDIARIES** are organizations that assist in moving goods and services from producer to industrial and consumer users.
         a. They are organizations in the middle of a series of organizations that join together to help distribute goods.
         b. A **CHANNEL OF DISTRIBUTION** consists of marketing intermediaries who join together to transport and store goods in their path.
         c. A **WHOLESALER** is a marketing intermediary that sells to other organizations.
         d. A **RETAILER** is an organization that sells to ultimate consumers.
      2. Channels of distribution enhance communication flows and the flow of money and title to goods.

   B. WHY MARKETING NEED INTERMEDIARIES
      1. Manufacturers don't always need marketing intermediaries to sell their goods to consumer and B2B markets.
      2. In the past, intermediaries performed certain functions better than most manufacturers. These functions include transportation, storage, selling, and advertising.
      3. **BROKERS** are marketing intermediaries who bring buyers and sellers together and assist in negotiating an exchange, but do not take title to the goods.

   C. HOW INTERMEDIARIES CREATE EXCHANGE EFFICIENCY
      1. Intermediaries create exchange efficiency by decreasing the number of contacts needed to establish marketing exchanges.
      2. Not only are intermediaries more efficient, but they are more effective than manufacturers as well.
      3. Intermediaries were often better at performing their functions than a manufacturer could be.
      4. Recently, technology has made it possible for manufacturers to reach consumers much more efficiently.
         a. Some manufacturers reach consumers directly on the Internet.
         b. Retailers are now so closely linked with manufacturers that they can get delivery several times a day.
      5. Wholesalers are not yet obsolete, but must change their functions to remain viable.

   D. THE VALUE VERSUS THE COST OF INTERMEDIARIES
      1. Some people think that if we could get rid of intermediaries, we could greatly reduce the cost of the things we buy.
      2. The text uses the example of Fiberiffic to illustrate how marketing intermediaries facilitate the movement of goods.

3. Values discussed include: the value of not driving to Michigan to buy a box of cereal, the value of saving time and effort by not having to drive to a wholesaler's on the outskirts of town.
4. The text emphasizes three basic facts about intermediaries:
   a. Intermediaries can be eliminated, but their activities cannot be eliminated.
      1) Today many activities are being performed on the Internet, and intermediaries are being eliminated.
      2) The term for eliminating intermediaries is disintermediation.
   b. Intermediaries have survived in the past because they perform functions more effectively and efficiently than most manufacturers.
   c. Intermediaries add costs to products, but these costs are offset by values they create.

II. THE UTILITIES CREATED BY INTERMEDIARIES

   A. **UTILITY** is an economic term for the value, or want-satisfying ability, that is added to goods or services by organizations because the products are made more useful or accessible to consumers.

   B. FORM UTILITY
      1. **FORM UTILITY** consists of taking raw materials and changing their form so that they become useful products.
      2. Producers create it; marketers perform the five other forms of utility (time, place, possession, information, and service).

   C. TIME UTILITY
      1. Intermediaries, such as retailers, add **TIME UTILITY** to products by making them available when they are needed.

   D. PLACE UTILITY
      1. Intermediaries add **PLACE UTILITY** to products by having them where people want them.

   E. POSSESSION UTILITY
      1. Intermediaries add **POSSESSION UTILITY** by doing whatever is necessary to transfer ownership from one party to another, including providing credit.
      2. Activities include delivery, installation, guarantees, and follow-up service.
      3. For those who don't want to own goods, possession utility makes it possible for them to use goods through renting.

   F. INFORMATION UTILITY
      1. Intermediaries add **INFORMATION UTILITY** by opening two-way flows of information between marketing participants.

   G. SERVICE UTILITY
      1. Intermediaries add **SERVICE UTILITY** by providing fast, friendly service during and after the sale and teaching customers how to best use products.
      2. Service utility is fast becoming the most important utility for retailers.

   H. For consumers to receive the maximum benefit from marketing intermediaries, the organizations must work together.

III. WHOLESALE INTERMEDIARIES

A. Differences between wholesalers and retailers.
   1. Some producers won't sell directly to retailers but only to wholesalers.
   2. Some organizations sell much of their merchandise to other intermediaries, but also sell to ultimate consumers.
   3. A **RETAIL SALE** is the sale of goods and services to consumers for their own use.
   4. A **WHOLESALE SALE** is the sale of goods and services to businesses and institutions for use in the business or to be resold to others.

B. MERCHANT WHOLESALERS
   1. **MERCHANT WHOLESALERS** are independently owned firms that take title to goods that they handle.
   2. Full-service wholesalers perform all eight distribution functions: transportation, storage, risk bearing, credit, market information, grading, buying, and selling.
   3. Limited-function wholesalers perform only selected functions, but do them especially well.
   4. **RACK JOBBERS** furnish racks or shelves full of merchandise to retailers, display products, and sell on consignment.
   5. **CASH-AND-CARRY WHOLESALERS** serve mostly smaller retailers with a limited assortment of products.
      a. Cash-and-carry wholesalers also sell to the general public in warehouse clubs.
      b. One function of these clubs is to provide small businesses with merchandise and supplies at low prices.
   6. **DROP SHIPPERS** solicit orders from retailers and other wholesalers and have the merchandise shipped directly from a producer to a buyer.
   7. A **FREIGHT FORWARDER** puts many small shipments together to create a single, large shipment that can be transported more cost-efficiently to the final destination.

C. BUSINESS-TO-BUSINESS (B2B) WHOLESALING
   1. AOL, eBay and Yahoo are building business online.
   2. The B2B market is bigger than the consumer market.

IV. RETAIL INTERMEDIARIES

A. A retailer is a marketing middleman that sells to consumers.
   1. The U.S. has about 2.3 million retail stores.
   2. About 11 million people work for retail organizations.

B. HOW RETAILERS COMPETE
   1. Price competition
      a. Discount stores such as Wal-Mart succeed with low prices.
      b. Service organizations, such as Southwest Airlines, also compete on price.
   2. Service competition
      a. Retail service involves putting the customer first.
      b. Consumers are frequently willing to pay a little more if the retailer offers outstanding service.
      c. The benchmark companies are Dayton's, Lord & Taylor, Dillard's, and Nordstrom.
   3. Location competition, many services compete effectively by having good locations.
   4. Selection competition

- a. Selection is the offering of a wide variety of items in the same product category, such as Toys R Us.
- b. **CATEGORY KILLER STORES** offer wide selection at competitive prices.
- c. Smaller retailers compete with category killers by offering more selection within a smaller category of items.
- d. Service organizations that compete successfully on selection include Blockbuster Video and most community colleges.
  5. Entertainment competition, some stores and malls make shopping fun.

C. RETAIL DISTRIBUTION STRATEGY
1. Different products call for different retail distribution strategies.
2. **INTENSIVE DISTRIBUTION** puts products into as many retail outlets as possible, including vending machines.
3. **SELECTIVE DISTRIBUTION** is the use of only a preferred group of the available retailers in an area.
4. **EXCLUSIVE DISTRIBUTION** is the use of only one retail outlet in a geographic area.

V. NONSTORE RETAILING

A. E-TAILING
1. An **E-TAILER** is a firm that is selling goods or services to the ultimate consumers over the Internet.
2. Getting customers is only half the battle, the other half is delivering the goods, providing helpful service, and keeping your customers.
   a. Some e-tailers fail at the second half.
3. The latest trend is for traditional retailers to go online.
4. Companies who want to compete in the future will have a real store presence and an online presence.

B. TELEMARKETING
1. **TELEMARKETING** is the sale of goods and services by telephone.

C. VENDING MACHINES, KIOSKS, AND CARTS
1. The benefit of vending machines is their convenient location.
2. Carts and kiosks have lower costs than stores, so they can offer lower prices.

D. DIRECT SELLING
1. Direct selling is selling to consumers in their homes or where they work.
2. Because so many women now work, many companies are sponsoring parties at workplaces and on weekends and evenings.

E. MULTILEVEL MARKETING
1. Each MLM salesperson works as an independent contractor.
2. They earn commissions on their own sales and create commissions for the upliners who recruited them.
3. They also receive commissions from downliners who they recruit to sell.
4. Multilevel marketing has been successful around the world.
5. The main attraction of multilevel marketing is the low cost of entry.
6. Be careful not to confuse multilevel marketing with pyramid schemes that are illegal.

F. DIRECT MARKETING
1. One of the fastest-growing aspects of retailing is direct marketing, includes any marketing activity that directly links manufacturers or intermediaries with the ultimate consumer.
2. Direct retail marketing includes direct mail, catalog sales, telemarketing, and on-line shopping.
3. Examples are L.L. Bean, Lands' End, Dell Computers, and Gateway 2000.
4. Direct marketing has become popular because it is more convenient for consumers.
5. Interactive online selling is expected to provide major competition for retail stores in the future.

VI. BUILDING COOPERATION IN CHANNEL SYSTEMS

A. Firms are often linked together in formal relationships to form efficient distribution systems.

B. A **CORPORATE DISTRIBUTION SYSTEM** is one in which all the organizations in the channel are owned by one firm.

C. **CONTRACTUAL DISTRIBUTION SYSTEM** is one in which members are bound to cooperate through contractual agreements.
1. In franchising system (such as McDonald's, KFC, Baskin-Robbins, and AAMCO), the franchisee agrees to all of the rules, regulations, and procedures established by the franchiser.
2. In wholesaler-sponsored chains (Western Auto and IGA food stores), each store agrees to use the name, participate in chain promotions, and cooperate even though each store is independently owned.
3. Retail cooperatives (Associated Grocers) are like wholesaler-sponsored chains except they initiate the relationships.

D. ADMINISTERED DISTRIBUTION SYSTEM
1. The management by producers of all the marketing functions at the retail level is called an **ADMINISTERED DISTRIBUTION SYSTEM**.
2. Retailers cooperate because they get so much free help.

E. SUPPLY CHAINS
1. The **SUPPLY CHAIN** is the sequence of linked activities performed by various organizations to move goods from the sources to ultimate consumers.

VII. SUPPLY-CHAIN MANAGEMENT

A. **SUPPLY CHAIN MANAGEMENT(SCM)** is the process of managing the movement of raw materials, parts, work in progress, finished goods, and related information through all the organizations involved in the supply-chain; managing the return of such goods, if necessary; and recycling materials when appropriate.
1. Outbound logistics have been the biggest problem for new online retailers.

VIII. CHOOSING THE RIGHT DISTRIBUTION MODE AND STORAGE UNITS

A. Modes
1. One concern is selecting a transporting mode that will minimize costs and ensure a certain level of service.

2. The largest percentage of goods is shipped by RAIL.
   a. Railroad shipment is best for bulky items.
   b. Railroads continue to handle about 35 to 40% of the total volume of goods in the U.S.
   c. Piggyback refers to shipping the cargo-carrying part of a truck on a railroad car.
3. The second-largest surface transportation mode is motor vehicles with a little over 25% of the volume.
   a. Trucks can deliver almost any commodity door-to-door.
   b. Now piggybacking methods involve railroad cars 20 feet high called double-stacks.
4. Water transportation carries 15 to 17% of the total.
   a. When truck trailers are placed on ships, the process is called fishyback.
5. About 21% of the total volume moves by pipeline.
   a. Pipelines are used primarily for transporting petroleum and petroleum products.
   b. There have been experiments with sending other solids in pipelines.
6. Only a small part of shipping is done by air.
   a. The primary benefit is speed.
   b. The air freight industry is starting to focus on global distribution.

B. INTERMODAL SHIPPING
   1. **INTERMODAL SHIPPING** uses multiple modes of transportation to complete a single long-distance movement of freight.

C. THE STORAGE FUNCTION
   1. Storage accounts for 25 to 30% of physical distribution costs.
   2. A storage warehouse stores products for a relatively long time.
   3. Distribution warehouses gather and redistribute products (UPS).

D. **MATERIALS HANDLING** is the movement of goods within a warehouse, factory, or store.

E. WHAT ALL THIS MEANS TO YOU
   1. There are many new jobs becoming available in the area of supply-chain management.

LEARNING THE LANGUAGE OF BUSINESS

Match each of the following key terms with the appropriate definition.

A. administered distribution system
B. brokers
C. cash-and-carry wholesaler
D. category killer stores
E. channel of distribution
F. contractual distribution system
G. corporate distribution system
H. drop shippers
I. e-tailers
J. exclusive distribution
K. form utility
L. freight forwarder
M. information utility
N. intensive distribution
O. intermodal shipping
P. marketing intermediaries
Q. materials handling
R. merchant wholesalers
S. place utility
T. possession utility
U. rack jobber
V. retailer
W. retail sale
X. selective distribution
Y. service utility
Z. supply chain
AA. supply chain management (SCM)
BB. telemarketing
CC. time utility
DD. utility
EE. wholesaler
FF. wholesale sale

____ 1. The process of managing the movement of raw materials, parts, work in progress, finished goods, and related information through all the organizations involved in the supply chain; managing the return of such goods, if necessary; and recycling materials when appropriate.

____ 2. Organizations that assist in the movement of goods and services form producer to industrial and consumer users.

____ 3. Adding value to products by making them available when they're needed.

____ 4. Adding value to products by opening two-way flows of information between marketing participants.

____ 5. Distribution system in which all the organizations in the channel are owned by one firm.

____ 6. Distribution system in which members are bound to cooperate through contractual agreements.

Lesson 21   Page 228

____ 7. Distribution system in which all the marketing functions at the retail level are managed by producers.

____ 8. The distribution strategy that puts products into as many retail outlets as possible, including vending machines.

____ 9. Distribution strategy that uses only a preferred group of the available retailers in an area.

____ 10. The distribution strategy that uses only one retail outlet in a given geographic area.

____ 11. Marketing intermediaries such as wholesalers and retailers who join together to transport and store goods in their path (channel) from producers to consumers.

____ 12. A marketing intermediary that sells to consumers.

____ 13. A marketing intermediary that sells to other organizations.

____ 14. A full-service wholesaler that furnishes racks or shelves full of merchandise to retailers, displays products, and sells on consignment.

____ 15. A limited-function wholesaler that serves mostly smaller retailers with a limited assortment of products.

____ 16. Taking raw materials and changing their form so that they become useful products.

____ 17. A limited-function wholesaler that solicits orders from retailers and other wholesalers and has the merchandise shipped directly from a producer to a buyer.

____ 18. Adding value to products by having them where people want them.

____ 19. Selling goods and services to ultimate customers over the Internet.

____ 20. The movement of goods within a warehouse, factory, or store.

____ 21. Providing fast, friendly service during and after the sale and by teaching customers how to best use products over time.

____ 22. Marketing intermediaries who bring buyers and sellers together and assist in negotiating an exchange but don't own the goods.

____ 23. The sale of goods and services by telephone.

____ 24. Large stores that offer wide selection at competitive prices.

____ 25. An organization that puts many small shipments together to create a single large shipment that can be transported cost-efficiently to the final destination.

____ 26. The use of multiple modes of transportation to complete a single long-distance movement of freight.

____ 27. Independently owned firms that take title to own the goods they handle.

____ 28. An economic term that refers to the value or want-satisfying ability that's added to goods or services by organizations when the products are made more useful or accessible to consumers than before.

____ 29. Doing whatever is necessary to transfer ownership from one party to another, including providing credit, delivery, installation, guarantees, and follow-up service.

____ 30. The sale of goods and services to consumers for their own use.

____ 31. The sale of goods and services to businesses and institutions for use in the business or to wholesalers or retailers for resale.

____ 32. The sequence of linked activities that must be performed by various organizations to move goods from the source of raw materials to ultimate consumers.

SELF-TEST

1. The part of the supply chain management that has been the biggest problem for new online retailers has been:
   A) inbound logistics.
   B) materials handling.
   C) factory processes.
   D) outbound logistics.

2. Retailers who have stores at convenient locations are trying to add value by:
   A) using a horizontal distribution strategy.
   B) using a broad resource allocation strategy.
   C) providing place utility.
   D) achieving market concentration.

3. Kumquat Computers is a major computer manufacturer that also owns all of the organizations in the channel of distribution for its computers, including a chain of Kumquat Direct retail stores. Kumquat is using a:
   A) franchise distribution system.
   B) corporate distribution system.
   C) administered distribution system.
   D) retail cooperative system.

4. Compared to railroads and trucks, the biggest advantage offered by air transport is that it is:
   A) faster.
   B) more dependable.
   C) lower in cost.
   D) able to reach more destinations.

5. Kidder Manufacturing wants to ship a large quantity of its goods across the country. They have contacted Wayback Shipping, Inc. to find out what the shipment would cost. Wayback has shown Kidder how it can arrange to use a combination of barges, trains, and trucks to complete the shipment at a low cost. Grunwell's strategy is an example of:
   A) on-line shipping.
   B) intermodal shipping.
   C) supply chain shipping.
   D) multilevel distribution.

6. Which type of wholesale organization would be most useful to a small manufacturer which has shipments that are too small to fill a truck or railcar?
   A) Rack jobbers.
   B) Cash-and-carry wholesalers.
   C) Piggy-backers.
   D) Freight forwarders.

Lesson 21

7. Comstock Coal Distributors does not mine coal itself. In fact, the firm does not even store or handle coal. Instead, Comstock solicits orders for low sulfur coal from other firms, then purchases the required amount from suppliers and directs them to ship the coal to its customers. Comstock is a:
   A) drop shipper.
   B) resource delivery facilitator.
   C) cash-and-carry wholesaler.
   D) limited distribution broker.

8. Category killer stores compete primarily on the basis of:
   A) selection and price.
   B) quality and service.
   C) location and product promotion.
   D) credit and image.

9. Delacroix Shoes produces top-quality high-fashion shoes, designed for the person concerned about style. Delacroix gives only a few preferred retailers in a given market area the right to market its product. Delacroix Shoes uses:
   A) intensive distribution.
   B) selective distribution.
   C) exclusive distribution.
   D) limited function distribution.

10. E-tailing, telemarketing, direct selling, and multilevel marketing are all examples of:
    A) full-service wholesaling.
    B) limited-service wholesaling.
    C) nonstore retailing.
    D) exclusive distribution systems.

ANSWER KEY

LEARNING THE LANGUAGE OF BUSINESS

1. AA
2. P
3. CC
4. M
5. G
6. F
7. A
8. N
9. X
10. J
11. E
12. V
13. EE
14. U
15. C
16. K
17. H
18. S
19. I
20. Q
21. Y
22. B
23. BB
24. D
25. L
26. O
27. R
28. DD
29. T
30. W
31. FF
32. Z

SELF-TEST

Answer	Page #
1. D	Page: 479
2. C	Page: 467
3. B	Page: 477
4. A	Page: 481
5. B	Page: 481
6. D	Page: 470
7. A	Page: 469-470
8. A	Page: 472
9. B	Page: 473
10. C	Page: 473-475

LESSON 22

UNDERSTANDING MONEY

ASSIGNMENTS

1. Review the Learning Goals and read the Lesson Overview for this lesson.

2. Read Chapter 21 pp. 646-670 in Understanding Business, 6th edition by Nickels, McHugh, and McHugh.

3. Watch the video Understanding Money.

4. Review the textbook material.

5. Match the key terms with the correct definitions in the Learning the Language of Business exercise.

6. Take the Self-Test.

7. Use the Answer Key to check your answers and review when necessary.

LEARNING GOALS

After you watch the video, read the textbook, and study this lesson, you should be able to:

1. Explain what money is and how its value is determined.

2. Describe how the Federal Reserve controls the money supply.

3. Trace the history of banking and the Federal Reserve System.

4. Classify the various institutions in the U.S. banking system.

5. Explain the importance of the Federal Deposit Insurance Corporation and other organizations that guarantee funds.

6. Discuss the future of the U.S. banking system.

7. Evaluate the role and importance of international banking and the role of the World Bank and the International Monetary Fund.

LESSON NOTES

The PROFILE at the beginning of this chapter focuses on Alan Greenspan, Chairman of the Federal Reserve, one of the most powerful positions in the country. Greenspan has control over the nation's money supply.

I. THE IMPORTANCE OF MONEY.

A. The American economy depends upon money: its availability, its value relative to other currencies, and its cost.
1. Money is so important that many institutions have evolved to manage money and to make it available to you when you need it.
2. The banking system is so complex because the flow of money from country to country is as free as the flow from state to state.
3. What happens to any major country's economy has an effect on the U.S. economy and vice versa.

B. WHAT IS MONEY?
1. **MONEY** is anything that people generally accept as payment for goods and services.
2. **BARTER** is the trading of goods and services for other goods and services directly.
   a. Many people today still barter goods and services, but transactions are difficult.
   b. People need some object that's more portable, divisible, durable, and stable so they can trade without having to carry the actual goods.
   c. Coins meet all the standards for more useful money.
3. The standards for useful money:
   a. Portability - Coins were easier to take to market than goods.
   b. Divisibility - Different-sized coins could be made to represent different values.
   c. Stability - Everybody agreed on the value of coins so the value of money became relatively stable.
   d. Durability - Coins last for years.
   e. Difficulty counterfeiting - The government has had to go to extra lengths to make real dollars readily identifiable.
4. Coins and paper money thus became units of value and a means of making exchanges easier.
   a. Most countries have their own coins and paper that they use as money.
   b. However, they are not always equally stable, the text uses the example of Russian money.

C. CHANGING THE CURRENCY IN EUROPE
1. Historically European nations each had their own money, which hindered trade.
2. Eleven European nations have decided upon one common currency, the Euro.

D. WHAT IS THE MONEY SUPPLY?
1. The **MONEY SUPPLY** is the amount of money there is to buy available goods and services.
2. There are several definitions of the money supply (M-1, M-2, and so on).
   a. **M-1** includes currency (coins and paper bills), money that's available by writing checks, and money held in traveler's checks; that is money that is quickly and easily raised.
   b. **M-2** includes everything in M-1 plus the money in savings accounts and money in money market accounts, mutual funds, certificates of deposit, and the like; that is money that may take a little more time to obtain than currency.
   c. M-2 is the most commonly used definition of money.

E. WHY DOES THE MONEY SUPPLY NEED TO BE CONTROLLED?
   1. The money supply needs to be controlled because the prices of goods and services can be somewhat managed by controlling the amount of money available in the economy.
   2. If too much money is available prices go up, inflation.
   3. If too little money were available, prices would go down, resulting in recession.
   4. The money supply tools have an effect on employment and economic growth and decline.

F. THE GLOBAL EXCHANGE OF MONEY
   1. A falling dollar means that the amount of goods and services you can buy with a dollar goes down.
   2. A rising dollar means that the amount of goods and services you can buy with a dollar does up.
   3. What makes the dollar weak or strong is the position of the U.S. economy relative to other economies.
      a. When the economy is strong, people want to buy dollars and the value relative to other economies rises.
      b. When a country's economy is perceived as weakening, people no longer desire its currency and the currency's value falls.

II. CONTROL OF THE MONEY SUPPLY

A. It is important to have an organization that controls the money supply to try to keep the U.S. economy from growing too fast or too slowly.
   1. The Federal Reserve System (the fed) is the organization in charge of monetary policy.
   2. The head of the Federal Reserve Alan Greenspan, is one of the most influential people in the world.

B. BASICS ABOUT THE FEDERAL RESERVE
   1. The Federal Reserve System consists of five major parts:
      a. The Board of Governors administers and supervises the 12 Federal Reserve System banks.
         1) There are seven members who are appointed by the President.
         2) The primary function is to set monetary policy.
      b. The Federal Open Market Committee has 12 voting members and is the policy-making body.
      c. The 12 Federal Reserve Banks.
      d. Three advisory councils.
         1) The advisory councils offer suggestions to the board and the FOMC.
         2) The councils represent the various banking districts, consumers, and member institutions.
      e. The member banks of the system.
   2. The Federal Reserve:
      a. Buys and sells foreign currencies.
      b. Regulates various types of credit.
      c. Supervises banks.
      d. Collects data on the money supply and other economic activities.
   3. The tools used to regulate the money supply include, reserve requirements, open-market operations, and the discount rate.

C. THE RESERVE REQUIREMENT
   1. The **RESERVE REQUIREMENT** is a percentage of commercial bank's checking and savings accounts that must be physically kept in this bank (for example, as cash in the vault) or a non-interest-bearing deposit at the local Federal Reserve district bank.
   2. Changing the reserve requirement is the Fed's most powerful tool.
   3. When the Fed increases the reserve requirement, banks have less money for loans and make fewer loans, which tends to reduce inflation.
   4. When the Fed decreases the reserve requirement, banks have more money available for loans and make more loans, which tends to stimulate the economy, risking inflation.
   5. Because this tool is so potent, and can cause such major changes in the U.S. economy, it is rarely used.

D. OPEN-MARKET OPERATIONS
   1. **OPEN-MARKET OPERATIONS** (a commonly used tool) involves the buying and selling of U.S. government securities by the Fed with the goal of regulating the money supply.
   2. When the fed wants to decrease the money supply, it sells government securities.
   3. When the fed wants to increase the money supply, it buys government securities from individuals, corporations, or organizations willing to sell.

E. THE DISCOUNT RATE
   1. The Fed is called the banker's bank.
   2. Member banks can borrow money from the Fed and then pass it on to their customers.
   3. The **DISCOUNT RATE** is the interest rate that the Fed charges for loans to member banks.
   4. Increasing the discount rate discourages banks from borrowing and consequently reduces the number of available loans, resulting in a decrease in the money supply.
   5. Decreasing the discount rate encourages banks borrowing and increases the amount of funds available for loans, resulting in an increase in the money supply.

F. THE FEDREAL RESERVE'S CHECK-CLEARING ROLE
   1. The Fed helps process checks.
   2. The whole banking industry is affected by actions taken by the Federal Reserve System.

III. THE HISTORY OF BANKING AND THE NEED FOR THE FED

A. Early banking history
   1. There were no banks in early colonial America.
      a. Strict laws limited the number of coins that could be brought to the colonies.
      b. Colonists were forced to barter.
   2. Massachusetts issued its own paper money in 1690 and soon other colonies did as well.
      a. Land banks made loans to farmers.
      b. England stopped these practices by 1741.
   3. Alexander Hamilton convinced Congress to form a Central Bank in 1791.
      a. The bank had so much opposition that it closed in 1811.
      b. An attempt to replace the bank in 1816 failed again by 1836.
   4. By the time of the Civil War, banking was a mess.
      a. Different banks issued different currency.
      b. Often the coins were worth more as gold or silver than as coins.
   5. The chaos reached a climax in 1907 when many banks failed.

      6. People withdrew their funds from the bank until there was no cash left and money could no longer be given to depositors.
      7. To avoid another cash shortage, the Federal Reserve System was formed.
         a. All Federally chartered banks must join; state chartered banks may join.
         b. The Federal Reserve became the bankers' bank.

  B. THE GREAT DEPRESSION
      1. The stock market crash of 1929 led to bank failures in the early 1930s.
      2. In 1933 and 1935, the federal government passed laws to strengthen the banking system.
      3. One move established federal deposit insurance.

  C. THE FEDERAL RESERVE AND THE BANKING INDUSTRY
      1. During the 1990s, there were many debates about the Fed's actions.
         a. In the early 1990s the Fed pumped up the money supply and lowered interest rates to get the economy moving.
         b. The Fed increased short-term interest rates in the mid-1990s, threatening the stock market.
         c. In 2000 and 2001 the Fed cut interest rates to get the economy going and the stock market moving up again.
      2. Businesses are concerned because higher bank rates mean a higher cost of borrowing.
      3. Stagflation is the combination of slow growth and inflation.

IV. THE AMERICAN BANKING SYSTEM

  A. The American banking system consists of commercial banks, savings and loan associations, credit unions, mutual savings banks, and **NONBANKS** (nondeposit institutions that perform several banking functions).

  B. COMMERCIAL BANKS
      1. A **COMMERCIAL BANK** is a profit-making organization that receives deposits from individuals and corporations in the form of checking and savings accounts and uses some of these funds to make loans.
      2. Commercial banks have two types of customers: depositors and borrowers.
      3. Commercial banks make a profit if the revenue generated by loans exceeds the interest paid to depositors.

  C. SERVICES PROVIDED BY COMMERCIAL BANKS
      1. A **DEMAND DEPOSIT** is the technical name for a checking account, from which the owner can withdraw the money on demand at any time.
      2. In the past, checking accounts paid no interest, but interest-bearing checking accounts (NOW and Super NOW accounts) have grown in recent years.
      3. A NOW (Negotiable Order of Withdrawal) account pays an annual interest rate, but imposes a minimum balance.
      4. A Super NOW account pays higher interest and requires a large minimum balance.
      5. A **TIME DEPOSIT** is the technical name for a savings account for which the bank requires prior notice before withdrawal.
         a. A **CERTIFICATE OF DEPOSIT (CD)** is an account that earns a guaranteed interest rate for a fixed period of time.
      6. Some other services include credit cards and ATMS.
         a. Automated teller machines (ATMs) give customers the convenience of 24-hour banking.

- b. Commercial banks may also offer credit cards, brokerage services, financial counseling, automatic payment of bills, safe deposit boxes, tax-deferred IRAs, travelers' checks, and overdraft privileges.

D. SERVICES TO BORROWERS
1. Banks screen loan applicants carefully to ensure that the loan plus interest will be paid back on time.
2. Small businesses and minority businesses often search out banks that cater to their needs.

E. SAVINGS AND LOAN ASSOCIATIONS (S&Ls)
1. A **SAVINGS AND LOAN ASSOCIATION (S&L)** is a financial institution that accepts both savings and checking deposits and provides home mortgage loans.
    a. S&Ls are often known as thrift institutions since their original purpose was to promote consumer thrift and home ownership.
    b. Thrifts were permitted to offer slightly higher interest rates to attract funds.
    c. These funds were then used to offer long-term fixed rate mortgages.
2. In the early 1980s S&Ls ran into trouble.
    a. To help relieve the pressure, the federal government permitted S&LS to offer NOW and Super NOW accounts, to allocate up to 10% of their funds to commercial loans, and to offer mortgage loans with adjustable interest rates.
    b. S&Ls became similar to commercial banks.

F. CREDIT UNIONS
1. **CREDIT UNIONS** are nonprofit, member-owned financial cooperatives that offer a full variety of banking service.
2. Credit unions offer members interest-bearing checking accounts at relatively high rates, short-term loans at relatively low rates, financial counseling, life insurance, and home mortgage loans.
3. As not-for-profit institutions, credit unions enjoy an exemption from federal income taxes.

G. OTHER FINANCIAL INSTITUTIONS (NONBANKS)
1. **NONBANKS** are financial organizations that accept no deposits, but offer many of the services provided by banks.
    a. Nonbanks include life insurance companies, pension funds, brokerage firms, and commercial finance companies.
    b. The diversity of financial services offered by nonbanks has caused banks to expand their services.
2. Life insurance companies provide financial protection for policyholders that periodically pay premiums.
3. **PENSION FUNDS** are amounts of money designated by corporations, nonprofit organizations, or unions to cover part of the financial needs of members when they retire.
    a. Pension funds typically invest in low-return but safe corporate stocks or government securities.
    b. Many large pension funds are becoming a force in U.S. financial markets.
4. Brokerage firms are organizations that buy and sell securities for their clients, but have begun to offer more bank type services.
5. **COMMERCIAL AND CONSUMER FINANCE COMPANIES** are institutions that offer short-term loans to individuals at higher interest rates than commercial banks.
    a. The primary customers are new businesses and individuals with no credit history.
    b. One should be careful when borrowing from such institutions because the interest rates can be quite high.
6. Corporate financial systems are financial services offered to customers of major corporations such as GE, Sears, and GM.

V. HOW THE GOVERNMENT PROTECTS YOUR FUNDS

  A. As a result of the depression of the 1930s, several organizations evolved to protect your money.
     1. The three major sources of financial protection are the FDIC, the SAIF, and the NCUA.
     2. All three insure deposits in individual accounts up to $100,000.

  B. THE FEDERAL DEPOSIT INSURANCE CORPORATION (FDIC)
     1. **THE FEDERAL DEPOSIT INSURANCE CORPORATION (FDIC)** is an independent government agency that insures accounts in banks against bank failures (up to a limit of $100,000 per account).
     2. If a bank were to fail, the FDIC would arrange to have its accounts transferred to another bank.
     3. The idea is to maintain confidence in banks so that others don't fail if one fails.

  C. THE SAVINGS ASSOCIATION INSURANCE FUND (SAIF)
     1. **THE SAVINGS ASSOCIATION INSURANCE FUND (SAIF)** (Formerly Federal Savings and Loan Insurance Corporation), insures holders of accounts in savings and loan associations.

  D. NATIONAL CREDIT UNION ADMINISTRATION (NCUA)
     1. The National Credit Union Administration (NCUA) provides up to $100,000 coverage per depositor.
     2. Additional protection can be obtained by holding accounts jointly or in trust.

VI. THE FUTURE OF BANKING

  A. Banks as we've traditionally known them will change.

  B. ELECTRONIC BANKING ON THE INTERNET
     1. The nation's top 25 retail banks now offer customers access to their accounts online.
     2. Banking services can also be performed online.
     3. New Internet banks have been created.
        a. These save on overhead and thus offer higher interest rates and cheaper services.
        b. Online banking is less satisfying to many customers than traditional banking.
     4. ATMs of the future will provide far more services than they do today.

  C. USING TECHNOLOGY TO MAKE BANKING MORE EFFICIENT
     1. The whole banking system is on the brink of a major revolution.
        a. The way things were done was expensive.
        b. One step in the past was to issue credit cards.
        c. The next step was to create the electronic exchange of money.
     2. **ELECTRONIC FUNDS TRANSFER (ETF) SYSTEM** is a computerized system that electronically performs financial transactions such as making purchases, paying bills, and receiving paychecks.
     3. Some people don't use checks they transfer funds through the Feds Automatic Clearing House using **ELECTRONIC CHECK CONVERSIONS (ECC).**
        a. There is less paper to handle.
     4. A **DEBIT CARD** is used to facilitate the transactions by taking money from a checking account.
     5. **SMART CARDS** combine a credit card, debit card, and other functions together.

6. Direct deposits and direct payments involve preauthorized deposits and payments that occur automatically.

VII. INTERNATIONAL BANKING AND BANKING SERVICES

A. Banks help businesses conduct business in other countries by providing three services.
   1. A **LETTER OF CREDIT** is a promise by the bank to pay the seller a given amount if certain conditions are met.
   2. A **BANKER'S ACCEPTANCE** promises that the bank will pay some specified amount at a particular time.
   3. Money exchange is the exchange of one country's currency for another country's currency.

B. LEADERS IN INTERNATIONAL BANKING
   1. In the future, many crucial financial issues will be international in scope.
   2. Today's money markets are global markets.
   3. Banking is no longer a domestic issue.
   4. What has evolved is a world economy financed by international banks.

C. THE WORLD BANK AND THE INTERNATIONAL MONETARY FUND (IMF)
   1. The World Bank and the IMF are twin pillars that support the structure of the world's banking community.
   2. The **WORLD BANK** is responsible for financing economic development.
      a. It is also known as the International Bank for Reconstruction and Development.
      b. Today, most of the money is lent to poor nations to raise productivity and raise the standard of living.
   3. The **INTERNATIONAL MONETARY FUND (IMF)** was established to assist the smooth flow of money among nations.
      a. It requires members to allow their currency to be exchanged for foreign currencies freely and keep the IMF informed about changes in monetary policy.
      b. The IMF is not primarily a lending institution, rather an overseer of member countries monetary and exchange rate policies.
   4. The IMF's goal is to maintain a global monetary system that works best for all nations.

LEARNING THE LANGUAGE OF BUSINESS

Match each of the following key terms with the appropriate definition.

A. banker's acceptance
B. barter
C. certificate of deposit
D. commercial and consumer finance companies
E. commercial bank
F. credit unions
G. debit card
H. demand deposit
I. discount rate
J. electronic check conversion (ECC)
K. electronic funds transfer system (EFTS)
L. Federal Deposit Insurance Corporation (FDIC)
M. International Monetary Fund (IMF)
N. letter of credit
O. M-1
P. M-2
Q. money
R. money supply
S. nonbanks
T. open-market operations
U. pension funds
V. reserve requirement
W. savings and loan association (S&L)
X. Savings Association Insurance Fund (SAIF)
Y. smart cards
Z. time deposit
AA. World Bank

____ 1. What people will generally accept as payment for goods and services.

____ 2. The sum of all the funds that the public has immediately available for buying goods and services.

____ 3. Money that is quickly and easily raised (currency, checks, travelers' checks, and the like).

____ 4. Money included in M-1 plus money that may take a little more time to raise (savings accounts, money market accounts, mutual funds, certificates of deposit, and the like).

____ 5. An electronic funds transfer tool that serves the same function as checks: it withdraws funds from a checking account.

____ 6. A profit-making organization that receives deposits from individuals and corporations in the form of checking and saving accounts and uses some of these funds to make loans.

____ 7. Nonprofit, member-owned financial cooperatives that offer basic banking services such as accepting deposits and making loans; they may also offer life insurance and a limited number of home mortgages.

_____ 8. Financial institutions that accept both savings and checking deposits and provide home mortgage loans.

_____ 9. Institutions that offer short-term loans to businesses or individuals who either can't meet the credit requirements of regular banks or else have exceeded their credit limit and need more funds.

_____ 10. The trading of goods and services for other goods and services directly.

_____ 11. An independent U.S. government agency that insures bank deposits.

_____ 12. Part of the FDIC that insures holders of accounts in savings and loan associations.

_____ 13. Financial organizations that accept no deposits, but offer many of the services provided by regular banks (pension funds, insurance companies, commercial finance companies, consumer finance companies and brokerage houses).

_____ 14. Amounts of money designated by corporations, nonprofit organizations, or unions to cover part of the financial needs of members when they retire.

_____ 15. A computerized system, which electronically performs financial transactions such as making, purchases, paying bills, and receiving paychecks.

_____ 16. The interest rate that the Fed charges for loans to member banks.

_____ 17. A percentage of member-bank funds that must be deposited in the Federal Reserve System.

_____ 18. The technical name for a savings account for which the bank requires prior notice before withdrawal.

_____ 19. The technical name for a checking account; the money can be withdrawn on demand at any time by the owner.

_____ 20. An electronic funds transfer tool that is a combination credit card, debit card, phone card and more.

_____ 21. An electronic funds transfer tool that converts a traditional paper check into an electronic transaction at the cash register.

_____ 22. A time-deposit account that earns interest to be delivered at the end of the certificate's maturity date.

_____ 23. A promise that the bank will pay some specified amount at a particular time.

_____ 24. A promise by a bank that a given amount will be paid if certain conditions are met.

_____ 25. The buying and selling of U.S. government securities by the Fed with the goal of regulating the money supply.

_____ 26. Organization that assists the smooth flow of money among nations.

_____ 27. The bank primarily responsible for financing economic development; also known as the International Bank for Reconstruction and Development.

SELF-TEST

1. A large decrease in the money supply would tend to:
   A) reduce the supply of gold held by the federal government.
   B) create shortages that would cause prices of goods and services to rise.
   C) throw the economy into a recession.
   D) reduce the size of the federal government's deficit.

2. When the Fed buys U.S. government securities, the:
   A) size of the federal deficit falls.
   B) discount rate rises.
   C) money supply increases.
   D) banking system loses reserves.

3. In order to stimulate the economy during a recession, the Fed could:
   A) cut taxes.
   B) increase the discount rate.
   C) reduce the reserve requirement.
   D) sell government securities.

4. The nation of Downturn has experienced very little economic growth over the past few years, yet at the same time it has experienced relatively high rates of inflation. The type of situation Downturn is experiencing is called:
   A) stagflation.
   B) unflation.
   C) deflation.
   D) disinflation.

5. Commercial banks, savings and loan associations and credit unions are similar in that they all:
   A) specialize in loaning money for home mortgages.
   B) are nonprofit organizations.
   C) are owned by their depositors.
   D) accept deposits and make loans.

6. During the early 1980s, the federal government responded to the severe problems plaguing savings and loan associations by:
   A) allowing S&Ls to offer a variety of financial services that made them more like commercial banks.
   B) nationalizing the savings and loan industry.
   C) providing interest-free loans to S&Ls who were short on reserves.
   D) declaring a moratorium on S&L debt payments, and limiting the amount of funds depositors could withdraw from an S&L in any given 24-hour period.

7. A major reason the FDIC and the FSLIC were established was to:
   A) restore confidence in banking institutions.
   B) serve as clearinghouses for transactions involving commercial banks and savings and loans.
   C) provide federally guaranteed insurance to small businesses at low cost.
   D) help the Federal Reserve enforce reserve requirements.

8. Xavier has $73,220 deposited in various individual accounts at his local credit union. He and his wife also have a joint savings account worth $34,500. The total amount for which the NCUA would insure these deposits would be:
   A) $0, because the NCUA does not insure individual credit union deposits.
   B) $73,220
   C) $100,000
   D) $107,720

9. Hal no longer receives a paycheck; instead, he has his employer deposit his pay directly into his account at the Mortonville Bank. He also has a card issued by his bank that looks like a credit card. When he shops at his local supermarket and department store, the retailer puts the card in a slot, and the appropriate amount of money is transferred from Hal's account to the store's account. Hal is making use of a(n):
   A) funds exchange network.
   B) NOW account.
   C) debit card.
   D) automatic funds deposit system.

10. Which of the following institutions would be most likely to lend funds to a less developed country to finance an economic development project?
    A) The International Monetary Fund.
    B) The World Bank.
    C) The International Development Administration.
    D) The International Reserve Bank.

ANSWER KEY

LEARNING THE LANGUAGE OF BUSINESS

1. Q
2. R
3. O
4. P
5. G
6. E
7. F
8. W
9. D
10. B
11. L
12. X
13. S
14. U
15. K
16. I
17. V
18. Z
19. H
20. Y
21. J
22. C
23. A
24. N
25. T
26. M
27. AA

SELF-TEST

Answer	Page #
1. C	Page: 650
2. C	Page: 652-653
3. C	Page: 652-653
4. A	Page: 656
5. D	Page: 656-660
6. A	Page: 659
7. A	Page: 661
8. D	Page: 661-662
9. C	Page: 664
10. B	Page: 666-667

LESSON 23

MANAGING SHORT-TERM FINANCING

ASSIGNMENTS

1. Review the Learning Goals and read the Lesson Overview for this lesson.

2. Read Chapter 19 pp. 582-597 in Understanding Business, 6th edition by Nickels, McHugh, and McHugh.

3. Watch the video Managing Short-term Financing.

4. Review the textbook material.

5. Match the key terms with the correct definitions in the Learning the Language of Business exercise.

6. Take the Self-Test.

7. Use the Answer Key to check your answers and review when necessary.

LEARNING GOALS

After you watch the video, read the textbook, and study this lesson, you should be able to:

1. Explain the importance of finance.

2. Describe the responsibilities of financial managers.

3. Tell what financial planning involves and define the three key budgets of finance.

4. Recognize the financial needs that must be met with available funds.

5. Distinguish between short-term and long-term financing, and between debt capital and equity capital.

6. Identify and describe several sources of short-term financing.

LESSON NOTES

The PROFILE at the beginning of this chapter focuses on Joy Covey, former CFO of Amazon.com. Joy is a different type of financial manager who seems to break all the typical stereotypes. Joy is a strong supporter of the "profitless corporation," a term use to describe a grow first, profit later philosophy. She followed a simple formula, grow the business and increase efficiencies. The demise of many dot.com firms indicates that profits still count. The ideas of risk, complexity, and uncertainty clearly define the role of financial manager.

I. THE ROLE OF FINANCE AND FINANCIAL MANAGERS

   A. Comparing the accountant and the financial manager.
      1. The role of an accountant is like a skilled technician who takes measures of a company's health and writes a report.
      2. **FINANCIAL MANAGERS** use the data prepared by accountants and make recommendations to top management regarding strategies for improving the company's financial strength.
      3. A manager cannot make sound financial decisions without understanding accounting information.
      4. The need for careful financial management remains an ongoing challenge in a business throughout its life.
      5. The three most common ways for firms to fail financially are:
         a. Undercapitalization, or not enough funds to start with.
         b. Poor control over cash flow, or cash in minus cash out.
         c. Inadequate expense control.

   B. THE IMPORTANCE OF UNDERSTANDING FINANCE
      1. The text describes a small organization called Parsley Patch, begun on a shoestring budget.
      2. When the owners expanded into the health-food market, sales took off.
      3. Neither woman understood cash flow procedures or how to control expenses, and profits did not materialize.
      4. They eventually hired a CPA and an experienced financial manager, and soon they earned a comfortable margin on operations.

   C. Financial understanding is important to anyone who wants to invest in stocks and bonds or plan a retirement fund.

II. WHAT IS FINANCIAL MANAGEMENT?

   A. **FINANCE** is the function in a business responsible for acquiring funds for the firm, managing funds within the firm, and planning for the expenditure of funds on various assets.
      1. Without a carefully calculated business plan, the firm has little chance for survival.
      2. **FINANCIAL MANAGEMENT** is the job of managing a firm's resources so it can meet its goals and objectives.
         a. Most organizations will designate a manager in charge of financial operations.
         b. Financial management could also be put in the hands of the company treasurer or vice president of finance.
      3. The fundamental task is to obtain money and then plan, use, and control that money effectively.

   B. Credit and collections are important responsibilities of financial managers.

1. Financial managers are responsible for collecting overdue payments and minimizing bad debts.
2. These functions are particularly critical to small and medium-size businesses, which have smaller cash or credit cushions.

C. Tax management is the analyzing of tax implications of various managerial decisions in an attempt to minimize the taxes paid by the business.
  1. As tax laws change, finance specialists must carefully analyze the tax implications of various decisions in an attempt to minimize taxes paid.
  2. Businesses of all sizes must concern themselves with managing taxes.

D. It is the internal auditor, usually a member of the firm's finance department, who checks on the financial statements to make sure that all the transactions are appropriate.
  1. Without such audits, accounting statements would be less reliable.
  2. It is important that internal auditors be objective and critical of any improprieties or deficiencies.

III. FINANCIAL PLANNING

A. Financial planning involves analyzing short-term and long-term money flows to and from the firm.
  1. The major objective of financial planning is to optimize profits and make the best use of the firm's money.
  2. The steps involved in financial planning are:
     a. Forecasting both long-term and short-term financial needs.
     b. Developing budgets to meet those needs.
     c. Establishing financial control to see how well the company is following the financial plans.

B. FORECASTING FINANCIAL NEEDS
  1. A **SHORT-TERM FORECAST** is a prediction of revenues, costs, and expenses for a period of one year or less.
  2. A **CASH FLOW FORECAST** is a prediction of cash inflows and outflows in future periods, usually months or quarters.
     a. The inflows and outflows of cash are based on expected sales revenues and on various costs and expenses.
     b. A firm often uses its past financial statements as a basis for projecting expected sales and various costs and expenses.
  3. A **LONG-TERM FORECAST** is a prediction of revenues, costs, and expenses for a period longer than 1 year, sometimes extending 5 or 10 years into the future.
     a. This forecast plays a crucial part in the company's long-term strategic plan.
     b. The long-term financial forecast gives top management some sense of the income or profit potential possible with different strategic plans.

C. WORKING WITH THE BUDGET PROCESS
  1. A budget is a financial plan.
     a. A budget becomes the primary basis and guide for the firm's financial operations.
     b. Most firms compile yearly budgets from short-term and long-term financial forecasts.
  2. There are usually several budgets in a company.
     a. A **CAPITAL BUDGET** is a spending plan for assets whose returns are expected to occur over an extended period of time, more than a year.
     b. A **CASH BUDGET** projects cash balances at the end of given periods.

        c. An **OPERATING (MASTER) BUDGET** summaries the firm's other budgets; it is a projection of dollar allocations to various costs and expenses needed to run or operate the company, given projected revenue.
    3. Financial planning often determines:
        a. What long-term investments are made.
        b. When specific funds will be needed.
        c. How the funds will be generated.

  D. ESTABLISHING FINANCIAL CONTROLS
    1. **FINANCIAL CONTROL** means that the actual revenues, costs, and expenses are periodically reviewed and compared with projections.
    2. Most companies hold at least monthly financial reviews as a way to ensure financial control.
    3. Such controls provide feedback to help reveal which accounts are varying from the financial plans.
    4. Some financial adjustments to the plan may be made.

IV. THE NEED FOR OPERATING FUNDS

  A. In business, the need for operating funds never seems to cease.
    1. Continuous sound financial management is essential because the capital needs of a business change over time.
    2. Funds must be available to finance specific operational needs.

  B. MANAGING DAILY BUSINESS OPERATIONS
    1. Funds must be made available to meet these daily cash expenditures without compromising the investment potential of the firm's money.
    2. Money has time value, $200 today is more valuable that $200 a year from today.
    3. Financial managers often try to keep cash expenditures to a minimum to free funds for investment in interest-bearing accounts.
    4. Efficient cash management is particularly important to small firms.

  C. MANAGING ACCOUNTS RECEIVABLE
    1. Making credit available helps keep current customers happy and attracts new customers.
    2. The major problem with credit purchasing is that as much as 25% of a company's assets can be tied up in accounts receivable.
    3. The firm needs to use some of its available funds to pay for the goods or services already given to customers.
    4. In order to collect this money as soon as possible, financial managers offer such incentives as cash or quantity discounts to purchasers who pay their account by a certain time.
    5. One way to decrease the time and expense of collecting accounts receivable is to accept bank credit cards such as MasterCard or Visa.

  D. OBTAINING NEEDED INVENTORY
    1. To satisfy customers, businesses must maintain inventories that involve a sizable expenditure of funds.
    2. A carefully constructed inventory policy assists in managing the use of the firm's available funds and maximizing profitability.
    3. JIT inventory may help reduce the funds companies must use to maintain inventories.

  E. MAJOR CAPITAL EXPENDITURES

1. **CAPITAL EXPENDITURES** are major investments in long-term assets such as land, buildings, equipment, or research and development.
2. The purchases of major assets require huge expenditures.
   a. It is critical that the firm weighs all possible options before it commits a large portion of its available resources.
   b. Financial managers must evaluate the appropriateness of capital expenditures.

V. ALTERNATIVE SOURCES OF FUNDS

A. Short-term versus long-term funds
   1. **SHORT-TERM FINANCING** refers to the need for capital that will be repaid within one year and helps finance current operations.
   2. **LONG-TERM FINANCING** refers to capital needs for major purchases that will be repaid over a specific time period longer than one year.

B. Methods of raising capital
   1. **DEBT CAPITAL** refers to funds raised through various forms of borrowing that must be repaid.
   2. **EQUITY CAPITAL** is money raised from within the firm or through the sale of ownership in the firm.

VI. OBTAINING SHORT-TERM FINANCING

A. Everyday operation of the firm calls for careful management of short-term financial needs.

B. TRADE CREDIT
   1. The most widely used source of short-term funding, trade credit, is the least expensive and most convenient form of short-term financing.
   2. **TRADE CREDIT** is the practice of buying goods now and paying for them later.
   3. Terms such as, 2/10, net 30 means that the buyer can take a 2 percent discount for paying within 10 days and the total bill is due in 30 days if the discount is not taken.

C. PROMISSORY NOTES
   1. For organizations with a poor credit rating or history of slow payment, the supplier may insist that the customer sign a promissory note.
   2. A **PROMISSORY NOTE** is a written contract with a promise to pay.

D. FAMILY AND FRIENDS
   1. It is better not to borrow from friends and relatives.
   2. Entrepreneurs have come to rely less and less on family and friends for funding.
   3. If you borrow from family or friends it is best to:
      a. Agree on the terms at the beginning.
      b. Write out the agreement.
      c. Pay them back in the same way you would pay a bank loan.

E. COMMERCIAL BANKS AND OTHER FINANCIAL INSTITUTIONS
   1. Banks are highly sensitive to risk and often reluctant to loan money to small business.
      a. The most promising ventures are sometimes able to get bank loans.
      b. The person in charge of finance should keep in close touch with the bank and see the banker periodically.
      c. How much a business borrows and for how long depend on the kind of business it is and how quickly the merchandise purchased with a bank loan can be resold or used to generate funds.

- d. Sometimes a business gets so far into debt that the bank refuses to lend it more funds.
    1) Often the business fails.
    2) This result can be chalked up to cash flow problems.
- e. By anticipating times when many bills will come due, a business can begin early to seek funds and prepare for the crunch.
2. DIFFERENT FORMS OF BANK LOANS
    - a. A **SECURED LOAN** is a loan that is backed by collateral.
        1) **PLEDGING** means using accounts receivable as security.
        2) **INVENTORY FINANCING** means that inventory is used as collateral.
    - b. An **UNSECURED LOAN** is a loan that is not backed by collateral, it is the most difficult to get, only highly regarded customers are approved.
    - c. **LINE OF CREDIT** means that bank will lend the business a given amount of unsecured short-term funds, provided the bank has the funds available.
        1) A line of credit is not guaranteed.
        2) The purpose of a line of credit is to speed the borrowing process.
        3) As businesses mature and become more financially secure, the amount of credit often is increased.
        4) **REVOLVING CREDIT AGREEMENT** is a line of credit that is guaranteed.
    - d. **COMMERCIAL FINANCE COMPANIES** make short-term loans to borrowers that offer tangible assets as collateral.
        1) Commercial finance companies are willing to accept higher degrees of risk than commercial banks.
        2) Interest rates charged are usually higher than banks.

F. FACTORING
1. **FACTORING**, the process of selling accounts receivable for cash, is relatively expensive.
2. A factor is a market intermediary that agrees to buy the accounts receivable from the firm at a discount for cash.
3. The factor then collects and keeps the money that was owed the firm.
4. Factoring is very popular among small businesses.
5. Factoring is not a loan it is the sale of an asset.
6. Factoring charges are much lower if the company assumes the risk for those accounts that don't pay at all.

G. COMMERCIAL PAPER
1. **COMMERCIAL PAPER** consists of unsecured promissory notes in amounts of $25,000 and up that mature in 270 days or less.
2. Commercial paper is unsecured and is sold at a public sale, so only financially stable firms are able to sell it.

LEARNING THE LANGUAGE OF BUSINESS

Match each of the following key terms with the appropriate definition.

A. capital budget
B. capital expenditures
C. cash budget
D. cash flow forecast
E. commercial finance companies
F. commercial paper
G. debt capital
H. equity capital
I. factoring
J. finance
K. financial control
L. financial management
M. financial managers
N. inventory financing
O. line of credit
P. long-term financing
Q. long-term forecast
R. operating (master) budget
S. pledging
T. promissory note
U. revolving credit agreement
V. secured loan
W. short-term financing
X. short-term forecast
Y. trade credit
Z. unsecured loan

____ 1. The function in a business responsible for acquiring funds for the firm, managing funds within the firm, and planning for the expenditure of funds on various assets.

____ 2. Management of the firm's resources so it can meet its goals and objectives.

____ 3. Financing that will be repaid over a specific time period longer than one year.

____ 4. Financing that will be repaid within one year.

____ 5. A loan that is backed by something valuable.

____ 6. The practice of buying goods now and paying for them later.

____ 7. Organizations that make short-term loans to borrowers that offer tangible assets as collateral.

____ 8. Using accounts receivable or other assets as collateral for a loan.

____ 9. A loan that is not backed by any specific assets as collateral.

____ 10. Major investments in long-term assets such as land, buildings, equipment, or research and development.

_____ 11. A short-term corporate equivalent of an IOU that is sold in the marketplace by a firm; it matures in 270 days or less.

_____ 12. Selling accounts receivable for cash.

_____ 13. Using inventory as collateral or security for a loan.

_____ 14. A process that periodically compares the actual revenue, costs, and expenses with projections.

_____ 15. The amount of unsecured short-term credit a bank will lend a borrower that is agreed to ahead of time.

_____ 16. Funds raise by borrowing money through the sale of bonds or from banks and other lending institutions.

_____ 17. Managers who make recommendations to top executives regarding strategies for improving the financial strength of a firm.

_____ 18. The budget that ties together all the firm's other budgets; it is the projection of dollar allocations to various costs and expenses needed to run the business, given projected revenues.

_____ 19. Projects the cash balance at the end of a given period.

_____ 20. A line of credit that is guaranteed by the bank.

_____ 21. The firm's spending plans for major asset purchases that often require large sums of money.

_____ 22. A prediction of cash inflows and outflows in future periods.

_____ 23. A prediction of revenues, costs, and expenses for a period longer than 1 year, sometimes extending 5 or 10 years into the future.

_____ 24. A prediction of revenues, costs, and expenses for a period of one year or less.

_____ 25. A written contract with a promise to pay.

_____ 26. Funds raised within the company or from selling ownership in the firm.

SELF-TEST

1. Sarah intends to major in finance and find employment in corporate financial management. As a finance major, Sarah probably will be required to take several courses in:
   A) marketing.
   B) psychology.
   C) sociology.
   D) accounting.

2. As a management consultant, Lamont has found that regardless of how good its product is, a firm has little chance of success without a(n):
   A) financial plan.
   B) outside consultant.
   C) auditor.
   D) warranty.

3. Elizabeth is a member of her firm's finance department. She spends her workday studying current tax law and any proposed changes that might occur in tax laws. Her company is concerned about taxes because of increasing liabilities. Elizabeth is involved in:
   A) tax accounting.
   B) tax management.
   C) tax deferrals.
   D) tax allocation.

4. Liberty Electronics is uncertain about revenues, costs, and expenditures for the coming year. This firm would benefit from developing a:
   A) master budget.
   B) consolidated income statement.
   C) short-term forecast.
   D) statement of cash flows.

5. Financial managers are responsible for financial planning. Sound financial planning involves three key steps. Which of the following is not one of the three key steps financial managers would take in the process of financial planning?
   A) Forecasting both short-term and long-term financial needs.
   B) Developing budgets to meet anticipated needs.
   C) Preparing the income statement and balance sheet.
   D) Establishing financial control to see how well the company is following the financial plans.

6. Firms use operating funds to finance all of the following activities except:
   A) making depreciation payments.
   B) obtaining needed inventory.
   C) managing accounts receivable.
   D) meeting the needs of daily business operations.

7. Enterprise Chemicals has not offered a cash discount for early payment to one of its major credit customers, Feel Well Enterprises. For this reason, Feel Well waits to pay its bills until the last possible date. Feel Well does this because of:
   A) the time value of money.
   B) tax benefits they receive from late payment.
   C) its negative attitude toward buying on credit.
   D) Enterprise's accounting system.

8. Clark, president of Cycles to Go, is concerned that his business may not have enough cash to pay for salaries and supplies at the end of the month. He anticipates that this situation will change as warm weather approaches. He wants to borrow some funds to meet his immediate needs, and intends to repay the amount borrowed in a few months. Clark is interested in obtaining:
   A) intermediate financing.
   B) contingency financing.
   C) short-term financing.
   D) long-term financing.

9. Wisconsin Scientific recently sold shares of ownership in an attempt to raise funds to finance the firm's research and development projects. Wisconsin Scientific is seeking to acquire long-term financing through the use of:
   A) debt capital.
   B) equity capital.
   C) venture capital.
   D) dividend capital.

10. Farmers Savings and Loan agreed to extend Eckhart's Orchards $200,000 of unsecured short-term funds to help with harvesting, planting, or other needs, if the bank has funds available. Eckhart's has obtained a:
    A) line of credit.
    B) pledge agreement.
    C) factor statement.
    D) trade voucher.

ANSWER KEY

LEARNING THE LANGUAGE OF BUSINESS

1. J
2. L
3. P
4. W
5. V
6. Y
7. E
8. S
9. Z
10. B
11. F
12. I
13. N
14. K
15. O
16. G
17. M
18. R
19. C
20. U
21. A
22. D
23. Q
24. X
25. T
26. H

SELF-TEST

	Answer	Page #
1.	D	Page: 584
2.	A	Page: 586
3.	B	Page: 586
4.	C	Page: 586
5.	C	Page: 586
6.	A	Page: 590-592
7.	A	Page: 590
8.	C	Page: 592
9.	B	Page: 593
10.	A	Page: 595

LESSON 24

MANAGING LONG-TERM FINANCING

ASSIGNMENTS

1. Review the Learning Goals and read the Lesson Overview for this lesson.

2. Read Chapter 19 pp. 598-605 and Chapter 20 pp. 610-641 in Understanding Business, 6th edition by Nickels, McHugh, and McHugh.

3. Watch the video Managing Long-Term Financing.

4. Review the textbook material.

5. Match the key terms with the correct definitions in the Learning the Language of Business exercise.

6. Take the Self-Test.

7. Use the Answer Key to check your answers and review when necessary.

LEARNING GOALS

After you watch the video, read the textbook, and study this lesson, you should be able to:

1. Identify and describe several sources of long-term financing.

2. Examine the functions of securities markets and investment bankers.

3. Compare the advantages and disadvantages of issuing bonds, and identify the classes and features of bonds.

4. Compare the advantages and disadvantages of issuing stock, and outline the differences between common and preferred stock.

5. Describe the various stock exchanges and how to invest in securities markets and explain various investment objectives such as long-term growth, income, cash, and protection from inflation.

6. Analyze the opportunities bonds offer as investments.

7. Explain the opportunities stocks and mutual funds offer as investments and the advantages of diversifying investments.

8. Discuss specific high-risk investments, including junk bonds, buying stocks on margin and commodity trading.

9. Explain securities quotations listed in the financial section of a newspaper, and describe how stock market indicators like the Dow Jones Average affect the market.

LESSON NOTES

I. OBTAINING LONG-TERM FINANCING

   A. The financial plan specifies the amount of funding that the firm will need over various time periods and the most appropriate sources of those funds.
      1. In setting long-term financing objectives, the firm generally asks three major questions:
         a. What are the organization's long-term goals and objectives?
         b. What are the financial requirements needed to achieve these goals and objectives?
         c. What sources of long-term capital are available, and which best fit our needs?
      2. Long-term capital is used to buy fixed assets such as plant and equipment and to finance any expansions of the organization.
      3. Long-term financing usually comes from two sources: debt capital or equity capital.

   B. DEBT FINANCING
      1. Debt capital is funds that come to the firm from borrowing through lending institutions or from the sale of bonds.
         a. With debt financing, the company has a legal obligation to repay the amount borrowed.
         b. Long-term loans are usually repaid within 3 to 7 years, but may extend to 15 or 20 years.
         c. A **TERM-LOAN AGREEMENT** is a promissory note that requires the borrower to repay the loan in specified installments.
         d. A major advantage is that interest paid on a long-term debt is tax deductible.
      2. Long-term loans are often more expensive than short-term loans because larger amounts of capital are borrowed and the repayment date is less secure.
         a. Most long-term loans require some form of collateral.
         b. Lenders will also often require certain restrictions on a firm's operations.
         c. The greater risk a lender takes in making a loan, the higher rate of interest it requires, known as the **RISK/RETURN TRADE-OFF**.
      3. If an organization is unable to obtain its long-term financing needs from a lending institution, it may decide to issue bonds.
         a. A bond is a company IOU, a binding contract through which an organization agrees to specific terms with investors in return for investors lending money to the company.
         b. **INDENTURE TERMS** are the terms of agreement in a bond.

   C. SECURED AND UNSECURED BONDS
      1. A bond is a long-term debt obligation of a corporation or government.
      2. Investors in bonds measure the risk involved in purchasing a bond with the return (interest) the bond promises to pay.
      3. A **SECURED BOND** is issued with some form of collateral, such as real estate, or equipment.
      4. An **UNSECURED BOND** is one that is backed only by the reputation of the organization and bondholders' trust in the issuer.

   D. EQUITY FINANCING
      1. Equity financing comes from the owners of the firm.
         a. It involves selling ownership in the firm in the form of stock, or using retained earnings the firm has reinvested in the business.
         b. A business can also seek equity financing from venture capitalist.

E. SELLING STOCK
1. One way to obtain needed funds is to sell ownership shares (stock) in the firm to the public.
2. Purchasers of stock become owners in the organization.
3. Shares of stock the company decides not to offer for sale are known as unissued stock.
4. Companies can only issue stock for public purchase if they meet requirements set by the Security and Exchange Commission (SEC).
5. The terminology and intricacies of selling stock to raise funds are discussed in the next chapter.

F. RETAINED EARNINGS
1. Retained earnings is the profit the company keeps and reinvests in the firm.
2. This is often a major source of long-term funds.
3. Retained earnings are usually the most favored source of meeting long-term capital needs because:
    a. The company saves interest payments, dividends, and underwriting fees.
    b. There is no dilution of ownership.
4. The major problem is that many organizations do not have sufficient retained earnings.

G. VENTURE CAPITAL
1. The hardest time for a business to raise money is when it is just starting.
2. Venture capital firms are one of the sources of start-up capital for new companies.
3. **VENTURE CAPITAL** is money that is invested in new companies with great profit potential.
4. The venture capital industry began about 50 years ago as an alternative investment vehicle for wealthy families.
    a. The venture capital industry grew significantly in the 1980s.
    b. For the fastest-growing firms, the number one source of funds is venture capital.
5. The venture capital firm generally wants a stake in the ownership of the business and expects a very high return on their investment.
6. The search for venture capital begins with a good business plan.
7. Financing a firm's long-term needs clearly involves a high degree of risk.

H. MAKING DECISIONS ON USING LEVERAGE
1. **LEVERAGE** is raising needed funds through borrowing to increase the firm's rate of return.
2. While debt increases the risk of the firm, it also enhances the firm's ability to increase profitability.
3. If the firm's earnings are larger than the interest payments on the funds borrowed, stockholders earn a higher rate of return than if equity financing were used.
4. It is up to each firm to determine exactly what is a proper balance between debt and equity financing.
5. The average debt of a large industrial corporation ranges between 33 and 40% of its total assets.

I. The next chapter looks at stocks and bonds and other investment topics both as financing tools and as investment options.

Chapter 20

I. THE FUNCTIONS OF SECURITIES MARKETS

   A. Markets serve two major functions.
      1. They assist businesses in finding large amounts of long-term funding.
      2. They provide private investors with a place to buy and sell investments.

   B. Primary and secondary markets
      1. The primary markets handle the sale of new securities.
         a. Corporations make money on the sale of their securities only once.
         b. The first time a stock is sold it is called an **INITIAL PUBLIC OFFERING (IPO).**
      2. The secondary market is where securities are sold subsequent to the initial public offering.
      3. Long-term funding is very important to business.

   C. THE ROLE OF INVESTMENT BANKERS
      1. **INVESTMENT BANKERS** are specialists that assist in the issue and sale of new securities.
         a. They assist with the preparation of the extensive financial analysis necessary to gain SEC approval.
         b. They underwrite stocks and bonds.
      2. The investment banker buys the entire issue at a discount and resells it at full price.
      3. Individuals or **INSTITUTIONAL INVESTORS,** which are large organizations such as, pension funds, invest their own funds or the funds of others in the securities.

II. DEBT FINANCING THROUGH SELLING BONDS

   A. Debt
      1. A **BOND** is a corporate certificate indicating that a person has lent money to the corporation.
         a. Legal obligation to pay regular interest.
         b. Pay principle at prescribed time.

   B. LEARNING THE LANGUAGE OF BONDS
      1. The borrower pays **INTEREST** to the bondholder.
         a. Also called the coupon rate.
      2. The interest rate may vary.
         a. Based upon the issuer's reputation.
         b. The state of the economy.
         c. Going rate of interest in the market.
         d. Based upon similar bonds.
      3. Bond quality is rated by such companies as: Standard & Poor's and Moody's Investment Service.
      4. Once set the interest rate does not change.
      5. The amount of debt represented on the bond is called the **DENOMINATION.**
         a. Almost all bonds are in multiples of $1000.
      6. The face value of the bond is the **PRINCIPAL.**
      7. The **MATURITY DATE** is when the issuer must pay the bond in full.

   C. ADVANTAGES AND DISADVANTAGES OF ISSUING BONDS
      1. Advantages include:
         a. Bondholders are creditors, not owners.
         b. Interest is tax deductible.
         c. A temporary source of funds.

2. Disadvantages include:
   a. Increased debt.
   b. Interest is a legal obligation.
   c. Face value must be repaid at maturity.

D. DIFFERENT CLASSES OF BONDS
   1. A **DEBENTURE BOND** is a bond with no collateral.
   2. A secured bond has collateral.

E. SPECIAL BOND FEATURES
   1. Many firms create a **SINKING FUND**, which is a provision of a bond that requires the issuer to retire on a periodic basis, some part of the bond principle prior to maturity.
      a. A sinking fund attracts investors because it provides for an orderly retirement of the bonds.
      b. It reduces the risk.
      c. It supports the market price.
   2. A **CALLABLE BOND** is one that gives the issuer the right to pay off the bond before it matures.
   3. A **CONVERTIBLE BOND** is one that the bondholder can convert into shares of the company's common stock.

III. EQUITY FINANCING THROUGH SELLING STOCK

A. LEARNING THE LANGUAGE OF STOCK
   1. A **STOCK CERTIFICATE** is evidence that a holder owns part of the firm through the shares of **STOCK**.
      a. Many stock certificates are held electronically.
   2. The stock certificate may have a dollar amount assigned to it, the **PAR VALUE**.
   3. The stockholder may receive **DIVIDENDS**, which are a part of the firms profits distributed to shareholders.

B. ADVANTAGES AND DISADVANTAGES OF ISSUING STOCK
   1. The advantages include:
      a. The owner never needs to be repaid.
      b. There is no legal obligation to pay dividends.
      c. Selling stock can improve the balance sheet.
   2. The disadvantages include:
      a. The owner has the right to vote on issues.
      b. Dividends are paid from profits.
      c. Some decisions might be made just to keep the stockholders happy.

C. ISSUING SHARES OF PREFERRED STOCK
   1. **PREFERRED STOCK** gives its owner preference in the payment of dividends.
      a. Preferred stock doesn't have voting rights.

D. SPECIAL FEATURES OF PREFERRED STOCK
   1. Preferred stock can be callable, convertible, and cumulative.
      a. A **CUMULATIVE PREFERRED STOCK** accumulates unpaid dividends.

E. ISSUING SHARES OF COMMON STOCK
   1. **COMMON STOCK** is the most basic form of ownership in a firm; it confers voting rights and the rights to share in the firm's profits through dividends, if offered by the firm's board of directors.
   2. Common shareholders have **PREEMPTIVE RIGHTS**, which is the right to purchase any new shares of common stock the firm decides to issue.

IV. STOCK EXCHANGES

　A. The exchanges
　　1. A **STOCK EXCHANGE** is an organization whose members can buy and sell securities for companies and investors.
　　2. The New York Stock Exchange (NYSE) has 1366 member seats.
　　3. Stock exchanges operate all over the world.

　B. U.S. EXCHANGES
　　1. The largest stock exchange in the U.S. is the NYSE.
　　　a. Founded in 1792 it is a floor-based exchange.
　　　b. The NYSE lists about 3,100 companies.
　　　c. Referred to as the "Big Board."
　　2. The American Stock Exchange (AMEX) is the second largest in the U.S., both the NYSE and the AMEX are national exchanges.
　　3. There are regional exchanges in Chicago, San Francisco, Philadelphia, Cincinnati, Spokane and Salt Lake City.
　　4. The **OVER-THE-COUNTER (OTC) MARKET** exchange provides a means to trade stocks not listed on the national exchanges.
　　5. Brokers in the OTC market communicate with each other through an electronic system called the **NATIONAL ASSOCIATION OF SECURITIES DEALERS AUTOMATED QUOTATIONS (NASDAQ)**.

　C. SECURITIES REGULATIONS
　　1. The Securities and Exchange Act of 1934 created the **SECURITIES AND EXCHANGE COMMISSION (SEC),** which is a federal agency that has responsibility for regulating the various exchanges.
　　　a. Companies trading on the exchanges must register.
　　　b. The Act set guidelines for companies to follow.
　　　c. The condensed version of the registration is a **PROSPECTUS**, which must be sent to potential investors.

V. HOW TO INVEST IN SECURITIES MARKETS

　A. Investing
　　1. First, find a stock or bond to invest in.
　　2. Contact a **STOCKBROKER** that is a registered representative who works as a marketing intermediary to buy and sell securities for clients.
　　3. The stockbroker places the order with an exchange member who goes to the exchange, negotiates a price, and completes the transaction.
　　4. Then the trade is reported to your stockbroker.
　　5. You are then given confirmation.
　　6. Large firms have automated systems.

　B. INVESTING ONLINE
　　1. Investors can use online services to trade securities.
　　2. In 2000 one-fifth of all stockholders had online accounts.

　C. CHOOSING THE RIGHT INVESTMENT STRATEGY
　　1. Key investment decisions often center on personal objectives.
　　2. Here are five key criteria for selecting investment options to achieve your objectives.
　　　a. The investment risk.
　　　b. The return or yield on your investment.
　　　c. The duration or length of the investment.

d. The liquidity of the investment.
e. The tax consequences of the investment.
3. If you are unsure contact a financial planner.

VI. INVESTING IN BONDS

A. Bonds
1. U.S. government bonds offer a low risk and guaranteed income.
2. Bonds don't have to be held to maturity.
3. Read about a bonds rating before buying.

VII. INVESTING IN STOCKS AND MUTUAL FUNDS

A. Buying stocks
1. Since 1925 the average annual return on stocks has been about 12%.
2. The market price and the growth potential of a stock depend on the corporation's performance.
   a. **CAPITAL GAINS** are the difference between the purchase and sale price of a stock.
3. Some stocks have expectations of earnings growth, these are called **GROWTH STOCKS**.
4. Stocks that offer investors a high dividend are called **INCOME STOCKS**.
5. Stocks of high quality, which generate consistent growth and regular dividends are called **BLUE CHIP STOCKS**.
6. A **PENNY STOCK** is a stock that sells for less than $2 and is considered a risky investment.
7. The instructions you give your stockbroker when buying a stock immediately at the best price possible is a **MARKET ORDER**.
8. If the order restricts the purchase or sale to a specific price it is a **LIMIT ORDER**.

B. STOCK SPLITS
1. Stocks are often purchased in **ROUND LOTS** of 100 shares.
2. If the purchases are less than 100 shares at a time, they are called **ODD LOTS**.
3. **STOCK SPLITS** are an action a company takes that gives stockholders two or more shares for each one they own.
   a. This lowers the market price of the stock and increases the market for the stock.

C. INVESTING IN MUTUAL FUNDS
1. A **MUTUAL FUND** is an organization that buys stocks and bonds and then sells shares in those security portfolios to the public.
2. Buying shares in a mutual fund is probably the best way for a small investor to get started.
3. Most funds can be bought directly to save commission charges.
4. Internet trading has made buying mutual funds easier than ever.
5. A no-load fund has no buying or selling commissions.
6. A load-fund charges a commission.
7. The key thing about mutual funds is that they spread out the risk.

D. DIVERSIFFING INVESTMENTS
1. **DIVERSIFICATION** is buying several different investment alternatives to spread the risk of investing.
2. It is important to remember the risk/return trade-off and be aware that some investments carry rather heavy risks.

VIII. INVESTING IN HIGH-RISK INVESTMENTS

   A. INVESTING IN HIGH-RISK (JUNK) BONDS
      1. High-risk and potentially high-return bonds are called **JUNK BONDS**.
         a. Interest rates on junk bonds are attractive but companies may not be able to pay the debts off.
         b. If the company can't pay the bond is "junk."

   B. BUYING STOCKS ON MARGIN
      1. **BUYING ON MARGIN** is buying stocks by borrowing some of the purchase cost from the brokerage firm.
         a. The margin is the amount of money the investor must invest.
         b. The margin rate is 50%.

   C. INVESTING IN COMMODITIES
      1. Commodities are usually high-risk investments.
      2. Commodities are articles of commerce.
      3. Estimates state that 75 to 80 percent of investors who speculate in commodities lose money.
      4. A **COMMODITY EXCHANGE** is a security exchange that specializes in buying and selling precious metals and minerals, foreign currencies, gasoline and agricultural products.
      5. Many companies use the **FUTURES MARKETS** where they purchase and sell goods for delivery sometime in the future.

IX. UNDERSTANDING INFORMATION FROM SECURITIES MARKETS

   A. Sources of information
      1. Newspapers, the Wall Street Journal, Investor's Daily, etc.

   B. UNDERSTANDING BOND QUOTATIONS
      1. The price of a bond is quoted as a percentage of $1000.
      2. The interest rate is frequently followed by an s.
         a. For example: a 9% bond due in 2015 would be 9s of 15.

   C. UNDERSTANDING STOCK QUOTATIONS
      1. Stocks are usually quoted in 16ths of a dollar.
         a. For example: 65 9/16, would be $65.5625.
      2. Some of the exchanges are converting from fractions to decimal quotes.
      3. A typical stock quote would read from left to right:
         a. High and low price over the last 52 weeks.
         b. Abbreviated company name or stock symbol.
         c. Last dividend per share paid.
         d. Dividend yield.
         e. The price/earnings ratio P/E.
         f. The number of shares in 100s traded that day.
         g. The high, low, and close of the day.
         h. The net change from the previous day.

   D. UNDERSTANDING MUTUAL FUNDS QUOTATIONS
      1. Typical quotations read like this from left to right:
         a. The funds name.
         b. The funds net asset value. (NAV)
         c. Sale price.

d. Net change in the net asset value from the previous day.

E. STOCK MARKET INDICATORS
1. The **DOW JONES INDUSTRIAL AVERAGE** is a frequently mentioned indicator; it is the average cost of 30 selected industrial stocks, used to give an indication of the direction of the movement of the stock market over time.
   a. The Dow periodically substitutes in new stocks when it is appropriate.
   b. Critics of the Dow say that a 30-company sample is too small.
2. The Standard & Poor's 500 is preferred by many critics of the Dow.
   a. The S&P 500 tracks 400 industrial, 40 financial, 40 utility, and 20 transportation stocks.
3. It is wise as an investor to stay informed.
   a. Remember your personal financial objectives and needs change over time.
   b. Markets can be volatile.

F. THE MARKET'S ROLLER-COASTER RIDE
1. During the last 100 years the stock market has had its ups and downs.
   a. Including some major ones.
2. Analysts believe the major fall of October 19, 1987 was due to program trading.
   a. **PROGRAM TRADING** is giving instructions to computers to automatically sell if the price dips to a certain point to avoid potential losses.
   b. Rules were changed after the 1987 fall to avoid such deep drops.
      1) If the market drops 350 points, trading is halted for 30 minutes to allow investors to regroup.

G. INVESTING IN THE 21st CENTURY MARKET
1. Global market changes may affect investing.
2. The potential competition between the exchanges may affect the market.
3. Diversification will still be the watchword.

LEARNING THE LANGUAGE OF BUSINESS

Match each of the following key terms with the appropriate definition.

A. indenture terms
B. leverage
C. risk/return tradeoff
D. secured bonds
E. term-loan agreement
F. unsecured bonds
G. venture capital
H. blue chip stocks
I. bond
J. buying on margin
K. callable bond
L. capital gains
M. commodity exchange
N. common stock
O. convertible bond
P. cumulative preferred stock
Q. debenture bonds
R. denomination
S. diversification
T. dividends
U. Dow Jones Industrial Average
V. futures market
W. growth stocks
X. income stocks
Y. initial public offering (IPO)
Z. institutional investors
AA. interest
BB. investment bankers
CC. junk bonds
DD. limit order
EE. market order
FF. maturity date
GG. mutual fund
HH. National Association of Securities Dealers Automated Quotation system (NASDAQ)
II. odd lots
JJ. over-the-counter (OTC) market
KK. par value
LL. penny stock
MM. preemptive right
NN. preferred stock
OO. principal
PP. program trading
QQ. prospectus
RR. round lots
SS. Securities and Exchange Commission (SEC)
TT. sinking fund
UU. stockbroker
VV. stock certificate
WW. stock exchange
XX. stock splits
YY. stocks

Lesson 24 Page 267

____ 1. A promissory note that requires the borrower to repay the loan in specified installments.

____ 2. Bonds which are not backed by any collateral.

____ 3. Raising needed funds through borrowing

____ 4. Money that is invested in new companies that have great profit potential.

____ 5. The most basic form of ownership of firms; it includes voting rights and dividends, if dividends are offered by the firm.

____ 6. Bonds backed by some tangible asset that is pledged to the investor if the principal is not paid back.

____ 7. The principle that the greater risk a lender takes in making a loan, the higher the interest rate required.

____ 8. The terms of agreement in a bond

____ 9. A nationwide electronic system, which communicates over-the-counter trades to, brokers.

____ 10. Exchange that provides a means to trade stocks not listed on the national exchanges.

____ 11. Giving instructions to computers to automatically sell if the price of stock dips to a certain price to avoid potential losses.

____ 12. A bond that gives the issuer the right to pay off the bond before its maturity.

____ 13. Federal government agency which has responsibility for regulating the various exchanges.

____ 14. Shares of ownership in a company.

____ 15. Stocks of high-quality companies.

____ 16. A stock that sells for less than $2.

____ 17. Stocks that offer a high dividend.

____ 18. An organization that buys stocks and bonds and then sells shares in those securities to the public.

____ 19. A condensed version of economic and financial information prepared for the SEC that must be sent to purchasers.

____ 20. The purchase of stocks by borrowing some of the purchase cost from the brokerage firm.

____ 21. Stock that gives owners preference in the payment of dividends and an earlier claim on assets if the business is sold but that does not include voting rights.

____ 22. Common stockholders' right to purchase any new shares of common stock the firm decides to issue.

____ 23. Giving stockholders two or more shares of stock for each one they own.

____ 24. A dollar amount assigned to shares of stock by the corporation's charter. The par value is printed on the front of a stock certificate and is used to compute the dividends of preferred stock.

____ 25. A bond that is unsecured.

____ 26. High-risk, high-interest bonds.

____ 27. The face value of a bond.

____ 28. The payment the issuer of a bond makes to bondholders for the use of borrowed money.

____ 29. Provision of a bond, which requires the issuer to retire (put in a trust fund), on a periodic basis, some part of the bond principal prior to maturity.

____ 30. The date on which the issuer of a bond must pay the principal of the bond to the bondholder.

____ 31. The part of the firm's profits that goes to stockholders.

____ 32. The purchase and sale of goods for delivery sometime in the future.

____ 33. Instructions to a broker to purchase stock at a specific price, if and when that price becomes possible.

____ 34. Purchases of 100 shares of stock at a time.

____ 35. Instructions to a broker to buy stock at the best price obtainable in the market now.

____ 36. Securities exchange which specializes in the buying and selling of precious metals and minerals (e.g., silver, foreign currencies, gasoline) and agricultural goods (e.g., wheat, cattle, sugar).

____ 37. The average cost of 30 specific industrial stocks; used to give an indication of the direction of the market over time.

____ 38. A corporate certificate indicating that a person has loaned money to a firm.

____ 39. Stocks of companies whose earnings are expected to grow faster than other stocks or the overall economy.

____ 40. A bond that can be converted into shares of common stock.

____ 41. Preferred stock, which accumulates unpaid dividends.

____ 42. Large investors such as pension funds, mutual funds, insurance companies, and banks.

____ 43. Buying several different investments to spread the risk.

____ 44. A registered representative who works as a market intermediary to buy and sell securities for clients.

____ 45. Purchases of less than 100 shares of stock at a time.

____ 46. The first public offering of a corporation's stock.

____ 47. The amount of debt represented by one bond.

____ 48. Evidence of stock ownership that specifies the name of the company, the number of shares it represents, and the type of stock being issued.

____ 49. The positive difference between the purchase price of a stock and its sale price.

____ 50. An organization whose members can buy and sell securities for companies and investors.

SELF-TEST

1. Which of the following is a common source of long-term financing for a corporation?
   A) A revolving credit agreement.
   B) Commercial paper.
   C) A bond issue.
   D) Trade credit.

2. Molly Manufacturing is going to sell $75 million of common stocks. In this situation, the firm will need the services of:
   A) a savings and loan association.
   B) a commercial bank.
   C) a credit union.
   D) an investment banker.

3. _____ are usually the most favored source of meeting long-term financing needs, since the company saves interest payments, dividends, and any possible underwriting fees by using this source.
   A) Secured bonds
   B) Debentures
   C) Warrants
   D) Retained earnings

4. Seattle Industries recently offered bonds for sale to the public. They offered an interest rate on the bonds of 9% to investors for the twenty-year life of the bonds. Seattle must remember that:
   A) bonds represent an ownership role in the company.
   B) bond interest must be paid regularly.
   C) bond interest is paid immediately after dividends.
   D) bond principal must be paid on owner demand.

5. After ten years, Connecticut Industries has finally decided to offer stock to the general public. This will permit them to raise needed capital. However, Connecticut must remember that:
   A) stock always has to be repaid at a future date.
   B) dividends are legally required on a quarterly basis.
   C) the company's debt position will be adversely affected.
   D) stockholders can have a strong say in company operations.

6. The stock exchange that has the greatest number of firms' securities listed is the:
   A) Over-the-counter market.
   B) New York Stock Exchange.
   C) American Stock Exchange.
   D) Chicago Board of Trade.

7. Abraham found a $1000 face value bond that belongs to his father. She checked in the Wall Street Journal and found the bond was currently selling for $1220. This bond is selling at a(n):
   A) discount.
   B) premium.
   C) excess trade-off.
   D) investment preference.

8. Jason called his stockbroker and placed an order for 100 shares of Utah Industries stock if and when the price falls to $25 per share. Jason placed a(n):
   A) market order.
   B) odd-lot order.
   C) limit order.
   D) conditional order.

9. Samad has always been interested in investing in stocks, but he can't afford the cost of blue chip stocks or even some growth stocks that sell at over $10 per share. Samad might consider investing in:
   A) time deposits.
   B) penny stocks.
   C) treasury stock.
   D) proxies.

10. In reviewing the firms whose stocks are used in the Dow Jones Industrial Average, we discover:
    A) the same 30 stocks have always been used.
    B) different companies are used each year.
    C) substitute stocks are used when deemed appropriate.
    D) there is an even mix between big and small companies.

ANSWER KEY

LEARNING THE LANGUAGE OF BUSINESS

1. E
2. F
3. B
4. G
5. N
6. D
7. C
8. A
9. HH
10. JJ
11. PP
12. K
13. SS
14. YY
15. H
16. LL
17. X
18. GG
19. QQ
20. J
21. NN
22. MM
23. XX
24. KK
25. Q

26. CC
27. OO
28. AA
29. TT
30. FF
31. T
32. V
33. DD
34. RR
35. EE
36. M
37. U
38. I
39. W
40. O
41. P
42. Z
43. S
44. UU
45. II
46. Y
47. R
48. VV
49. L
50. WW

SELF-TEST

Answer		Page #
1.	C	Page: 599
2.	D	Page: 613
3.	D	Page: 600-601
4.	B	Page: 615
5.	D	Page: 617
6.	A	Page: 620
7.	B	Page: 625-626
8.	C	Page: 627
9.	B	Page: 627
10.	C	Page: 636

Lesson 24

LESSON 25

ACCOUNTING FOR MANAGMENT

ASSIGNMENTS

1. Review the Learning Goals and read the Lesson Overview for this lesson.

2. Read Chapter 18 pp. 548-575 in Understanding Business, 6th edition by Nickels, McHugh, and McHugh.

3. Watch the video Accounting for Management.

4. Review the textbook material.

5. Match the key terms with the correct definitions in the Learning the Language of Business exercise.

6. Take the Self-Test.

7. Use the Answer Key to check your answers and review when necessary.

LEARNING GOALS

After you watch the video, read the textbook, and study this lesson, you should be able to:

1. Understand the importance of financial information and accounting.

2. Define and explain the different areas of the accounting profession.

3. Distinguish between accounting and bookkeeping, and list the steps in the accounting cycle.

4. Explain the differences between the major financial statements.

5. Describe the role of depreciation, LIFO, and FIFO in reporting financial information.

6. Detail how computers are used to record and apply accounting information in business.

7. Explain the importance of ratio analysis in reporting financial information.

LESSON NOTES

The PROFILE at the beginning of this chapter focuses on Scott Little of the Hard Rock Café. By the late 1990s the theme-dining business that was thriving just years earlier, was now in trouble. In response to the changing market the Hard Rock Café speculated that a change in financial management might be needed. The HRC lacked the ability to analyze its financial information, thus the entry of Scott Little. His objective was to compile company-wide information for sound decision making. He broke down the barriers between the accounting and finance departments, as well as others. Today the financial information is shared directly with managers, down to the restaurant level. Controlling costs, managing cash flows, understanding profit margins, and reporting finances accurately are keys to the survival of any business, large or small.

I. THE IMPORTANCE OF FINANCIAL INFORMATION

   A. Accounting information is the heartbeat of business.
      1. Most of us know almost nothing about accounting from experience.
      2. However, you have to know something about accounting if you want to understand business.
      3. It is almost impossible to run a business effectively without being able to read, understand, and analyze accounting reports and financial statements.

   B. Accounting reports and financial statements are as revealing of the health of a business as pulse rate and blood pressure reports are in revealing the health of a person.

II. WHAT IS ACCOUNTING?

   A. **ACCOUNTING** is the recording, classifying, summarizing, and interpreting of financial events and transactions to provide management and other interested parties with the information they need to make better decisions.
      1. Financial transactions include buying and selling goods and services, acquiring insurance, using supplies, and paying taxes.
      2. An accounting system is the methods used to record and summarize accounting data into reports.

   B. Purpose of accounting:
      1. To help managers evaluate the financial condition and the operating performance of the firm so they may make better decisions.
      2. To report financial information to people outside the firm such as owners, suppliers, and the government.

   C. Accounting is the measurement and reporting of financial information to various users regarding the economic activities of the firm.

III. AREAS OF ACCOUNTING

   A. Accounting has been called the language of business, but it also is the language used to report financial information about nonprofit organizations.

   B. MANAGERIAL ACCOUNTING
      1. **MANAGERIAL ACCOUNTING** is used to provide information and analyses to managers within the organization to assist them in decision making.
      2. Managerial accountants:
         a. Measure and report costs of production, marketing, and other functions.

Lesson 25

    b. Prepare budgets.
    c. Check whether or not units are staying within their budgets.
    d. Design strategies to minimize taxes.
   3. A **CERTIFIED MANAGEMENT ACCOUNTANT** is a professional accountant who has met certain educational and experience requirements and been certified by the Institute of Certified Management Accountants.

  C. FINANCIAL ACCOUNTING
   1. The information provided by **FINANCIAL ACCOUNTING** is used by people outside of the organization (owners and prospective owners, creditors and lenders, employee unions, customers, governmental units, and the general public).
    a. These external users are interested in the organization's profits and other financial information.
    b. Much of this information is contained in the company's **ANNUAL REPORT**, a yearly statement of the financial condition and progress of an organization covering a one-year period.
   2. It is critical for firms to keep accurate financial information.
    a. A **PRIVATE ACCOUNTANT** is one who works for a single company or organization.
    b. A **PUBLIC ACCOUNTANT** is one who provides services for a fee to a number of companies.
    c. CPAs help firms by:
     1) Designing an accounting system for a firm.
     2) Helping select the correct computer and software to run the system.
     3) Analyzing the financial strength of an organization.
   3. The accounting profession assures users of financial information that financial reports of organizations are accurate.
    a. The independent Financial Accounting Standards Board (FASB) defines what are generally accepted accounting principles (GAAP) that accountants must follow.
    b. If financial reports are prepared in accordance with GAAP, users know the information is reported professionally.
   4. A **CERTIFIED PUBLIC ACCOUNTANT (CPA)** is an accountant who has passed a series of examinations established by the American Institute of Certified Public Accountants (AICPA) and met the state's requirements for education and experience.

  D. AUDITING
   1. **AUDITING** is the job of reviewing and evaluating the records used to prepare the company's financial statements.
    a. Internal accountants often perform internal audits.
    b. Public accountants also conduct independent audits of accounting records.
   2. An **INDEPENDENT AUDIT** is an evaluation and unbiased opinion about the accuracy of company financial statements.
   3. An accountant who has a bachelor's degree, experience in internal auditing, and has passed an exam can earn standing as a **CERTIFIED INTERNAL AUDITOR**.

  E. TAX ACCOUNTING
   1. Federal, state, and local governments require submission of tax returns that must be filed at specific times and in a precise format.
   2. A **TAX ACCOUNTANT** is trained in tax law and is responsible for preparing tax returns and developing tax strategies.
   3. As the burden of taxes grows, the role of the tax accountant becomes more important.

IV. ACCOUNTING VERSUS BOOKKEEPING

  A. **BOOKKEEPING** is the recording of business transactions.

1. Bookkeeping is part of accounting, but accounting goes far beyond the mere recording of data.
2. Accountants classify, summarize, interpret, and report data to managers.
3. They suggest strategies for improving the financial condition of the company.

B. What bookkeepers do:
1. The first task of bookkeepers is to divide all the firm's transactions into meaningful categories.
2. Then they record the data from the original transaction documents (sales slips, etc.) into record books called journals.
3. A **JOURNAL** is a book where accounting data is first entered.

C. **DOUBLE-ENTRY BOOKKEEPING** is the system of recording each transaction in two places.
1. Bookkeepers can check one list against the other to make sure they add up to the same amount.
2. In double-entry bookkeeping, two entries in the journal are required for each company transaction.

D. A **LEDGER** is a specialized accounting book in which information from accounting journals is accumulated into specific categories and posted so that managers can find all the information about one account in the same place.

E. THE SIX-STEP ACCOUNTING CYCLE
The **ACCOUNTING CYCLE** results in the preparation of the financial statements: the balance sheet and the income statement.
Step 1. Analyzing and categorizing documents.
Step 2. Recording the information into journals.
Step 3. Posting that information into ledgers. (These first three steps are continuous.)
Step 4. Preparing a **TRIAL BALANCE**, which summarizes all the data in the ledgers to see that the figures are correct and balanced.
Step 5. Preparing an income statement and balance sheet.
Step 6. Analyze the financial statements and determine the financial health of the company.

V. UNDERSTANDING KEY FINANCIAL STATEMENTS

A. A **FINANCIAL STATEMENT** is the summary of all transactions that have occurred over a particular period.
1. These indicate a firm's financial health.
2. Two key financial statements are:
   a. The balance sheet reports the firm's financial condition on a specific date.
   b. The income statement reports revenues, expenses, and profits (or losses) for a period of time.
3. The balance sheet is a snapshot, while the income statement is a motion picture.

B. THE BALANCE SHEET
1. A **BALANCE SHEET** is the financial statement that reports a firm's financial condition at a specific time.
   a. The term balance sheet implies that the report shows a balance between two figures, a company's assets and its liabilities and owners equity.

C. THE FUNDAMENTAL ACCOUNTING EQUATION
1. The **FUNDAMENTAL ACCOUNTING EQUATION** is:
   assets = liabilities + owners' equity

2. The fundamental accounting equation is the basis for the balance sheet.
3. The assets are equal to, or are balanced with, the liabilities and owners' equity.

D. THE ACCOUNTS OF THE BALANCE SHEET
   1. **ASSETS** are economic resources owned by the company.
      a. Assets include productive, tangible items that help generate income, as well as intangibles of value.
      b. **LIQUIDITY** refers to how fast the assets can be converted into cash.
      c. **CURRENT ASSETS** can be converted to cash within one year.
      d. **FIXED ASSETS** are such things as equipment, buildings, and land, they are relatively permanent.
      e. **INTANGIBLE ASSETS** include items of value such as patents and copyrights that have no real physical form.

E. LIABILITIES AND OWNERS' EQUITY ACCOUNTS
   1. **LIABILITIES** are what the business owes to others.
      a. Current liabilities are payments due in one year or less.
      b. Long-term liabilities are payments not due for one year or longer.
      c. Accounts payable are monies owed for merchandise and services purchased on credit but not paid for yet.
      d. Notes payable, are short-term or long-term promises for future payment.
      e. Bonds payable are money loaned to the firm that it must pay back.
   2. Equity
      a. The value of things you own (assets) minus the amount of money you owe others (liabilities) is called **OWNERS' EQUITY**.
      b. Businesses not incorporated identify this as a capital account.
      c. For corporations, the owners' equity account records the owners' claims to funds they have invested in the firm, plus earnings kept in the business and not paid out.

F. THE INCOME STATEMENT
   1. The **INCOME STATEMENT** summarizes all of the resources that came into the firm from operating activities, money resources that were used up, expenses incurred in doing business, and what resources were left after all costs and expenses, including taxes, were paid.
      a. **NET INCOME or NET LOSS** is the revenues minus the expenses.
      b. The income statement reports the results of operations over a particular period of time.
      c. The income statement formula:
         revenue - cost of goods sold = gross margin (gross profit)
         gross margin - operating expenses = net income before taxes
         net income before taxes - taxes = net income (or loss)
      d. The income statement includes valuable financial information for stockholders and employees.
      e. The income statement is arranged according to generally accepted accounting principles:
         revenue
         - cost of goods sold
         gross margin
         - operating expenses
         net income before taxes
         -taxes
         Net income (or loss)

G. REVENUE
   1. **REVENUE** is the value of what is received for goods sold, services rendered, and other financial sources.
      a. There is a difference between revenue and sales.

       b. Most revenue comes from sales, but there could be other sources of revenue, such as rents earned, interest earned, and so forth.
       c. Net income can also be called net earnings, or net profit.

H. COST OF GOODS SOLD (COST OF GOODS MANUFACTURED)
1. **COST OF GOODS SOLD (COST OF GOODS MANUFACTURED)** measures the cost of merchandise sold or cost of raw materials or parts and supplies used for producing items for resale.
2. The cost of goods sold includes the purchase price plus any costs associated with obtaining and storing the goods.
3. **GROSS MARGIN** is how much the firm earned by buying and selling, or making and selling merchandise.
4. In a service firm, there may be no cost of goods sold.
5. In either case, the gross margin doesn't tell you everything you must subtract expenses.

I. OPERATING EXPENSES
1. Operating **EXPENSES** include rent, salaries, supplies, utilities, insurance, and depreciation of equipment.
2. After all expenses are deducted, the firm's net income before taxes is determined.
3. After allocating for taxes, you get to the bottom line, the net income (or perhaps net loss) the firm incurred from operations.
4. Businesses need to keep track of how much money they earn, spend, how much cash they have on hand, and so on.

J. THE IMPORTANCE OF CASH FLOW ANALYSIS
1. **CASH FLOW** is simply the difference between cash flowing in and cash flowing out of the business.
2. A major financial cause of small-business failure today is inadequate cash flow.
    a. Businesses often get into cash flow problems when they are growing quickly, borrowing heavily, and receiving payment from customers slowly.
    b. They are selling their goods and services, but aren't getting paid in time to turn around and pay their own bills.
    c. In order to meet the demands of customers, more and more goods are bought on credit.
    d. When the credit limit has been reached, the bank may refuse the loan.
    e. Too often, the company goes into bankruptcy because there was no cash available when it was most needed.
3. By keeping a banker informed about sales, profits, and cash flow, a small-business person makes sure of good financial advice.

K. THE STATEMENT OF CASH FLOWS
1. In 1988, the Financial Accounting Standards Board required that the statement of cash flows replace the statement of changes in financial position.
2. The **STATEMENT OF CASH FLOWS** reports cash receipts and disbursement related to the firm's major activities:
    a. Operations - Show cash transactions associated with running the business.
    b. Investments - Measures cash used in or provided by the firm's investment activities.
    c. Financing - Cash raised from the issuance of new debt or equity capital or cash used to pay business expenses, past debts, or company dividends.
3. Accountants analyze all of the cash changes that have occurred from operating, investing, and financing and determine the firm's net cash position.
4. The cash flow answers questions such as:
    a. How much cash came into the business from current operations?
    b. Was cash used to buy stocks, bonds, or other investments?
    c. Were some investments sold that brought in cash?
    d. How much money came in from issues stock?

VI. APPLYING ACCOUNTING KNOWLEDGE

   A. The major functions of recording transactions and preparing financial statements have largely been assigned to computers, but how you record and report data is also important.

   B. Depreciation
      1. Companies are permitted to recapture the cost of assets using depreciation as a business operation expense.
      2. **DEPRECIATION** is the systematic write-off of the cost of a tangible asset over its estimated life.
      3. Companies may choose from a number of techniques for calculating depreciation.
      4. Each method could result in a different net income.
      5. Accountants can offer financial advice and recommend ways of handling investments, depreciation, and other accounts.

   C. Handling inventory
      1. Inventories are a critical part of a company's financial statements and important in determining a firm's cost of goods sold.
      2. FIFO is the accounting technique for calculating cost of inventory based on **FIRST IN, FIRST OUT (FIFO)**.
      3. LIFO is the accounting technique for calculating cost of inventory based on **LAST IN, FIRST OUT (LIFO)**.
      4. The American Institute of Certified Public Accountants (AICPA) insists that complete information about the firm's financial operations be provided in financial statements.

VII. ACCOUNTANTS AND THE BUDGETING PROCESS

   A. A budget is a financial plan.
      1. A **BUDGET** sets forth management's expectations for revenues and, based on those financial expectations, allocates the use of specific resources.
      2. Financial statements form the basis for the budgeting process because past financial information is what is used to project future financial needs and expectations.

   B. Accountants often assist the financial managers in determining the organization's future financial needs.

VIII. THE IMPACT OF COMPUTER TECHNOLOGY ON ACCOUNTING

   A. Financial information and transactions may be recorded by hand or in a computer system.
      1. Most companies use computers since computers greatly simplify the task.
      2. As a business grows, the number of accounts a firm must keep and the reports that must be generated expand in scope.
      3. Many small-business accounting packages address the specific accounting needs of a small business.

   B. Computers can record and analyze data and print out up-to-the-minute financial reports.
      1. It is possible to have continuous auditing, testing the accuracy and reliability of financial statements, because of computers.
      2. Software programs allow even novices to do sophisticated financial analyses.

   C. Computers do not make financial decisions.
      1. They are tools to help accountants determine the best strategies.

2. Small-business owners should hire or consult with an accountant before they get started in business.
3. Computers help make accounting work less monotonous.

D. The work of an accountant requires training and very specific competencies.

IX. USING FINANCIAL RATIOS

A. Accurate financial information forms the basis of the financial analysis performed by accountants.
  1. Financial ratios are helpful in analyzing the actual performance of the company compared to its financial objectives.
  2. They also provide insights into the firm's performance in comparison to other firms in the industry.

B. LIQUIDITY RATIOS
  1. Liquidity ratios measure the company's ability to pay its short-term debts.
  2. These short-term debts are expected to be repaid within one year.
  3. The current ratio is the ratio of a firm's current assets to its current liabilities.
     a. current ratio = $\dfrac{\text{current assets}}{\text{current liabilities}}$
     b. The ratio should be compared to competing firms within the industry.
  4. The acid-test ratio measures the cash, marketable securities, and receivables of the firm, to its current liabilities.
     a. acid-test ratio = $\dfrac{\text{cash + marketable securities + receivables}}{\text{current liabilities}}$
     b. This ratio is important to firms that have difficulty converting their inventory into quick cash.

C. LEVERAGE (DEBT) RATIOS
  1. Leverage (debt) ratios refer to the degree to which a firm relies on borrowed funds in its operations.
  2. The debt to owners' equity ratio measures the degree to which the company is financed by borrowed funds that must be repaid.
     a. debt to owners' equity ratio = $\dfrac{\text{total liabilities}}{\text{owners' equity}}$
     b. A ratio above 1 (or 100%) would show that a firm actually has more debt than equity.
  3. It is important to compare ratios to other firms in the same industry.

D. PROFITABILITY (PERFORMANCE) RATIOS
  1. Profitability (performance) ratios measure how effectively the firm is using its various resources to achieve profits.
  2. Management's performance is often measured by using profitability ratios.
  3. A new Accounting Standards Board rule went into effect at the end if 1997 requiring companies to report their quarterly earning per share two ways: basic and undiluted.
  4. Basic earnings per share (basic EPS) measures the amount of profit earned by a company for each share of common stock it has outstanding.
     a. Earnings help to stimulate growth and pay for stockholders' dividends.
     b. basic earnings per share = $\dfrac{\text{net income after taxes}}{\text{number of common shares outstanding}}$

5. Diluted earnings per share (diluted EPS) measures the amount of profit earned by a company for each share of outstanding common stock, but also takes into consideration stock options, warrants, preferred stock, and convertible debt securities which can be converted into common stock.
6. Return on sales is calculated by comparing a company's net income with its total sales.
   a. return on sales = $\dfrac{\text{net income}}{\text{net sales}}$
   b. Firms use this ratio to see if they are doing as well as other companies they compete against in generating income from sales.
7. Return on equity measures how much was earned for each dollar invested by owners.
   a. It is calculated by comparing a company's net income with its total owner's equity.
   b. return on equity = $\dfrac{\text{net income after taxes}}{\text{total owners' equity}}$
   c. The higher the risk involved in an industry, the higher the return investors expect on their investment.
8. There are other profitability ratios which are vital measurements of company growth and management performance.

E. ACTIVITY RATIOS
   1. Activity ratios measure the effectiveness of the firm's management in using the assets that are available.
   2. Inventory turnover ratio measures the speed of inventory moving through the firm and its conversion into sales.
      a. inventory turnover ratio = $\dfrac{\text{cost of goods sold}}{\text{average inventory}}$
      b. The more efficiently a firm manages its inventory, the higher the return.
      c. A lower than average inventory turnover ratio often indicates obsolete merchandise on hand or poor buying practices.
      d. Inventory control is needed to ensure proper performance.

F. Finance professionals use several other specific ratios to learn more about a firm's financial condition.

LEARNING THE LANGUAGE OF BUSINESS

Match each of the following key terms with the appropriate definition.

A. accounting
B. accounting cycle
C. annual report
D. assets
E. auditing
F. balance sheet
G. bookkeeping
H. budget
I. cash flow
J. certified internal auditor
K. certified management accountant
L. certified public accountant (CPA)
M. cost of goods sold (or cost of goods manufactured)
N. current assets
O. depreciation
P. double-entry bookkeeping
Q. expenses
R. First in, First out (FIFO)
S. financial accounting
T. financial statement
U. fixed assets
V. fundamental accounting equation
W. gross margin (gross profit)
X. income statement
Y. independent audit
Z. intangible assets
AA. journal
BB. ledger
CC. liabilities
DD. Last in, First out (LIFO)
EE. liquidity
FF. managerial accounting
GG. net income/net loss
HH. owners' equity
II. private accountant
JJ. public accountant
KK. revenue
LL. statement of cash flows
MM. tax accountant
NN. trial balance

_____ 1. The recording of business transactions.

_____ 2. The recording, classifying, summarizing, and interpreting of financial events and transactions to provide management and other interested parties the information they need to make better decisions.

_____ 3. A system of bookkeeping in which two entries in the journal are required for each company transaction.

Lesson 25 Page 283

____ 4. Recording device in which information from accounting journals is categorized into homogeneous groups and posted so that managers can find all the information about one account in the same place.

____ 5. Recording devices used for the first recording of all transactions.

____ 6. Totaling all of the debit balances and all of the credit balances in the ledgers to be sure debits equal credits.

____ 7. A six-step procedure that results in the preparation and analysis of the two major financial statements: the balance sheet and the income statement.

____ 8. An evaluation and unbiased opinion about the accuracy of company financial statements.

____ 9. The provision of information and analyses to managers within the organization to assist them in decision making.

____ 10. The summary of all transactions that have occurred over a particular period.

____ 11. Assets = liability + owners' equity; it is the basis for the balance sheet.

____ 12. Assets minus liabilities.

____ 13. Revenue minus expenses.

____ 14. The value of what is received for goods sold, services rendered, and other sources.

____ 15. How much the firm earned by buying and selling or making and selling merchandise.

____ 16. Accountants who pass a series of examinations established by the American Institute of Certified Public Accountants (AICPA) and meet the state's requirements for education and experience.

____ 17. Accountants who work for a single company.

____ 18. An Accountant who is trained in tax law and is responsible for preparing tax returns and developing tax strategies.

____ 19. An accountant who has a bachelor's degree, 2 years, of internal auditing experience, and has successfully passed an exam administered by the Institute of Internal Auditors.

____ 20. A professional accountant who has met certain educational and experience requirements and been certified by the Institute of Certified Management Accountants.

____ 21. An Accountant who provides accounting services to individuals or businesses on a fee basis.

____ 22. Report of cash receipts and disbursements related to the firm's major activities: operations, investments, and financing.

____ 23. Financial statement which reports the financial position of a firm on a specific date, it is composed of assets, liabilities, and owners' equity.

____ 24. Financial statement which reports revenues and expenses over a specific period of time, showing the results of operations during that period.

____ 25. A yearly statement of the financial condition and progress of an organization covering a one year period.

____ 26. A particular type of expense measured by the total cost of merchandise sold or cost of raw materials or parts and supplies used for producing items for resale.

____ 27. The difference between cash receipts and cash disbursements.

____ 28. The economic resources owned by the firm.

____ 29. Resources, including cash or noncash items, that can be converted to cash within one year.

____ 30. Items that are not included in the current and fixed assets categories. This catchall category includes items such as patents and copyrights.

____ 31. Resources of a permanent nature, such as land, buildings, furniture, and fixtures.

____ 32. The ease with which an asset can be converted to cash.

____ 33. Amounts owed by the organization to others.

____ 34. The systematic write-off of the value of an asset over its estimated useful life.

____ 35. Costs incurred in operating a business, such as rent, utilities, and salaries.

____ 36. The task of reviewing and evaluating the records used to prepare the company's financial statements.

____ 37. Accounting technique for calculating cost of inventory based on last in, first out.

____ 38. Accounting technique for calculating cost of inventory based on first in, first out.

____ 39. A financial plan that sets forth management expectations for revenues and based on those expectations, allocates the use of specific resources throughout the firm.

____ 40. Accounting information and analysis prepared for people outside the organization.

SELF-TEST

1. "Accounting is boring. I'll hire someone to do that for me so that I can focus my attention on satisfying my customers." Which of the following is an appropriate response to this complaint?
   A) Make sure you hire a good accountant.
   B) You'll need to understand the accountant's reports to successfully run your business.
   C) Most entrepreneurs would agree with your opinion.
   D) Thank goodness that someone likes to do that type of work.

2. Leonora works for a textbook publishing firm preparing budgets and reporting production costs. She works in the field of:
   A) managerial accounting.
   B) financial accounting.
   C) tax accounting.
   D) auditing.

3. Jose recently graduated with a degree in accounting. He plans to go to work for the American Cancer Society as an accountant. Jose will be working in:
   A) private accounting.
   B) public accounting.
   C) service accounting.
   D) independent accounting.

4. Sales receipts, purchase orders, and payroll records are all examples of accounting transactions that would be recorded by the:
   A) auditor.
   B) private accountant.
   C) bookkeeper.
   D) purchasing agent.

5. Brianne is a bookkeeper for Kitty Creations Limited. It is her job to take the firm's transactions and record them in books referred to as:
   A) credit accounts.
   B) asset components.
   C) journals.
   D) comparative ledgers.

6. Keith will be graduating from Southern State University this year. He has accumulated $10,000 dollars in student loans during his four years at college. An accountant would classify the loans as:
   A) assets.
   B) liabilities.
   C) owners' equity.
   D) intangibles.

7. Over the past month, Monica noted that she disbursed $6,347 in payments for operations in her travel agency and received $6,189 in cash receipts for services rendered. Monica had a:
   A) positive disbursement.
   B) negative cash flow.
   C) bad debt allowance.
   D) tax credit payment.

8. During a period of rising prices, FIFO (first in, first out) inventory valuation method will report _____ net income figures than would LIFO (last in, first out).
   A) higher
   B) lower
   C) more accurate
   D) less accurate

9. The Left Bank Bookstore wants to indicate to its shareholders how successful it has been. To do this, it would be helpful to report their:
   A) liquidity ratios.
   B) leverage ratios.
   C) activity ratios.
   D) profitability ratios.

10. The use of computers in accounting has:
    A) made it possible for most firms to operate without the expense of hiring accountants.
    B) reduced the pressure on managers in making financial decisions.
    C) increased the possibility for firms to have continuous auditing ability.
    D) made financial errors almost impossible to detect.

ANSWER KEY

LEARNING THE LANGUAGE OF BUSINESS

1. G
2. A
3. P
4. BB
5. AA
6. NN
7. B
8. Y
9. FF
10. T
11. V
12. HH
13. GG
14. KK
15. W
16. L
17. II
18. MM
19. J
20. K
21. JJ
22. LL
23. F
24. X
25. C
26. M
27. I
28. D
29. N
30. Z
31. U
32. EE
33. CC
34. O
35. Q
36. E
37. DD
38. R
39. H
40. S

SELF-TEST

	Answer	Page #
1.	B	Page: 550
2.	A	Page: 551
3.	A	Page: 552
4.	C	Page: 554
5.	C	Page: 554
6.	B	Page: 558
7.	B	Page: 562-564
8.	A	Page: 566
9.	D	Page: 570-571
10.	C	Page: 567-568

LESSON 26

MANAGING RISK

ASSIGNMENTS

1. Review the Learning Goals and read the Lesson Overview for this lesson.

2. Read the Appendix: Managing Risk pp. 700-708 in Understanding Business, 6th edition by Nickels, McHugh, and McHugh.

3. Watch the video Managing Risk

4. Review the textbook material.

5. Match the key terms with the correct definitions in the Learning the Language of Business exercise.

6. Take the Self-Test.

7. Use the Answer Key to check your answers and review when necessary.

LEARNING GOALS

After you watch the video, read the textbook, and study this lesson, you should be able to:

1. Distinguish between different kinds of risk and identify the four ways businesses manage risk.

2. Describe the guidelines used to determine insurable risks.

3. Explain the law of large numbers and other tools used by insurance companies to limit the cost of claims.

4. Distinguish between stock and mutual insurance companies.

5. Describe the various types of insurance coverage available to businesses and individuals.

6. Explain the risks involved with global warming, acid rain and other environmental concerns

LESSON NOTES

I. THE INCREASING CHALLENGE OF RISK MANAGEMENT

   A. The management of risk is a major issue for businesses.

   B. Earthquakes, flood, fire, airplane crashes, riots, and car crashes destroy property and injure people.

   C. Businesspeople must pay to restore the property and compensate those who are injured.

   D. Other incidents might involve businesspeople in lawsuits.

   E. HOW RAPID CHANGE AFFECTS RISK MANAGEMENT
      1. Changes occur so fast in business today that it is difficult to keep up with all the risks.

II. MANAGING RISK

   A. **RISK** refers to the chance of loss, the degree of probability of loss, and the amount of possible loss.
      1. There are two different kinds of risk.
         a. **SPECULATIVE RISK** involves a chance of either profit or loss.
            1) An entrepreneur takes speculative risk on the chance of making a profit.
         b. **PURE RISK** is the threat of loss with no chance for profit.
            1) Pure risk involves the threat of fire, accident, or loss.
            2) If such events occur a company loses money; but if the events do not occur, the company gains nothing.
      2. Pure risk threatens the very existence of some firms.
      3. Once such risks are identified, firms can:
         a. Reduce the risk.
         b. Avoid the risk.
         c. Self-insure against the risk.
         d. Buy insurance against the risk.

   B. REDUCING RISK
      1. A firm can reduce risk by establishing loss-prevention programs.
      2. Examples of these programs are fire alarms, smoke detectors, and so on.
      3. An effective risk management strategy starts with a good loss-prevention program.
      4. High insurance rates have forced some people to avoid risks, and in extreme cases go out of business.

   C. AVOIDING RISK
      1. Many risks cannot be avoided.
      2. Some companies avoid avoiding risk by not accepting hazardous jobs and by out-sourcing certain functions.

   D. SELF-INSURING
      1. Many companies have turned to self-insurance because they either can't find or can't afford conventional property/casualty policies.
      2. Using **SELF-INSURANCE**, firms set aside money to cover routine claims and buy only catastrophe policies.
      3. Self-insurance is most appropriate when a firm has several widely distributed facilities.
      4. A risky strategy for self-insurance is for a company to go bare; paying claims straight out of its budget.

5. A less risk alternative is the forming of risk retention group-insurance pools that share similar risks.

E. BUYING INSURANCE TO COVER RISK
1. Well-designed, consistently enforced risk-prevention programs reduce the probability of claims, but accidents do happen.
   a. Some insurance protection is provided by the federal government.
   b. Most risks must be covered by individuals and businesses on their own.

2. What risks are uninsurable?
   a. An **UNINSURABLE RISK** is one that no insurance company will cover.
   b. You cannot insure market risks, political risks, some personal risks, and some risks of operation.

3. What risks are insurable?
   a. An **INSURABLE RISK** is one that the typical insurance company will cover.
   b. Insurance companies use these guidelines:
      1) The policyholder must have an **INSURABLE INTEREST**.
      2) The loss should be measurable.
      3) The chance of loss should be measurable.
      4) The loss should be accidental.
      5) The risk should be dispersed.
      6) The insurance company can set standards for accepting risk.

F. The law of large numbers
1. An **INSURANCE POLICY** is a written contract between the insured and an insurance company that promises to pay for all or part of a loss.
2. A **PREMIUM** is the cost of the policy coverage to the insured or the fee charged by the insurance company.
3. The object of an insurance company is to make a profit.
4. What makes the acceptance of risk possible is the law of large numbers.
5. The **LAW OF LARGE NUMBERS** states that if a large number of people or organizations are exposed to the same risk, a predictable number of losses will occur during a given period of time.
   a. These figures are used to determine the appropriate premiums to assume the risk.
   b. Many insurance companies are charging high premiums for the anticipated costs associated with more court cases and higher damage awards

G. Rule of indemnity
1. The **RULE OF INDEMNITY** says that a person or organization cannot collect more than the actual loss from an insurable risk.
2. One cannot gain from risk management; one can only minimize loses.

H. Sources of insurance
1. A **STOCK INSURANCE COMPANY** is owned by stockholders.
2. A **MUTUAL INSURANCE COMPANY** is owned by its policyholders.
   a. A mutual insurance company does not earn profits for its owners.
   b. It is a not-for-profit organization, and any excess funds go to the policyholder in the form of dividends.

III. TYPES OF INSURANCE
A. There are many types of insurance that are available to cover various losses.
1. Property losses result from fires, accidents, theft, or other perils.

2. Liability losses result from property damage or injuries suffered by others for which the policyholder is held responsible.

B. HEALTH INSURANCE
1. Businesses and nonprofit organizations may offer their employees an array of health care benefits to choose from.
2. **HEALTH MAINTENANCE ORGANIZATIONS (HMOs)** are health care organizations that require members to choose from a restricted list of doctors.
    a. HMOs offer a full range of health care benefits with emphasis on helping members to stay healthy.
    b. HMOs employ or contract with doctors, hospitals, and other systems, and members must use those providers.
    c. This system is called managed care and is less expensive, but members sometimes complain about not being able to choose doctors.
    d. To save money, HMOs usually must approve treatment before it is given.
3. PREFERRED PROVIDER ORGANIZATIONS (PPOs) are similar to HMOs except they allow members to choose their own physicians.
    a. PPOs also contract with hospitals and physicians, but you do not have to go to those physicians.
    b. Members usually have to pay a deductible before the PPO will pay any bills.
    c. You usually have to pay part of the bill, called co-insurance.
    d. The benefit of such plans is that you can choose your own physician.
    e. Both HMOs and PPOs can cost much less than comprehensive individual health insurance policies.

C. DISABILITY INSURANCE
1. Disability insurance replaces part of your income if you become disabled and unable to work.
2. Experts recommend this type of insurance: the chances of becoming disabled are much higher than the chance of dying.

D. WORKERS' COMPENSATION
1. Worker's compensation insurance guarantees the payment of wages, medical care, and rehabilitation services for employees who are injured on the job.
2. Employers in all 50 states are required to provide this insurance.
3. The cost of insurance varies by the company's safety record, its payroll, and the types of hazards faced by workers.

E. LIABILITY INSURANCE
1. Professional liability insurance covers people who are found liable for professional negligence.
2. Product liability insurance provides coverage against liability arising out of products sold.

F. OTHER BUSINESS INSURANCE
1. Risk management is critical in all firms.
2. Remember that risk is often matched by opportunity and profits.
3. Entrepreneurs often buy life insurance that will pay partners and others what they will need to keep the business going.

G. LIFE INSURANCE FOR BUSINESSES
1. Everything said about life insurance in Chapter 22 applies to businesspeople as well.
2. The best coverage for most individuals is tem insurance.

H. INSURANCE COVERAGE FOR HOME-BASES BUSINESSES
1. Homeowner's policies usually don't have adequate protection.

2. Few of us are experts on insurance, so check with an insurance agent regarding a home-based business.

IV. THE RISK OF DAMAGING THE ENVIRONMENT

A. The risk of environmental harm reaches international proportions.

B. The Chernobyl nuclear power plant in the former Soviet Union highlights this risk.

C. Many feel there is a need for a more careful evaluation of environmental risks.

D. Risk management means evaluating global risks and prioritizing these risks so that international funds can be spent where they can do the most good.

LEARNING THE LANGUAGE OF BUSINESS

Match each of the following key terms with the appropriate definition.

A. health maintenance organizations (HMOs)
B. Insurable interest
C. Insurable risk
D. Insurance policy
E. law of large numbers
F. mutual insurance company
G. preferred provider organizations (PPOs)
H. premium
I. pure risk
J. risk
K. rule of indemnity
L. self-insurance
M. speculative risk
N. stock insurance company
O. uninsurable risk

____ 1. The chance of loss, the degree of probability of loss, and the amount of possible loss.

____ 2. A type of risk that involves a chance of either profit or loss.

____ 3. The threat of loss with no chance for profit.

____ 4. Putting funds away to cover routine claims rather than buying insurance to cover them.

____ 5. Risk that a typical insurance company will not cover.

____ 6. Risk that a typical insurance company will cover.

____ 7. Possibility of policyholder to suffer a loss.

____ 8. A written contract between the insured and an insurance company that promises to pay for all or part of a loss.

____ 9. The fee charged by an insurance company for an insurance policy.

____ 10. Principle, which states that if a large number of people or organizations are exposed to the same risk, a predictable number of losses, will occur.

____ 11. Insurance restriction which states that an insured person or organization cannot collect more than the actual loss from and insurable risk.

____ 12. Insurance company owned by stockholders, just like any other investor-owned company.

____ 13. Insurance firm owned by its policyholders.

____ 14. Health care organizations that require policyholders to choose from a restricted list of doctors and hospitals.

____ 15. Health care organizations similar to HMOs, but that allow policyholders to choose their own physicians.

SELF-TEST

1. Some businesses will set aside money to cover routine claims and buy "catastrophe" policies to cover big losses. This is an example of which of the following?
   A) avoiding the risk.
   B) self-insuring against the risk.
   C) reducing the risk.
   D) a loss-prevention program.

2. Hector had been asked to serve on the board of a major pharmaceutical firm. He reluctantly declined, citing the firm's lack of liability coverage for outside members of the board of directors. Hector's decision indicates that he:
   A) will self-insure against a loss from legal action taken against the pharmaceutical firm.
   B) feels that the potential loss from legal action against this firm is an uninsurable risk.
   C) insists that the firm follow the rule of indemnity.
   D) will mange his risk by avoiding the potential loss from a liability suit directed at the board of directors.

3. There have been a series of large judgements in product liability cases against companies producing hairdryers. If this trend continues, insurance companies will respond by _____ the premiums charged for liability insurance for hairdryer manufacturers.
   A) lowering
   B) canceling
   C) increasing
   D) underwriting

4. Constitutional Corporation is a mutual insurance company. This means that:
   A) it is a not-for-profit organization.
   B) it is owned by stockholders, just like any other investor-owned company.
   C) it is jointly owned by stockholders and the federal government.
   D) It provides several different types of insurance coverage.

5. One benefit of Preferred Provider Organizations (PPOs) compared to Health Maintenance Organizations (HMOs) is that PPOs :
   A) offer lower costs for members.
   B) require members to pay a deductible before coverage by the PPO begins.
   C) allow members to choose their own physicians.
   D) offer co-insurance where the PPO pays only part of the total health cost.

6. Amusement parks often have a minimum height restriction on some of their most thrilling rides. This risk management strategy is done in an effort to:
   A) minimize the speculative risk associated with an injury.
   B) reduce the risk associated with a potential accident.
   C) self-insure against a catastrophic accident.
   D) create the perception of a more exciting ride.

7. Harold owns several gas stations. He realizes that among the several risks associated with this type of business is the risk of minor damage to cars from dirty or contaminated fuel. He also understands the potential of a major loss associated with a fire at one of his gas stations. In an effort to minimize his insurance cost and yet have a reasonable risk management program, Harold is considering self-insurance. Which of the risks mentioned earlier would best fit the self-insuring strategy of managing risk?
   A) Neither of the risks should be self-insured.
   B) Both of them are equally good candidates to be self-insured.
   C) The smaller, more routine, losses associated with the damage caused by dirty or contaminated fuel.
   D) The larger, catastrophic losses of a major fire.

8. Demetrius was turned down when he attempted to buy a life insurance policy on his former Introduction to Business instructor. The insurance company felt that he did not meet the criteria to establish an insurable interest. His attempt to insure the life of his former instructor was probably turned down because:
   A) the chance of the loss could not be measured.
   B) the loss could not be measured.
   C) the insurance company did not have history of providing life insurance on college instructors.
   D) The loss would not be accidental.

9. The objective of stock insurance companies is to make a profit. How can they make a profit?
   A) They profit when the premiums they charge equal the cost of covering losses for their policyholders.
   B) They profit when the premiums they charge are less than the cost of covering losses for their policyholders.
   C) Their profits are assured by the federal government since the service they provide is critical to our economy.
   D) They profit when the premiums they charge are greater than the cost of covering losses for their policyholders.

10. Bill, a professional hockey player, is upset when he discovers that his twin brother, a grade school PE teacher, pays 50% less for disability insurance that he does. What is the most likely explanation for this difference?
    A) Bill's policy is with a different insurance company.
    B) The likelihood of a disabling injury is greater for Bill than his brother.
    C) Bill's brother is healthier than Bill.
    D) The law of large numbers establishes that Bill and his brother have similar risks over a given period of time.

ANSWER KEY

LEARNING THE LANGUAGE OF BUSINESS

1. J
2. M
3. I
4. L
5. O
6. C
7. B
8. D
9. H
10. E
11. K
12. N
13. F
14. A
15. G

SELF-TEST

Answer	Page #
1. B	Page: 702
2. D	Page: 702
3. C	Page: 704
4. A	Page: 704
5. C	Page: 704-705
6. B	Page: 701
7. C	Page: 702
8. B	Page: 703
9. D	Page: 703
10. B	Page: 705